Anti-Money Laundering Transaction Monitoring Systems Implementation

Wiley and SAS Business Series

The Wiley and SAS Business Series presents books that help senior level managers with their critical management decisions.

Titles in the Wiley and SAS Business Series include:

Financial Institution Advantage and the Optimization of Information Processing by Sean C. Keenan

Fraud Analytics Using Descriptive, Predictive, and Social Network Techniques: A Guide to Data Science for Fraud Detection by Bart Baesens, Veronique Van Vlasselaer, and Wouter Verbeke

Hotel Pricing in a Social World: Driving Value in the Digital Economy by Kelly A. McGuire

Intelligent Credit Scoring: Building and Implementing Better Credit Risk Scorecards (Second Edition) by Naeem Siddiqi

JMP Connections: The Art of Utilizing Connections in Your Data by John Wubbel

Leaders and Innovators: How Data-Driven Organizations Are Winning with Analytics by Tho H. Nguyen

On-Camera Coach: Tools and Techniques for Business Professionals in a Video-Driven World by Karin Reed

Mobile Learning: A Handbook for Developers, Educators, and Learners by Scott McQuiggan, Lucy Kosturko, Jamie McQuiggan, and Jennifer Sabourin

Next Generation Demand Management: People, Process, Analytics, and Technology by Charles W. Chase

The Patient Revolution: How Big Data and Analytics Are Transforming the Health Care Experience by Krisa Tailor

A Practical Guide to Analytics for Governments: Using Big Data for Good by Marie Lowman

Profit-Driven Business Analytics: A Practitioner's Guide to Transforming Big Data into Added Value by Wouter Verbeke, Cristian Bravo, and Bart Baesens

Profit from Your Forecasting Software: A Best Practice Guide for Sales Forecasters by Paul Goodwin

Project Finance for Business Development by John E. Triantis

SAS Data Analytic Development: Dimensions of Software Quality by Troy Martin Hughes

For more information on any of the above titles, please visit www .wiley.com.

Anti-Money Laundering Transaction Monitoring Systems Implementation

Finding Anomalies

Derek Chau

Maarten van Dijck Nemcsik

WILEY

Published by John Wiley & Sons, Inc., Hoboken, New Jersey.

Published simultaneously in Canada.

For general information on our other products and services or for technical support, please contact our Customer Care Department within the United States at (800) 762-2974, outside the United States at (317) 572-3993, or fax (317) 572-4002.

Wiley publishes in a variety of print and electronic formats and by print-on-demand. Some material included with standard print versions of this book may not be included in e-books or in print-on-demand. If this book refers to media such as a CD or DVD that is not included in the version you purchased, you may download this material at http://booksupport.wiley.com. For more information about Wiley products, visit www.wiley.com.

Library of Congress Cataloging-in-Publication Data

Names: Yip, Derek Chau Chan, 1978- author. | Nemcsik, Maarten van Dijck, 1972- author.
Title: Anti-money laundering transaction monitoring systems implementation : finding anomalies / Derek Chau Chan Yip, Maarten van Dijck Nemcsik.
Description: First Edition. | Hoboken : Wiley, 2020. | Series: Wiley and SAS business series | Includes index.
Identifiers: LCCN 2020032916 (print) | LCCN 2020032917 (ebook) | ISBN 9781119381808 (cloth) | ISBN 9781119381969 (adobe pdf) | ISBN 9781119381938 (epub)
Subjects: LCSH: Money laundering—Prevention.
Classification: LCC HV8079.M64 Y57 2020 (print) | LCC HV8079.M64 (ebook) | DDC 363.25/968—dc23
LC record available at https://lccn.loc.gov/2020032916
LC ebook record available at https://lccn.loc.gov/2020032917

Cover image: Derek Chau
Cover design: Wiley

10 9 8 7 6 5 4 3 2 1

Contents

About the Authors

Chau Chan Yip (Derek), is a principal consultant in SAS Hong Kong. He has twenty years of IT system integration and implementation experience. He has participated in several complex and large-scale projects. He leads the SAS AML consulting team in Hong Kong overseeing the delivery and support of over 30 SAS AML sites. Derek designed a tool for analyzing and tuning transaction monitoring scenario thresholds. This tool was deployed in six financial institutes in Hong Kong, and he led the team in providing scenario review service recommending the thresholds, customer segmentation, and other adjustments to the AML transaction monitoring systems. He has also held advisory roles for some foreign delivery of this AML solution. Derek has an honors bachelor degree in computer science and computer engineering from the Hong Kong University of Science and Technology, and a master of science degree in computer science from the Chinese University of Hong Kong.

Maarten van Dijck Nemcsik, LLM, PhD, has worked for SAS since 2012 as a financial crimes and (tax) compliance domain expert and solution lead. Over the years he has implemented SAS AML, Customer Due Diligence, Enterprise Case Management, and SAS Visual Investigator. Maarten is currently part of the SAS Global Fraud & Security Business Intelligence Unit, being responsible for internal and external training courses for the implementation of the SAS financial crimes and compliance products and project implementation advisory and support. After obtaining a master's and PhD degree in the field of criminal law and procedure and working as a post doctorate in the field of Organized Crime research at the University of Tilburg, the Netherlands, Maarten worked as a security fraud intelligence officer for ABN AMRO Bank NV in Amsterdam and The Royal Bank of Scotland Group in London. Maarten has published in the field of organized and economic crime, anti-money laundering, and compliance in the diamond sector.

Acknowledgments

I would like to express my gratitude to a few people who have supported me in this endeavor.

I would like to thank:

- Maarten van Dijck Nemcsik, who offered to co-write this book with me, when he recognized in me an equal sense of passion for the difficult but often (ultimately) rewarding job of implementing complicated AML software.

- My manager, William Hou of SAS Hong Kong, who trusted me and gave me room to develop my knowledge on AML.

- Wallace Chow, who brought me the many opportunities on AML implementation experience.

- The consulting team in Hong Kong, who brought me various ideas for learning together.

- Frits Fraase Storm and Mohammed Farhatullah of SAS, who supported the production of this book.

- Jim West of SAS US, for allowing me to reference his material about customer segmentation and scenario threshold tuning.

- David Steward and Hugo Tolosa of SAS, for sharing their experiences in AML for different industries.

- K.F. Lam, for reviewing the book content and giving us very helpful feedback from a professional business user's view.

- Stacey Hamilton, Lauree Shepard, and Catherine Connolly of SAS Publishing, for their advice on writing, and their patience and perseverance.

- The SAS Product Management team and R&D, who produced SAS AML. Many of the ideas in this book are based on this software solution.

- My customers in Hong Kong and Greater China, who have been demanding better software solutions.

- My awesome wife, Cindy, and my son, Anton, for their support and giving me room to concentrate on this project.

Thank you all!

Derek

I am thankful for Derek for initiating this book and allowing me to embark on this project. Indeed, anti-money laundering is one thing, implementing software that helps (and satisfies) our SAS customers with being compliant with regulations in an effective and efficient way, is quite something else.

I would further like the thank Bryan Stines, my manager at SAS for giving me sufficient bandwidth for co-authoring this book and my wife, Ágnes, for her enduring patience and giving me the space to focus on this sideline project.

Lastly, I want to thank Emeritus Professor Petrus van Duyne, who introduced me to the world of money laundering research and helped me to develop a critical, yet not cynical, view on the regulatory effort to make financial institutions shoulder their part of the burden of fighting crime and abuse of our financial system.

Maarten

Preface

Over the past years, we have been supporting quite a significant number of AML and other financial crime-related implementation projects. We have been meeting with many customer project teams and end users, mainly across Asia Pacific, Europe, and the Middle East. From working with small financial institutions that operate strictly at a domestic level, to implementing our software in some of the largest financial groups worldwide . . . and almost everything in between. As each customer is different, so is each project and we have had to find solutions for a wide range of, sometimes peculiar, customer requirements. We are thankful to our customers for coming up with such a wide range of wishes and demands, as it challenges us not only as consultants but also as software developers, to continuously improve our software, but also our personal skills and our way of delivering tailor-made solutions to satisfaction.

SAS has a relatively low attrition rate, which is testament to SAS being one of the best employers worldwide (don't take our word for it, Google it!). But even then, as time passes, we see team members come and go and may ourselves move on to explore different pastures. With each skillful consultant that moves on in their career path, insights, expertise, and experience is bound to get lost. Back in 2016, Derek began thinking about preserving these insights, knowledge, and experience via writing and publishing. This initiative was well received within SAS, and a foundation was laid for this book . . . Derek's first one.

This was initially an individual effort, and not an easy task for a "technical" guy who, until now was happy conversing within his own comfort zone . . . the language of data and computers! After a while Maarten joined Derek and we have been working on the book ever since, in whatever time we could spare from both our busy jobs and, more importantly, family life.

Even at the time when social distancing wasn't even "a thing," we kept well apart from each other. Maarten working from Spain and Derek from Hong Kong. Never on a project together, or even a training. As technically savvy as we believe ourselves to be, (why else would we work in this field and for a company like SAS!) we were fine communicating strictly through electronic means. The time zone difference only became a bit of a hindrance when our SAS editorial support, namely Lauree Shepard, was based at the SAS mothership in Cary, North Carolina.

So, this book is about transaction monitoring implementation, which is, at the end of the day, inescapably a technical subject. In the world of today, technology is still very much in the fast lane. Four years have elapsed since 2016 and during the process we were worried about some of the content becoming outdated. That worry has still not dissipated entirely, but we are modestly confident that most of the information and guidance that we set out to share will still be relevant for those entering the field of AML software implementation. We hope that most of our insights as captured in the following chapters will hold some truth for now and in the foreseeable future. And we would like to thank you, as our (aspirant) reader . . . for placing your trust in us and this book.

CHAPTER 1

An Introduction to Anti-Money Laundering

THE EMERGENCE OF AML

Money laundering is generally understood as the concealment of an illegitimate source of assets, providing an apparent legal origin. People have various reasons to whitewash assets: they might want to conceal the original crime and not let their wealth become a whistleblower, or they may simply want to build up a reputation of being a successful and respectable member of the community. Since the late 1980s, there has been another reason to launder money. Law enforcement, initially as part of the US-driven war on drugs, started to clamp down on the financial aspect of crime and new laws were enacted globally to criminalize the laundering of assets itself, whilst at the same time making it much easier for law enforcement to seize assets and for the courts to include confiscation of assets, both as a penalty and a measure of redistributive justice. Against the backdrop of a publicly perceived rise in profit-driven crime, it was generally felt that criminals should be hit where it hurt the most: in their pockets. Criminalization of the act of money laundering and the emphasis on the law enforcement effort to go after the money are a natural extension of the age-old adage that no man should profit from his own crime. Consequently, money laundering touched upon the core beliefs about a just society, where advancing oneself by evading the rules is felt as unfair towards those citizens who abide by the law. As such, money laundering (as any criminal offence) is a crime against society, against the public . . . and there is a public duty to fight and prevent.

By the late 1990s, another dimension was added: the counteracting of the financing of terrorism, and this was further fueled by the US terrorist attacks on September 11, 2001. This dimension worked as a catalyst for the development of ever more stringent anti-money laundering regulations, adopted across the globe, and the emergence of what arguably can be called an entire new industry: Compliance. To a large degree, Compliance became a synonym for *AML* Compliance, AML standing for Anti-Money Laundering (and we will use this well-established acronym throughout the rest of this book), but even that is a pars pro toto, as it commonly also encompasses counter-terrorist financing (CTF).

There were two main factors that contributed to the emergence of AML Compliance. First, there is the down-to-earth fact that law enforcement simply did not and does not have the capability or the capacity to do what is needed to detect money laundering. This is why financial institutions were recruited to partake in law enforcement as *gatekeepers*. Second, there was the shift in public perception about the role of private companies as *Corporate Citizens* and the intrinsic notion of *good citizenship*, linked to widespread notions on corporate moral responsibility, sustainability, and good standing and reputation. This is why the financial institutions, to date, accept the operational and cost burden of AML. Obviously, there is a clear financial incentive for financial institutions to be compliant: the fines imposed by the regulatory watchdogs for non-compliance are enormous. But beneath this mundane motivator there seems to be a genuine acceptance by the financial industry of the role they have to play, as members of society at large, to disallow and prevent the abuse of their systems.

Accepting this role is one thing, it is quite another to live up to it. Being a money laundering prevention gatekeeper imposes all kind of practices that need to be established in order to keep compliant with all regulatory requirements. There is the practice of "know your customer" (KYC), which in a nutshell means establishing that a customer is who he claims to be. Then there is the practice of enhanced due diligence: risk assessing a financial institution's entire customer base on a continuous basis, specifically for the purpose of AML and CTF, and stepping up the monitoring effort or even reconsidering the relationship with the client in the case of high risk. Lastly, there is the practice of transaction monitoring: looking at behavior on the account to identify any suspicious[1] or unusual activity. When such activity is deemed to be found and cannot be refuted by further analysis or investigation, then the financial institution has the obligation to report this to the local Financial Intelligence Unit, which in most countries acts as the

---

[1] Whilst some jurisdictions allow for financial institutions to look for suspicious activities, other countries define this as an activity specifically for law enforcement and against the rule of law to task the banking sector with law enforcement tasks typically associated with the public domain. Whereas the semantic distinction between suspicious and unusual seem to point in the direction of the former compared to the latter, requiring a greater investigation effort by the financial institution, in reality, there does not seem to be much difference other than in the wording.

conduit between the financial institutions and law enforcement, and quite often acts in an investigative capacity itself.

It goes without saying that complying with AML along the lines of these three practices impose a huge administrative burden on the financial institutions, requiring significant investment in front, middle, and back office operations. This applies in particular to transaction monitoring where volumes of customers, accounts, and transactions are significant, and meaningful analysis cannot be done by human labor alone.

And this is where AML software enters the scene. Financial institutions not only deploy electronic means to detect suspicious or unusual activity because of the sheer scale of the data, but also because regulatory watchdogs require them to apply computerized forms of analysis to avoid inconsistency and too much reliance on the (frailty of) human capacity to do so. Whilst computer systems carry out the tasks they can do more efficiently than humans, there is still a role for human analysts and investigators to further verify the validity of the initial electronic analysis. Thus AML transaction monitoring is typically divided into three practices: electronic analysis of transactions and the subsequent generation of *alerts*, the assessment by a human analyst with regard to the validity of the alert(s), and the subsequent filing of a regulatory report if one or more related alerts cannot be refuted as false positives.

The end-to-end process of data collection involves electronic and then human analysis; further investigation of more complex cases; and reporting to the regulators and being able to explain to the regulator how risks have been assessed and mitigated appropriately. All of this constitutes a complex operation, driving up the (manufacturing) cost of financial services delivery and potentially upsetting customers, especially when these customers find themselves unjustifiably subject to a financial investigation, often with the added penalty of not being able to execute transactions and do business. Striking the balance between satisfying both the regulator (compliance), banking customers (services delivery), and shareholders (keeping operational costs down whilst maintaining a good reputation) is of utmost importance for financial institutions today. It is the AML transaction monitoring software that enables financial institutions to do this.

The aim of this book is to explain various aspects of AML transaction monitoring software and will mainly focus on the electronic analysis, both from a perspective of the logic applied in this analysis and the challenges faced during implementation of that software in terms of data integration and other technical aspects.

We, as authors of this book, share a history with SAS, representing a combined 17 years of experience in the implementation, configuration, and redesign of the SAS Compliance Software. SAS has been considered market leader in a number of significant areas relevant for the practice of AML: data integration, analytics, transaction monitoring, case analysis, and reporting.

For any AML software to be taken seriously, is by definition complex. This is because AML transaction monitoring is a multifaceted process. This book aims to provide further clarity mainly on the logic applied to the rules. We hope to provide a good starting point for the beginning AML scenario analyst and administrator. We also hope this will benefit AML alert analysts and investigators, so that they may understand a bit better the output of what we call the alerting engine in terms of the AML and CTF alerts. To that aim this book will put the technical and analytical detail in its business context.

One could legitimately ask if this would not play into the hands of those whose actions we try to detect and allow them to improve their ability to evade detection. We think this not to be the case. Whilst much of the rule-based approach is already in the public domain, the keys are in the actual thresholds financial institutions set as part of these rules for their specific customer segments.

AML AS A COMPLIANCE DOMAIN

Money laundering is commonly defined as the act of providing a seemingly legitimate source for illegitimate funds. In order to conceal the illegitimate origin, the proceeds of economic crimes need to be whitewashed. This will do two things for the criminal beneficiary. Firstly, it will cut the follow-the-money trail leading to the criminal acts, thus avoiding financial assets giveaways of the underlying crimes. But, secondly, even when it does and the criminal is successfully prosecuted and convicted for the criminal proceeds, when successfully laundered, the proceeds will not be subject to confiscation, since no link between these assets and the convicted can be proven. Even if the criminal is imprisoned, the criminal or their family will still be able to dispose of the assets and wealth build from a criminal life.

Anti-Money Laundering, therefore, is, in its widest sense, a worldwide framework of legislation and regulations to prevent abuse of the financial system for the purpose of money laundering, and the practices and processes to comply with this framework. AML attempts to put in barriers to prevent abuse of the financial system by those seeking to conceal the criminal origins of assets and/or the link to their (criminal) ultimate beneficial owners.

What the legislation and regulations have in common is that they require private sector organizations, defined as Financial Service Providers, to put in place a mechanism to prevent the abuse of the financial system by perpetrators of financial crimes. Underpinning this effort is the adage that criminals should not be allowed to profit from their (economic) crimes and respectable financial service providers should not facilitate criminals in doing so. Some hold the view that AML regulations seek to recruit the financial service providers in the active detection of economic crime through the detection of money laundering that is often associated with it.

Compliance and AML cover a wide domain that includes many subdomains, such as customer acceptance (KYC, name screening), customer due diligence, handling of politically exposed persons, ongoing risk assessment, real-time screening on remittance, transaction monitoring, sanctions screening, regulatory reporting, and more. Although there are tools and technologies available for each and all of those aspects, of equal importance is the awareness and understanding of the institutes' personnel about AML principles and regulations and how to apply these in everyday practice. The software is there to assist responsible staff to efficiently and effectively work through the vast amount of customer transaction data, sanctions, and watch lists, and to detect links and patterns that are impossible to see with a human-driven and/or naked eye approach.

Within the various subdomains, transaction monitoring often incurs the highest spending by financial institutes. A transaction monitoring system basically looks at the financial transactions of customers over time and identifies suspicious patterns. Virtually any monitoring rule can be implemented, given the relevant data available. It is an after-the-fact control, instead of preventive. At the time when unusual, suspicious, or otherwise alertable behavior is detected, the money has most likely already been transferred and beyond reach of the financial institution. Reporting to the authorities may, however, still provide useful indications of abnormal behavior for investigation and, thus, be a starting point for an investigation, especially when the alert from one bank can be triangulated with alerts by other banks. In most countries the alerts will end up with the Financial Intelligence Unit (FIU). This may lead to the unravelling of money laundering schemes and rings and possibly lead to prosecution and conviction of those responsible.

Central to AML is the concept of alerting. This has its origin in the gatekeeper function imposed on financial institutions by AML regulations. Counteracting money laundering and its predicate crimes is a task for law enforcement, governed by the rule of law. But in most jurisdictions, they lack the capability, capacity, and, more importantly, the legal backing to directly monitor the transactions of citizens. Financial institutions do, and one important driver of the AML regulations is to mobilize the financial institutions to contribute to the fight against crime by disallowing money launderers and criminals to reap the benefits of their criminal proceeds through the abuse of the financial institutions' infrastructure, products, or services. The main mechanism through which financial institutions contribute is by reporting suspicious or unusual behavior.[2]

Before they can submit a report, financial institutions must have identified a transaction or some behavior as reportable. This internal identification is commonly referred to as an alert. An alert, in this context, can be defined as something to draw attention to indications of possible money laundering or terrorist financing. There is no need

[2]Whilst some jurisdictions task the financial institutions under local AML legislation to detect *suspicious* behavior, in other jurisdictions the viewpoint is held that this belongs to the realm of law enforcement and therefore the financial institutions' involvement goes as far as identifying unusual behavior. This conceptual difference is often reflected in the naming of the reports: e.g. in the US, SAR stands for *Suspicious* Activity *Report*, and the name of the report in the Netherlands, literally translated, is *Unusual Transaction Report*.

to prove this (as that would bring the financial institution into the realm of law enforcement); it suffices to have assessed the likelihood of the alerted behavior pertaining to money laundering (or terrorist financing) as higher than average and worthy of further scrutiny.

Alerts are therefore indications that something may require further attention and those indications can both be human generated and machine generated. A typical scenario of human-generated alerts is when a front office, customer-facing bank employee observes something suspicious and decides to send an e-mail, pick up the phone, or submit an online form to make the Compliance department aware of his or her suspicions. Such notifications may come from employees, but also from customers, other financial institutions, law enforcement, or any other party. To further serve this kind of human alerting, many AML case management systems provide the option for end users to create alerts manually.

However, regulators these days require the majority of transactions to be analyzed individually and in the context of other transactions on the same account and by the same customer or customer group, and the sheer volume of data to be processed means that we can no longer rely on human vigilance alone. This is where software starts to come into the picture. For the past two decades, dedicated software has become increasingly sophisticated in how it analyses the bulk of transactions processed by the financial institutions on a daily basis.

Most commonly, this scrutiny takes place in two phases. The first is in the form of a high-level analysis. If reasons or conditions can be found that refute the hypothesis of money laundering (ML) or terror financing (TF), then the alert will be discarded as a false positive. If, however this cannot be done, the financial institution is obliged to further investigate the alert until a corroborated decision can be made to either report the activity to the regulator or to close the investigation without reporting.

Striking the balance between hit rate and alert productivity is vital to any AML operation driven by a commercially operating financial institution. It is here where a transaction monitoring system supporting a risk-based approach with a more advanced analytical approach, demonstrates its value. A robust system with a proper model in place, and backed by a capability to change the model and scenario thresholds based on analysis, keeps both the regulator satisfied (hit rate) and minimizes the operational cost of alert handling (alert productivity).

THE OBJECTIVES OF AML

Let us give some thought to the objectives from a financial institution's perspective in AML transaction monitoring. We take as an example a private sector, profit-driven financial institution, to whom compliance with legislation is merely a cost of doing business and has to be balanced with customer experience and satisfaction as one of the main drivers for being competitive and generating revenue by financial service delivery.

Regulatory Reporting

If you ask people working in the domain of AML transaction monitoring software about the purposes of such a system, many will respond along the lines of generating AML alerts. Others, who keep in mind the overall business context will say to report to the regulator. Indeed, the entire AML chain culminates in that one final objective: submitting regulatory reports. The financial institution's effort starts with the sourcing of the data and continues with the analysis of the data and the creation of alerts. During alert triage and the case investigation stage the financial institution will decide whether the findings are reportable in terms of the regulatory requirements imposed by the AML regulatory framework. If so, the relevant data must be submitted to the local regulatory authority, often in a format prescribed by the authority. Once submitted, feedback may be received on whether the report has been received correctly (this is technical and can be automated feedback from the recipient system talking to the sending system); other feedback will be around the content (or payload) of the report and may comprise a response from the FIU in terms of requests for further information. Evidently, this is an ongoing, never-ending process, but conceptually speaking many financial institutions consider their job done once the report has been submitted. The submission of the report represents the end of a cycle. At the surface level, when someone says the ultimate objective of the AML transaction monitoring system is to submit regulatory reports required by law to the relevant regulatory recipient, then technically that person would not be wrong. Of course, there is more to it.

Corporate Citizenship versus Profitability

AML regulations put the financial institution between a rock and hard place. Being compliant with legislation and regulations may be intrinsically important for a self-respecting financial institution that is serious about its role as a responsible corporate citizen, but abiding by the law itself does not generate revenue. Those with a more Machiavellian view on things may argue that financial institutions only comply with regulations from a perspective of sustainability and that any fight with the regulatory bodies is doomed to fail, and fines are so high that it endangers profitability, let alone continuity of the financial institution. In that case, satisfying the regulators, whilst avoiding costly fines, does not generate revenue. Revenue is generated by good customer service that customers can appreciate. Being reported to the regulator usually is not. Any financial institution that will see itself as a good corporate citizen is more than willing to comply with the law and even to accept some spillover of customers that are mistakenly or unnecessarily reported to the FIU. This becomes more of a problem if too many legitimate customers end up being reported.

Then there is the operational side of things. As most financial institutions are essentially profit-driven entities in a sometimes highly competitive market it is important to keep operational costs down. Most financial institutions are also publicly registered companies and shareholder value sometimes even trumps profitability in terms of key performance indicators. Shareholder value, by itself, has two sides: in most situations there is a strong correlation with profitability and economic performance, providing one more reason for financial institutions to keep operational costs, including those associated with AML operations, down. Regulatory fines by the regulatory watchdogs for being found insufficiently compliant can be huge and turn a profitable quarter or even year into a non-profitable one. On top of that, shareholder value may shrink upon the news of a major fine, let alone a multitude of fines. See Figure 1.1.

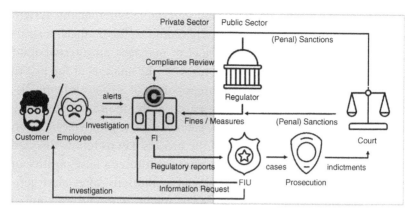

Figure 1.1 Interactions around a financial institution on AML.

To avoid fines, financial institutions, these days, are putting a high emphasis on getting their houses in order and having a robust Compliance program in place to satisfy the regulator. However, and somewhat ironically, the more stringent the scrutiny of transactions, the higher the operating costs, especially when proper scrutiny and avoiding the unnecessary reporting of legitimate customers, at some point in the process, entails human involvement. AML operations, both from a human resource and an IT perspective, come with high costs. All of which are eating into the bottom line and may affect both profitability and shareholder value. So, when it comes to the true objectives behind AML operations, from a publicly registered, profit-driven financial institution's perspective, it all comes down to getting the balance right between overreporting and underreporting and to do so in the most economical way. And *this* is *the* key objective of any AML automation.

About True and False Positives and Negatives

Automated AML transaction monitoring is a form of predictive analysis. Based on a limited set of data that, in itself, will never be conclusive on the subject of whether a transaction constitutes money laundering or is part of it, the system tries to filter those situations to point the analyst in the right direction. Ultimately, a human analyst will look at the generated alerts and determine whether the system correctly singled out that situation. This could be the financial institution's compliance analyst, his/her peer or manager, an internal audit team, a regulatory watchdog audit team, or the analysts of the FIU to whom the truly suspicious events are reported. If an alert is being discarded as not being relevant or not (sufficiently) indicative of money laundering, then we call this a *false positive*. A false positive can mean different things at various stages of the process. Let us follow through the most common process and see what constitutes a false positive at these various stages. For most financial institutions, after alert generation, the process starts with an AML analyst who performs initial *triaging*. This term is borrowed from military practices: after a mass casualty event the sparse group of medical aids will have to prioritize their efforts to maximize the number of lives they will save. They must quickly assess on-site who are beyond help (either dead or so heavily wounded that with the time and effort to stabilize and help them, a lot of others could have been helped but will die because efforts are concentrated on this more badly damaged person). Triaging in AML has nothing to do with saving lives, but the term is used to express that an analyst must first discard the obvious false positives and separate out those that require further investigation. Many Compliance departments (and the same goes for fraud investigation) distinguish between an alert and a case: the latter meaning that one or more alerts are singled out for further scrutiny and more time and effort is put into them to determine whether these alerts should or should not be reported to the FIU. When an analyst discards the alert, then from his/her perspective this will be a false positive, a false alarm so to speak. Both in AML and fraud it is widely accepted that 9 out of 10 alerts are false positives. At this stage, a true positive is when the alert might be potentially reportable and therefore either reporting will be decided or, as in most situations, a case will be launched to further investigate. To simplify: true positive = case. The case investigation can be done by the same analyst who now has decided to devote more time to it, but many financial institutions have created a separate role for that: the investigator or senior analyst. At this stage, the same question is again asked: are the alerts under investigation sufficiently out of line with what one would expect under the same circumstances to raise enough suspicion so that the authorities should be informed? Here a true positive means that the details of the transaction(s) of the account and account holders will have to be shared with the FIU. Here: positive alert = regulatory report. From one perspective, the better the analyst does his job, the higher the ratio between cases created and reports submitted. This process will repeat itself at the level of the FIU, which will research the incoming reports, tie them together where relevant and hand over to law enforcement, which in many countries are specialist financial investigations units. Here, true positive means a report worth further investigation by the FIU, and ultimately it will mean producing a case that prosecution will take to court. Ultimately a true positive alert in its truest sense means that the ultimate money launderers and other who benefit from the money laundering scheme are convicted in court and that the ruling is upheld in appeal. See Figure 1.2.

Obviously financial institutions are usually not concerned with this legal follow-up. At most, records are formally requested by the prosecution to serve as evidence in their case, the financial crimes unit works together with the bank's fraud prevention department in investigation, and/or bank employees are summoned to court to give testimony. For financial institutions, whether an alert is a true or false positive is determined at the early stages of triage, case investigation or submission of the reports. However, it is important to understand that the notion of a false positive and the false positive rate, as key

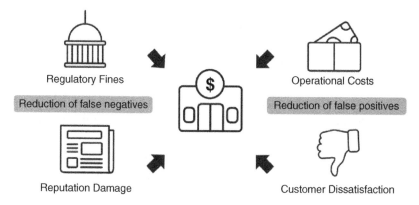

Figure 1.2 Financial Institutions have incentives to reduce both false positive and false negative alerts.

performance indicators for automated transaction monitoring, are multi-interpretable concepts and the team concerned with optimization of the system analytical performance will have to decide which measurement(s) they adopt as their key metric.

A high false positive rate indicates overreporting. While this may not necessarily be an issue for the regulator, as they would want financial institutions to stay on the safe side of things, it is a concern for the AML reporting chain, from financial institutions to FIUs, as too many false alerts may clog the system and actually draw away precious resources and capacity from more relevant investigations. From an operational and cost-efficiency perspective there is a big incentive for financial institutions to keep the false positives down and have a high true positive ratio. A key metric to express the quality of the system is detection rate: how many alerts are produced? But this detection rate must always be offset with the true and false positive rates. A high detection rate means nothing if the true positive alerts are still the proverbial needles in a haystack of false positives. At the moment, a 90% false positive rate, meaning that only 1 in 10 alerts is considered for further investigation, seems to be acceptable and is considered within the risk tolerance of many financial institutions and regulators alike.

Optimizing the analytical systems performance by looking at true or false positive is referred to as above-the-line analysis. This seems to imply there is also a below-the-line equivalent. Below-the-line analysis is concerned with the false *negatives*. A false negative is when the system failed to generate an alert in a situation where (often in hindsight) the Compliance analyst or investigator would have deemed the alert a true positive in the hypothetical case that was generated by the system.

Whereas true and false positive ratio are produced by the normal process of reviewing alerts by Compliance analysts and investigators, the analysis of the negatives requires a special effort and is usually only done periodically (or as a one-off) during a system optimization exercise. Below-the-line testing requires a lowering of the thresholds and then a review of the resulting additional alerts, to assess how many of these alerts *would* have been true positives, which makes them, in fact, false *negatives*. This exercise can be repeated with different threshold values. Depending on the number of false negatives, compared to the number of overall additional alerts, the financial institution may decide to lower the thresholds to have a better hit rate.

From a regulatory viewpoint, false negatives are an issue. The financial institution has to defend why it has set its scenario parameters so high as to knowingly miss out on a number of valid alerts. One reason is that catching those few extra true positives may come with significant overhead for the handling of the additional false positives. This may not be of concern to the regulator, but it certainly is for the financial institution, who seeks to minimize its operational costs.

Analytical software supports the activity of above- and below-the-line testing and helps to run what-if scenarios to optimize the threshold parameters and strike the right balance between effectiveness and efficiency, meaning the best ratio between true and false positives, and true and false negatives. This is the primary, if not sole purpose of any AML transaction monitoring system: getting the balance right in having the most cost-efficient tool that satisfies the regulator in terms of risk tolerance.

THE EVOLUTION OF AUTOMATED TRANSACTION MONITORING

In the field of AML transaction monitoring, technology is applied to support front and back office business processes with a specific business objective: being compliant with relevant legislation and regulations. Inherently these business objectives are predominantly driven by regulatory developments. These regulatory developments are, in turn, partially driven by a learning process on the part of the regulatory supervisors, which is enabled by the technological advancements and the increase in analytical capability. Regulatory developments are also driven by what regulators and law enforcement observe with who they target: the money launderers. Technology and the application of (advanced) analytics has the effect of tightening the net; however, a consequential effect is that those who seek to launder money through the system will adapt and survive. One can truly speak of an evolution whereby the various actors in this monetary and legislative eco-sphere react to each other's progress.

This evolution is increasingly determined and driven by advancements in technology: the introduction of electronic payments, online, and mobile banking on the one hand, and the increasing importance of data and data processing on the other hand. As can be seen in virtually all areas of commerce and corporate activity, everything is electronic-data driven. Transactions in financial institutions, even the ones that seemingly involve only cash, will be registered in a ledger, which these days is an electronic database.

This brings opportunities, but it also brings challenges. Big challenges. The first and foremost challenge concerns the volume of data, which is so big, that human, naked-eye scrutiny of this data is impossible and highly ineffective. Whilst this may seem an open door, it should be realized that even today some financial institutions rely, for parts of their transaction monitoring, on analysts who have as a day job to cast their eye on hardcopy printed lists of transactions, merely to see if they can catch any irregularities. These lists are at worst random samples of transactions and at best a tiny subset of the overall volume of transactions filtered out by very simplistic and crude rules, sometimes built in as a formula into the spreadsheet used for this purpose. Needless to say, this is a highly insufficient approach to transaction monitoring and most probably will not bear a regulatory approval, not today at least. But, apparently, it had done so in the past.

From a technology perspective we can distinguish between three areas of expertise that have enabled the evolution of AML transaction monitoring. These are data integration, analytics, and data visualization. The evolution of AML transaction monitoring followed a path along the lines of these areas, in this particular order. Whilst initially the concern was with how to link into the electronically available data and get all the data into one place for the use and analysis of the one specific goal of AML, the focus has now shifted to the analytics applied to that data to refine models and increase alert productivity. Whereas automated alerting has taken up an increasingly important role, most regulatory frameworks will not allow for a fully automated process, and the human element is still considered an essential component of any AML operation. To make sense out of the massive volumes of data and the information that can be drawn from it, data visualization is claiming its place.

Here, we also find an educational cycle between human and computer. While it is human expertise and knowledge that created the rules that instructed the computers, it is then with the aid of computers, databases, and electronic data analysis tools that humans learned much more about the data. The new insights are then reapplied in ever more elaborate and sophisticated models. Models are then trained by or with the help of electronic data, often enriched by human investigation, and gradually we move into the direction of self-learning machines that only need minimum input from humans to further train their own models and increase their own capability of separating the wheat from chaff.

From Rule-Based to Risk-Based

AML and, in particular, transaction monitoring are, on the one hand, driven by regulatory developments which, in a strongly simplified way of speaking, represent how the world should be, the realm of desirable. On the other hand, the transaction monitoring is also driven by the progress the world has made in computing. Computing power and the ability to analyze big data in increasingly shorter amounts of time represents the realm of the possible. The increase in sheer computing power has had and will have big implications for AML transaction monitoring, especially the sophistication in the detection of unusual or suspicious behavior.

We have discussed the move from a rule-based to a risk-based system. In a nutshell, this move was the result of the system being clogged by a vast volume of false positives because the initial rule, prescribed by the regulators, were far too crude. This to the dismay of the FIUs, which lacked the capacity to review hundreds of thousands of incoming reports. Financial institutions saw operational cost towering without any evident benefit, and customers found themselves the subject of alerting for no good reason at all. The financial institutions jointly indicated that the regulators should trust them and allow them to replace or at least augment the initial hardcoded rules with more sophisticated scenarios.

The name of the game became find the odd one out. If a bank's customer base predominantly consisted of oranges, and not so many apples, then under a rule-based regime, the apples were the ones reported on. Continuing this metaphor, under the risk-based regime, this shifted from finding the rotten orange amongst the healthy oranges and the rotten apple amongst the healthy apples. It further seeks to separate less rotten from severely rotten fruit. Of course, this is a simplification of the difference, but it serves to make clear that the ongoing evolution of transaction monitoring is one of continuing refinement of the way we can analyze data.

The risk-based approach incorporates a number of risk concepts that are utilized in different ways in transaction monitoring. Ultimately, transaction monitoring is looking at transaction risk: what is the likelihood that *this* transaction is concealed money laundering and therefore concealing criminal funds? The risk of the transaction is calculated on the basis of algorithms that incorporate other notions of risk. See Figure 1.3.

One of these notions is the risk that the parties to the transactions represent. If these are internal parties, i.e. *customers*, then a customer risk level, most commonly in terms of high, medium, or low, is established for the party. This customer risk may itself be based on a calculative score card or be the result of an investigation into the customer. Obviously, the latter is not done for all customers – that would be impractical – but for the high-value private and corporate customers,

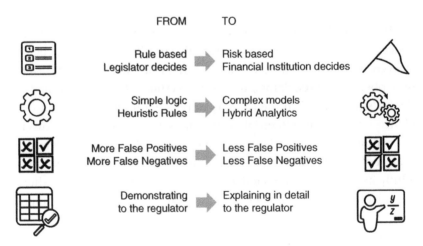

FROM   TO

Rule based ➡ Risk based
Legislator decides   Financial Institution decides

Simple logic ➡ Complex models
Heuristic Rules   Hybrid Analytics

More False Positives ➡ Less False Positives
More False Negatives   Less False Negatives

Demonstrating ➡ Explaining in detail
to the regulator   to the regulator

Figure 1.3 Evolution of transaction monitoring.

it is not uncommon to pinpoint a precise risk level if they are teetering on the edge of high risk. This is where the notions of Enhanced Due Diligence (EDD) and Special Due Diligence (SDD) come into play. The majority of customer risk is, however, calculated based on information gathered during account opening and throughout the lifespan of the customer relationship.

Most financial institutions are also risk assessing their own products. Product risk is often a separate category of risk that feeds into customer risk or directly finds its way to the transaction monitoring risk assessment. For example, purely domestic and common products, like a normal current or tax exempted savings account are assessed to represent low risk (for money laundering) and more exotic products with a foreign currency component or products that have been known to be favored by money launderers in the past may be allocated a higher risk level.

This brings us to a third risk dimension, that of country risk. Most regulatory frameworks require financial institutions to look at country risk separately. Most, if not all, financial institutions with cross-border activity maintain risk scores or levels for each country or territory. Sometimes these are simply copied from a subscription, but the larger financial institutions commonly have processes in place to assess or even calculate the risk level for all countries and territories worldwide. Under the rule-based system the non-governmental Financial Action Task Force (FATF) maintained a list of non-cooperative countries and territories and local regulations incorporated this as a blacklist. The list still exists, but over the years, countries featuring on this FATF list made sure they improved their AML regime and were subsequently taken off.

Countries may still appear on the so-called watchlists, alongside individuals, entities, and registered vessels. Watchlists arguably can be categorized as one of the risk factors. They feed into the customer risk, although most commonly they are used during the onboarding process of a customer and appearance on the list will prevent accounts being opened for the individual or entity. But also, transaction monitoring scenarios commonly include a number of rules that specifically look at parties and jurisdictions involved in a payment that are on watchlists.

Apart from these potential high-risk components of a transaction, there is a different notion of transaction risk that ties in with the assessment of the transaction as being unusual. The underlying premise is that the more unusual a transaction is for this customer or this account, the higher the ML risk. Determining whether a transaction is unusual has become an increasingly sophisticated process, in which ever more data is drawn into the equation. A transaction can be unusual from different angles and most transaction monitoring systems look at it from multiple perspectives.

First there is the perspective of being unusual compared to the usage of the account. Many algorithms look at how the account has been used and whether one or more transactions are (suddenly) deviating strongly from that pattern. One can look at the size of the transaction and the number of transactions in a given interval (velocity), but one has to account for more gradual increases or decreases of income and spending patterns, as these are in fact quite ordinary. One must account for seasonal variations: many individual customers and most retailers use their accounts more actively during the festive season, and sudden slumps or bursts are associated with vacation periods.

Further, the behavior on the account can, and often is, assessed in comparison with similar accounts to avoid comparing apples and oranges. High-net-worth customers will have a significantly different pattern from middle- and low-income customers. Retail business accounts may show very different patterns than those of manufacturing businesses. And even within retail, a low-end retailer in a busy shopping area will show a completely different income and outgoings stream than a more exclusive high-end retailer. Most financial institutions therefore divide their customer base into segments and either have separate rules in place specific to each segment or have set threshold parameters different across the thresholds. Those financial institutions that go a step further introduce the concept of peer groups: each customer or account is allocated to a group that is expected to behave similarly. A group profile is built, dynamically or statically, and transactions and summary profiles for the account are compared to the group profile. If there is a significant deviation, then an alert will be produced.

As we have mentioned above, the move from rule based to risk based brought about a shift in responsibility and accountability. In a rule-based system, there is hardly any responsibility for the financial institutions beyond simply ensuring the rules are applied. The price to pay was a tsunami of alerts and reports, most of them being false positives. A risk-based approach may stem the flood of false positives and reports to be filed, but at the cost of increased liability and the investment into a framework that justifies the (risk) approach taken. As we have seen above, the risk-based approach opens the field wide, as there are endless variations of the approach and countless decisions to be made. At any given time, the regulatory watchdog may review that system and assess its robustness. Financial institutions will have to be able to explain why they set up transaction monitoring the way they did. If country risk is part of the process, then it may have to explain separately how country risk levels are arrived at and what is done with that knowledge further downstream. And so this goes for all the other concepts of risk that together make up the risk-based approach. These approaches and the decisions need to be documented in a way that they explain to a relative outsider (regulatory auditors) how it all works and that it is sufficiently robust.

A lot of the mathematical logic is built into the transaction monitoring software. It is, however, the financial institutions who will need to understand the software as AML accountability cannot be deferred to the software supplier. Financial institutions are free to hire consultants from the software vendor to assist with regulatory review. However, from the perspective of regulatory scrutiny, it is always a good thing if the solution is white box as opposed to black box. Black box software conceals most or parts of its built-in logic, its inner mechanisms, most often to protect its intellectual property. The software vendor might fear that making their solution fully transparent exposes them to IP theft. For example, the customer itself may decide to end the contract and build a solution themselves based on what they have learned from the vendor's software. Not all software vendors have the same fear and, like SAS, take a white box approach and are willing to give the customer access to (virtually) any component of the system. This means that analysts, consultants, and coders can dive deep into the system to understand how and explain why the transaction monitoring system yields the result it does. Our common experience is that most financial institutions feel more at ease with a system that hides no secrets in terms of how risk is being calculated and used and how alerts are generated.

From Static to More Dynamic Transaction Monitoring

In the quest for reducing false positives and the detection of relevant, i.e. significant deviations from behavioral patterns on one or multiple accounts, the aim is to refine the mechanism by way of recognizing (more complex) patterns.

To put it simply, if every transaction is measured against the same fix threshold, such as any cash deposit of (the equivalent of) $10,000, this would be a very crude and most likely ineffective way to identify suspicious or unusual transactions. First, such a straightforward rule seems to assume that cash deposits are more likely to be done by money launderers than by law abiding citizens. It is true that, to a certain extent, crime economies are largely cash based. This is, for example, typically the case in drug trafficking, where across the entire chain from manufacturing through wholesale to retail distribution, cash seems to be the preferred method of payment. Much of that cash is cycled in the underworld drug economy, upstream in the supply chain, but many operational costs, such as pay-out of staff, purchasing of vehicles for transport, and hiring of warehouses, are also paid for in cash. From the net profit for the criminal entrepreneur some will be stashed as cash; some of it will be lent to others in cash, and paid back in cash; and for only part of it there will be a need to put it in a bank account. But many forms of crime are not predominantly cash based, such as many forms of fraud, and there is no need to siphon off profits held in cash and make large cash deposits. Also, cash deposits may be common in some perfectly legal trades, such as for new and second-hand cars. Putting up a fixed threshold will erect a type of barrier for cash-rich money launderers, but that will also affect a bank's legitimate customers in a cash-based industry and so will come at an operational and/or commercial cost. And to what effect? This barrier will be (and has been) quickly recognized and circumvented with structuring techniques, such as smurfing. Smurfing is the breakdown of large sums of money into (well) below threshold chunks and distributing it across multiple depositors who use multiple accounts to avoid unwanted attention. These days transaction monitoring systems will not only look for above-the-threshold deposits, but also for amounts that are just below it. This does not make the rule more sophisticated or more dynamic; it is still a fixed threshold, except that the one for internal alerting is a different one than the one that is communicated publicly. But such sub-rules are often combined with an additional threshold on a minimum number of such below-the-threshold deposits. By doing so the financial institution has taken its first step towards a more dynamic rule.

The simplest form of a dynamic rule is where the threshold is manually set and reviewed either periodically or even on a driven basis. The form brings relatively high operational costs and seems inefficient. The setting of the threshold needs to be described in some type of process to avoid arbitrariness and regulatory exposure. The second form of threshold setting is relatively rare for AML transaction monitoring and more often seen in the context of fraud and abuse incident response, and heavily driven by alert analysis and case investigation. A good example is the activation or refocusing of a geographic rule if it is suspected that a certain postcode area has become the habitat of a fraud or money laundering ring, with involvement of ATMs, or multiple accounts being set up at local branches. That postcode area will be temporarily set to high risk to allow more alerts to be created and analyzed, in order to identify the issues and mitigate the problem. The perpetrators are likely to move on to other areas, if not caught by law enforcement. Either way the risk for that area decreases and likely either the same or a new ring will pop its head up somewhere else, thus making the rule obsolete or dysfunctional without change.

Such manual dynamic rules are not common in the world of transaction monitoring, but those which adjust thresholds automatically, are. And they come in various degrees of complexity.

The modus operandi known as smurfing, as described above, is a good example of the need for more dynamic rules, supplementary to the fixed threshold rules, such as the one for cash deposits. To detect smurfing, one needs to zoom out from the micro event of the single transaction and take into consideration a range (or history) of transactions, preferably across a number of accounts potentially associated with a number of account holders. Let us set aside, for now, the complexity of identifying multiple customers (the "smurfs") with different accounts – these customers are not usually blue skinned (as the label given to them would suggest) so there is no straightforward way of telling whether they are all colluding as part of a wider smurfing scheme. There are ways of doing so, from a transaction monitoring perspective, but let us look into simpler cases first.

The simplest form of looking at transactions is dynamically. This means to look at transactions dynamically from the perspective of the account, namely the *history* of the account. One can either look for gradual or sudden changes on the account that may arouse suspicion, or for certain patterns *over time*. For the latter a lookback period is defined (usually an *x* number of days) and the thresholds need to be exceeded within that time frame. In the smurfing example the scenario could look like this:

> *Create an alert when over the past 7 days at least three cash deposits were made with an amount between the fixed threshold value ($10,000) and 95% of that amount ($ 9,499).*

Although this rule would look over time, it is not dynamic, as the principal threshold value is fixed and the secondary threshold is derived from that. It would be dynamic if the percentage of the lower threshold were made dependent on the number of cash transaction over that period. For example:

> *Create an alert when over the past 7 days at least three cash deposits were made with an amount between the fixed threshold value ($10,000) and 100 − CD(n) * 2% of that amount, with a minimum of 75%. CD(n) is the number of Cash Deposits.*

The more cash deposits are made to the account the lower the alerting threshold for the cash deposit. Such a rule could be applied to a single account, or to all accounts of one customer, or even to all accounts by all customers who are connected to each other by at least one joint account. This would give a much better and more dynamic chance of detecting smurfing activity.

Dynamics of much higher complexity are possible, whereby a range of analytical measurements is applied to an account to detect a pattern and predict within what range the next transaction will be in case of normal behavior. Transactions that exceed this dynamically calculated threshold will be considered unusual (for a particular account, given that history of the account). Such a rule, for example, would run like this:

> Create an alert when at least two cash deposits exceed the amount of two times the standard deviation for *cash deposits on that account for the last 28 days.*

Whilst still looking at cash deposits, this scenario compares the latest cash deposit with the others over the last 28 days and allows for one-off spikes as well as gradual increase. Although money launderers could still avoid alerting by gradually increasing their cash deposits, they would have to do so patiently and be aware of such a rule and, preferably, its threshold parameters.

Current practice is to have such dynamic rules supplementary to the fixed rules, and the fixed cash deposit threshold rule acts as a safety blanket, whilst the dynamic rule deals with those schemes that seek to circumvent the (known) fixed threshold rule.

How this makes sense can be seen when taking into consideration a mule account operation. In a typical mule operation money launderers seek to recruit account holders and use their accounts to channel funds. These accounts are attractive to criminals as they often already have an (untainted) history and account holders are classified as low risk. Typical examples are students, job starters, and low- or middle-income elderly, who are either naively ignorant or deliberately pretend to be to the true nature of the funds channeled through their accounts. For the dynamic rule described above to be effectively circumvented, the money launderers would have to know what normal behavior is for each of the recruited mule accounts. But this information is not easily disclosed without raising suspicion. If the accounts are recruited by means of earn-money-easy-from-your-home types of job advertisement, it would be easier to trick people into receiving and sending specific funds (as part of the job) than it would be for them to obtain and share with their employers the history on their account, especially that history from before they took the job. This would easily set off alarm bells. On a side note, obviously one of the reasons for the money launderers to recruit mules is because they do not have to worry about alarms bells going off, since certainly they would not have given away their true identity to the mule account holders.

More complex dynamic rules build profiles for accounts and potentially also peer groups (numerous accounts clustered together on the assumption that the behavior on them will be very similar) on a monthly, yearly, or even broader basis, whereby profiles are constructed automatically and expectation for the next days or months are set. Averages and transaction volumes and amounts could be set for incoming and outgoing payments and could be differentiated for payment types or channels.

The dynamic rules described so far do not consider the outcome of the alert analysis or investigation. In a way, the epitome of dynamic rules is where the line between automated parameter settings and rule creation converge. This brings us into the realm of machine learning.

Latest Trends: Machine Learning and Artificial Intelligence

In the last decade the notions of artificial intelligence (AI) and machine learning have gradually found their way to virtually every domain of automation, AML being no exception. The developments can be seen as ultimately replacing the human element in the processes, i.e. completely relying on machines, algorithms, and the self-learning capability of the software. They can also be viewed as augmenting humans involved in the process, whereby data will be processed in such a way that it allows the human worker to concentrate on that part of the work that requires judgment.

When thinking in terms of augmenting or even replacing the human element in AML processes, one must distinguish between (at least) two parts in the overall business process where humans play a role: the scenario design and optimization process, and the triage/investigation process. At face value, both seem to lend themselves to machine learning. But at closer look this seems less evident.

Let us start with the scenario design and optimization part of the process. This part is where the objective of detecting suspicious activity in the use of financial products and services – suspicious from an ML or TF perspective – is translated into scenarios and analytical models that can calculate the propensity of certain behavior based purely on the data that is fed into the system about the account holder, the account, the financial transactions related to that account, and the non-financial transactions (changes) to both account and account holder.

Transaction monitoring for AML purposes is, in its core, an industrial application of forecasting. Forecasting is a field in analytics whereby data is used to set up and train models to optimize the output of these models in terms of the desired end result. For money laundering this end result and the optimization thereof are, as discussed above, to maximize the hit-rate whilst at the same time minimizing false positives.

Analytical software, such as that developed by SAS, already assists analysts in analyzing data and training the models. This software, in the right hands, can be used to analyze data, identify statistically relevant indicators, and create new rules. Artificial intelligence (AI) is these days usually associated with neural networks as the analytical method that, backed by sufficient computing power, allows machines to become autodidacts. Neural networks as an advanced analytical technique made its introduction into the world of analytics some time ago. It has also entered the realm of applied analytics in AML.

Predominantly analytical software is used to optimize the performance of both new rules, through initial threshold settings, or existing rules, e.g. by doing what-if analysis on slight changes of the threshold settings and what is called below-the-line analysis. We will discuss these in more (technical) detail in following chapters. From an analytical perspective rule optimization is in fact the training of an analytical model. Training of models is either done supervised or unsupervised. Supervised training means that data is added that captures the outcome of the analysis in terms of something being either correct or incorrect. In training AML transaction monitoring models, the correct outcome is a productive alert; the incorrect outcome is an unproductive alert. Instead of alerts, one could also look at cases and the conclusions of the case investigation: submitting a regulatory report would count as the correct outcome; dismissing the case and closing it without follow-up action would be the incorrect outcome. The point is that these outcomes can tell the system what to look for specifically and the forecasting software can use that to find strong correlations in the data that are indicators of money laundering, or at least productive alerts. Forecasting software, which has been in use for more than a decade in the world of money laundering, is essentially a form of machine learning, whereby the outcome is fed back into system that (re)trains the models and that can suggest new rules or new settings to rules to optimize its productivity (which is the ratio between productive alerts versus non-productive alerts). If the feedback loop would be closed, meaning that alert and case disposition data would be automatically fed back into the system, and if the system would automatically retrain itself periodically and tweak the threshold parameters on the fly, then in fact this would be full-on machine learning.

However, financial institutions are reluctant, for good reasons, to close the feedback loop and automate this part. At the moment, even for those financial institutions that apply advanced analytics to train the models, rule optimization is still a periodic human-driven effort. The (re)training software is not considered sufficiently sophisticated to let the system be in charge of running multiple analyses *and* let the computer decide which set of threshold parameters work best. And probably the regulator who has to assess the robustness of the approach would refuse to sign off on a closed loop mechanism where a computer can tweak the detection scenarios without human interference. Instead, financial institutions choose to periodically engage in an exercise to manually retrain the models. The same analytical software is being used and the same methods applied, but all driven by analytical experts who evaluate the outcome together with domain experts. The decision to change threshold parameters, to deactivate a non-productive rule, or to introduce a completely new scenario is still made by humans.

Even if financial institutions were to move to a closed feedback loop system, transaction monitoring would still not be fully automated to the extent that human judgment would be fully taken out of the equation. The machine would still train itself on the basis of the supervision data, which is a column in the data set that tells it if the outcome is a correct or incorrect one. That final verdict for each alert or case, whether productive or non-productive, is being given by a human. It is the AML analyst, whose job is to look at alerts and the data contained in them, who has to decide whether to discard it as a false positive or continue investigating until a decision can be reached as to whether to file a regulatory report or not. The keystone holding the metaphorical arc of transaction monitoring together is the human analyst assessing the system generated alert as a true or false positive. And the same applies to below-the-line analysis where periodically thresholds are lowered to allow for the generation of alerts in situations that would not have been generated under the actual settings. These alerts are scrutinized by human analysts, just to see if the actual settings do not miss too many false negatives, i.e. situations that are indicative of money laundering but were not scooped up in the net of the thresholds.

Ultimately, one can foresee the in-house analyst's judgment being replaced by the external feedback from the recipient regulatory body. As long as the recipient FIU does not communicate to the financial institution that it receives too many false positives, or periodic reviews and investigations do not bring to surface situations where reports should have been filed but weren't, the financial institution could continue to trust their self-learning software to do a proper job. This day still seems far off.

Thus, whilst notions of machine learning and AI are not new to AML transaction monitoring and will claim an increasingly prominent position, there will still be a need in the foreseeable future for data analysts developing and training the models and optimizing the rules, and domain analysts investigating and assessing alerts as true or false positives.

Latest Trends: Blockchain

Some say that what the internet and the World Wide Web meant for the online exchange of information, blockchain will mean for the online exchange of value. If true, one can hardly overstate the importance of blockchain. And what will be its impact on money laundering and the software we offer to help our customers combat money laundering?

Blockchain is a technology and a process to decentralize and harden a ledger. Perhaps this is better explained by what blockchain is a reaction to. Up until blockchain, online or electronic transactions were always mitigated by a central guardian of the ledger, such as the bank holding your account or the clearing house processing batches of payments. What money sits where and goes from whom to whom is kept record of in a secure file or database, providing a single point of vulnerability to malicious actions. Tampering in some way with the one single electronic ledger would suffice to commit payment fraud. And it also requires a central agent who has de facto power over the transactions for all of its customers. Customers have to trust the banks. Blockchain seeks to mitigate the risk of tampering and take out the central agent. At its very core, blockchain seeks to provide a safe way of transferring value and keeping records in a world where trust is not presumed.

Blockchain technology rests on five principles:

1. The ledger is public: verified copies are freely downloadable.
2. It is distributed: many synched copies of the ledger exist across the world.
3. There is consensus: for transactions to be added (hence executed) a majority or threshold consensus must exist amongst the miners who verify the ledger with the new transactions and those miners are competing and not colluding.
4. There is transparency: the ledger will contain a full history of all transactions.
5. There is ownership: one has to own credits before these can be transferred, going short is not an option.

Ownership verification is possible due to the transparency of the full ledger. A batch of transactions to be added to the ledger is presented as a new block to be added to the existing ledger, the chain with the full history of transactions of the same currency. A block (of new transactions) will be presented to be added to the chain and each block contains a cryptographic puzzle based on the contents of the block but also of the entire ledger. This puzzle needs to be solved and the block will only be added to the chain if a predetermined number of checkers, called miners, agree on the outcome. Miners are self-subscribing participants that utilize vast computing power to solve the puzzle as quickly as their machines allow. The first who comes up with an answer that is similar to the answer found by the others, will get an incentive. For Bitcoin, for example, the first to solve the cryptographic puzzle, upon verification, will unlock a Bitcoin. Hence the mining metaphor. The more complex the cryptographic puzzle, the more computing power (and time) is needed to solve it. Recently it was estimated that the energy required for one Bitcoin transaction could provide electricity for almost 9 US households for a day. At the moment, Bitcoin has set the complexity of the encryption, so that on average every 10 minutes a new block is added to the chain. Once a new version has been confirmed it will discard any variations and all copies are synched to the one new version. With the next block presented this cycle repeats itself.

Blockchain is safe because it requires many miners to confirm a version before the chain (and all of its copies) is updated. This means that any alterations by fraudsters will have to be on the majority of copies, otherwise it will perish in this distributed verification process. Since there are many miners and these are unrelated and unlikely to collude, it is more difficult for fraudsters to tamper with the ledger. Also, computer glitches, creating different versions of the ledger are ironed out this way. Blockchain is also safe because the full ledger is public (anyone can obtain the latest copy online) and unchangeable. Any change to historic blocks will create a deviating version, meaning that the outcome of the cryptographic puzzle will change, and that version will not survive.

Blockchain is believed to revolutionize payments, or even broader, the exchange of value. Blockchain enables peer-to-peer transactions in a world where trust is lacking. It will also allow taking out the middleman, the financial institutions that currently operate as the guardian keepers of their own ledgers (as a global collective) process all transactions. Financial institutions fear that blockchain will do to them what online retail commerce has done to many brick-and-mortar stores. Blockchain, however, may be unstoppable and banks are now exploring ways to incorporate block chain into their ways of doing business. Nasdaq has opened a new trading platform, Linq, specifically for blockchain-based currency. In other words, blockchain is here probably to stay and it will be transforming the financial system;

hence, it will be transforming AML and Compliance. If blockchain is relevant for our own customers, which in the space of AML are mainly banks, then sooner rather than later it will become relevant to those providing software to support them.

The impact of blockchain on AML is threefold. Firstly, on a strictly technical level, it will transform the way (part of) the transactions are fed into the AML system. Rather than an extract from the core the chain itself will be offered. Would this really change the way data is loaded into our system through mapping and ETL? Not necessarily. Does it mean that there will be no limits regarding the history, as the blockchain will be available in its entirety? I am not convinced. For data management and volume and related performance reasons, it would be preferable to keep the flow of data constant and increase will only be permitted if related to organic growth (more transactions on a single day). It would almost make transaction monitoring easier, as blockchain itself has an inherent data quality control aspect to it. From a data integration point of view, blockchain's impact is probably limited to the data pertaining to the actual transaction, and not so much the other data, such as for accounts, customers, or households.

Secondly, there are many who fear blockchain will undermine the current AML effort, mainly because it seems to facilitate anonymous transactions. Whereas an intrinsic part of blockchain and blockchain safety is in its transparency, this is only relative transparency. Only within the chain can one see which transactions involved which accounts. Accounts are coined wallets, and are in fact secured IP addresses. Some cryptocurrencies allow for people and entities to open an account without proper identification or verification of the true identity behind those who own or operate the wallet. In a way this is not different from the, now forbidden, number accounts operated by Swiss and Austrian banks until a decade ago, or from the still existing practice in some tax havens where financial institutions are legally protected from disclosing the identity of the ultimate beneficial owners behind the accounts or corporate entities. In a way this does not seem an issue created by blockchain technology, but by how we use this technology. As a federal prosecutor stated in her Ted Talk: "most successful technology is often first adopted by criminals." Like with the conventional financial system, blockchain providers should ensure KYC at account opening. Like with conventional banking, the ledger itself may contain customer references that make the customer non-identifiable, as long as they keep these identities and can map them. It is a matter of legal debate and, if necessary, legislation to make sure blockchains used for financial purposes and cryptocurrency are considered or brought under the umbrella of regulatory governance.

Thirdly, naturally following on from the above, the transparency of the blockchain and the inherent security may also benefit AML. Granted, this transparency and the hardness of the public ledger primarily benefits fraud prevention and only to a lesser degree AML. Irregularities in the data loaded into the transaction monitoring system have never been a main concern: the correctness of the transaction data is almost never questioned, at least from an ML concern. Having the full history of the entire ledger freely available obviously will help investigators, both on the side of law enforcement and on the side of the financial service providers to trace back money to their original accounts. From a data visualization perspective, the full ledger seems to take care of data preparation and is probably easier than getting the same data over a similar period of time together from traditional core banking systems. The capacity to process, mine, and visualize Big Data may become a key factor, simply from a sheer data volume perspective. It is widely known that blockchain crypto mining requires vast amounts of computing resources, but that is primarily due to the way the decryption algorithms work. AML data analysis of the ledger is probably less resource intensive, but the sheer size of the ledger may cause issues. One possible solution could be not to analyze the ledger in full, but use it as source data and load the relevant data (or delta) into the core database as is currently common practice.

Should the Compliance Domain Prepare for Blockchain?

The answer is an unreserved Yes. There are too many voices raising blockchain and cryptocurrency as a game changer, for the financial industry to ignore. Customers are already asking what we can do for them in terms of blockchain, also within the subspace of AML and financial crimes. At least we should prepare ourselves by starting to understand blockchain and the impact it will have on existing and new (types of) financial institutions and the software used. Banks are now starting to explore blockchain technology, and regulators will also get involved in the conversation sooner rather than later. If anything, blockchain will present the Compliance domain with an opportunity to combine transaction monitoring analytics with big data and meaningful data visualization. AML, pushed by blockchain, will move into a space where multiple disciplines will come together . . . and right up the sleeve of data analytics.

Risk-Based Granularity and Statistical Relevance

For statistical analysis in general it applies that the more data, the better. This is particularly true when the data is structured. Financial institutions, even those of smaller size, produce high volumes of data, especially around their core commodity services and products. However, data density is not always equally spread. Large financial institutions stretch their arms widely and may also provide products and services tailored to niche markets, servicing only small and selective groups of customers. As a result, the statistical analysis may become less meaningful and lack statistical relevance.

In addition, the shift from rule- to risk-based system has introduced the notion of profiling: to determine if a transaction or a pattern of transactions is unusual, one must make sure the customer is compared against like customers. This can easily backfire; the more a financial institution knows about the specifics of a customer, the more it knows to what extent this customer can or cannot be meaningfully compared with others. Customer segmentation is necessary to meet the requirements of a risk-based approach, but a profiling that is too granular will come at the cost of data volume, to the extent that statistical relevance will become an issue.

A good example is trade-based money laundering, whereby price levels or volumes of traded goods are deliberately overstated in the contracts and not aligned with the underlying commercial reality, if there is one: the trade can also be wholly made up. This requires enough reference data that is comparable. In a trade of goods, a unit price is affected by type of goods (of course), country, season, expiry date, unit, and also trading contract terms. With all these parameters, it can hardly get enough data for reference. In one situation we studied two-year trade transactions. The largest few groups of unit price (same type of goods, same country, unit, etc.) had only 200 data points, not satisfactory for a statistical analysis; most other groups had much fewer data points. The move from a rule-based to a risk-based AML framework can also be reconstrued as a move from a strict formal know-your-customer to a genuinely know-the-business-of-your-customer. On the one end of the (rule-based) spectrum, financial institutions merely had to establish the veracity of a customer's identity (or the identity of their registered controlling persons) by way of a relatively superficial check of the ID documents. Since its early days KYC and ID verification as part of that has taken a flight of its own, which we will not discuss in this book. At the other end of the spectrum there is the notion that a financial institution, mainly through its account managers, knows all financial ins and outs of a business or an individual that they provide services for . . . and in case of any suspicion of irregularities the account manager should contact the Compliance or Security department. This turns every customer-facing employee into a part-time AML enforcement officer. This is very much a human-driven approach, effectuated through training, awareness, internal policies, and codes of conduct. Theoretically, there could be a data-driven approach if sufficient data would be gathered. This could be done if AML were to include external data, e.g. on demographics and/ or if financial institutions in a country would share data. However, the development to include external data for improved statistical accuracy is not driven by financial institutions as long as the law and regulations do not require them so. Other than in the field of fraud prevention, in AML there is no direct incentive for financial institutions to further increase the complexity of their AML operations beyond what at any given point in time suffices to meet regulatory demand. Even if data would be obtainable or become available, restraint may be required.

From a data-driven transaction monitoring software design and delivery perspective, commercial software vendors have to serve the interest of their commercial customers and optimize a system within the (risk and cost) appetite of the financial institution. Ultimately the financial institution, not the software or its vendor, is held responsible for compliance with law and regulations. It is therefore the financial institution's decision how and what to implement for the purpose of detection of money laundering in transaction monitoring.

Summary

With a history of over three decades, AML has made a long journey that has not yet come to an end. This journey has been one of learning and mutual education of the regulator and financial institutions governed by the regulatory framework.

In the childhood years of AML, simple rules based on known money laundering modus operandi associated with specific forms of crime led to an extremely high and unworkable number of false positives and Compliance departments and FIUs alike were overburdened and operating neither effectively nor efficiently.

The gradual shift to a risk-based system, which is still ongoing, opened the doors widely for a data-driven approach, where computer-driven analytics provide the answers to ever bigger data analysis and meaningful transaction monitoring and customer risk assessment, whilst at the same time reducing operational costs to an (already very high) minimum.

Whilst human judgment, for the foreseeable future, will remain to be an important factor, financial institutions and software vendors alike are introducing advanced technology in an increasing number of steps on the journey from transaction monitoring and regulatory reporting. Automated computing is not only introduced more widely across this chain, but also embedded more deeply than before.

Models, and how these are trained, are becoming ever more sophisticated, enabled by a parallel growth of computing power (at a relative low-cost increase or even decrease) and the ability to process higher volumes of data (we're talking billions of transactions these days) at higher levels of sophistication.

Financial institutions seek to meet ever more stringent regulatory requirements and avoid the huge regulatory fines and maintain acceptable levels of operational costs and resource demand. And they do so by investing in AML transaction monitoring and case management software that allows them to go bigger, better, faster . . . and still enable them to explain to the regulator that (and, equally important, *how)* they are doing a proper job as gatekeeper, protecting the financial system from (at least the most blatant) abuses by money launderers.

With the emergence of artificial intelligence and (deep) machine learning and with the introduction of cryptocurrency and blockchain, a new era is beginning for AML Compliance. Rather than invoking a paradigm shift in how we monitor transactions and risk-assess our customers, these developments, from a software manufacturing and implementation perspective, may well be a matter of scaling and absorbing the latest and greatest from the field of data management and analytics.

CHAPTER 2

Transaction Monitoring in Different Businesses

Money laundering and terrorist financing are criminal offences in most, if not all, jurisdictions worldwide. The scope of anti-money laundering pivots around two dimensions that are each delineated by a legal definition.

We touched upon the first dimension in Chapter 1: the definition of money laundering, and closely related to that, the list of predicate crimes, the proceeds of which may be subject to money laundering. As mentioned, this started in the late 1980s with the proceeds of trafficking of narcotic substances, and later evolved to also encompass human trafficking, proceeds from smuggling, and other profit-driven and/or economic crimes, such as fraud and corruption. Also, the financing of terrorism was brought under the regulatory compliance umbrella, although strictly not under the name of money laundering, but counter-terrorism financing.

The other dimension determining the scope of the regulatory compliance domain is formed by the group of entity types that are subject to regulatory compliance, as delineated by the definition of "financial institution." In the early days, only banks with a banking license fell under the regime of local AML regulations. It was not until the early 2000s that insurance companies were considered financial institutions under the AML regulatory framework. And even later, in Europe, with the introduction of the Third Anti-Money Laundering Directive a range of other business types were brought under that umbrella: money exchange businesses, (online) gambling businesses, and traders in high-value goods, such as operating in the diamond industry. (In parallel to this development and not completely unrelated, the notion of black diamonds or conflict diamonds emerged, and the diamond industry started to regulate itself through the Kimberley Process (2003). Also, professional service providers, such as legal firms and notaries, had to comply and demonstrate compliance with AML and CTF regulations.

From a regulatory oversight perspective, countries had to make a choice: Would regulatory compliance oversight be brought under the auspices of one regulatory body specialized in AML and CTF? Or would regulatory compliance be a (new) subdomain of existing oversight bodies specific to different industry sectors? An example of the first can be found in a number of European countries where AML regulatory oversight was brought under an existing watchdog, often named Financial Markets Authority.[1]

Some countries, such as the United Kingdom, have a hybrid system where one overarching AML watchdog oversees multiple – in the case of the UK no less than 22 – branch-specific supervisors.

Apart from an industry-specific overview, countries can adopt a model whereby different regulatory compliance domains are covered by different regulatory bodies. An example is the US, where the US Treasury FINCEN (Financial Crimes Enforcement Network) department is responsible for AML oversight and the recipient of the CTRs (Cash Transaction Reports), SARs (Suspicious Activity Reports), and DOEP (Designation of Exempt Person) reports. Then there is the Office of Foreign Assets Control (OFAC), which is responsible for issuing the sanctions list but also supervises compliance with the list. Whereas FINCEN is looking for unknown criminals and suspicious activity, OFAC deals with known criminals and the prevention of their abuse of the financial system. Then there is the US Securities Exchange Commission (SEC), which oversees the securities trade, including brokers and the exchanges. The SEC has been increasingly focusing on AML and violations of the US Bank Secrecy Act, training its staff to investigate and to bring charges in relation to these.

Seen from a distance, AML in the various industry sectors may be very similar. Risk-based approaches look for anomalies; behavior that, at face value, does not seem to fit into known and common patterns of other participants in the same industry. Whilst analytical software is capable of looking for anomalies regardless of the nature of the data or the industry or behavioral context these data represent, the actual patterns and anomalies may differ widely. From a modus operandi perspective, money laundering may look very different in an (online) casino compared to the insurance industry or retail banking. Trade-based money laundering has gradually emerged as a separate money laundering domain, together with correspondent banking. Regarding the latter, the days that financial institutions could trust

---

[1]For example, in the Netherlands the Autoriteit Financial Markten (AFM) and in France the Autorité des Marchés Financiers (AMF) literally translate to Financial Markets Authority.

other financial institutions – simply because they were registered as a financial institution and had a longstanding reputation as a trustworthy partner – are over.

Like modus operandi differ from industry to industry, so do the rules, even though, at the end of the day, the rules across various industry sectors may look much more similar than the modus operandi do. Differences in rules and regulatory requirements also relate to differences in compliance maturity of a sector. With each and every new money laundering directive, the EU added new industries and professions to the scope of AML. Every time a new directive was issued, it was followed by a wave of gradual change through the countries (who implement the directive and adopt new legislation or regulations at country level), through industry-specific oversight and advisory firms, to the organizations that become subject to the AML regime. It takes a few years, end-to-end, from the initial publication of the directive, through building awareness in the industry; through adoption of industry-specific regulations and the creation of policies, processes, and procedures in the new AML subjects; and the training of staff to an actual business-as-usual level of compliance. And even after that, both regulators and regulated evolve and the former start demanding more and more from the latter.

Apart from a gradual expansion by legislation of the group of the so-called gatekeepers, there is another, secondary, consequence to this widening of the AML regulatory scope for financial institutions servicing (corporate) customers in these sectors. Whilst, on the one hand, operators in these new areas of regulatory scrutiny have the obligation to implement AML policies and operations, on the other hand, traditional financial institutions, which have long since fallen under the AML regime, now have to change the way they look at their customers if they belong to any of these sectors now included in AML. In a manner of speaking, one could say a layered regulatory system has come into existence. This is well illustrated by the diamond mining and trading sector: whilst diamond sector players are now responsible for their own AML and anti-corruption operations, this by no means eases the risk assessment work to be done by those banks and insurers who have these players as their customers. On the contrary, if anything it has made the financial institution's job harder than before and by no means can the financial institution rely on the self-regulatory qualities of the diamond sector.[2]

As a result, the regulatory framework and the regulatory demands are more granular, and more sophisticated and complex in the area that has been subject to AML regulation for longer: retail banking. Let's have a closer look at the various industries and their differences from an AML perspective.

BANKING

Among the industry sectors discussed here, banks have the widest range of services. The 1980s saw the rise of the universal bank, a financial corporation with a presence in a high number of countries and offering a vast range of services to a wide-ranging customer base. From the most basic current accounts to juveniles and low-income households to very complex asset management services, to high-net-worth premium or platinum private individuals. From cash flow and factoring services to the retailer with a single market stall, to highly complex financing of mammoth deals by the large corporate manufacturers, the Unilevers, Samsungs, and Apples of this world. From small personal loans and consumer credit to Initial Public Offerings (IPOs), where privately owned companies and partnerships seek to capitalize on their success by going to market and raising money through shares. From an individual savings account to pension fund asset management and equity trading and brokerage and navigating capital markets through futures, derivates, and complex products like credit default swaps. Under capitalism, financial services delivery has evolved into an extremely wide-ranging and complex financial industry where dealing in risk (as that is, in essence, what banks do) is no longer necessarily attached to real-world material goods with intrinsic value.

AML has always focused primarily on retail and commercial banking, and most rules and regulations are written with these sectors in mind. And for good reason: this is where criminals and money launderers are known to use and abuse the financial system.

[2]See Dijck, M. V. (2008). Has clarity been brought to the diamond sector? A survey into AML and TF risk mitigation by diamond traders and their financiers. *Crime, Law and Social Change*, 52(1), 73–94. https://doi.org/10.1007/ s10611-008-9171-z

Being individuals themselves, criminals will eventually want to have the same financial services at their disposal as legitimate citizens with comparable wealth and assets. They will own private accounts for their personal everyday spending, savings accounts to safely stash any savings, credit cards for their convenience, ISA accounts to enjoy the tax cut on pension savings, and wealth management services, if they have money left to play around with and invest. The funds in these accounts, if of criminal origin, are most likely to be the end product of money laundering and have already gone through the whitewashing process. These funds are either integrated or being (further) integrated into the financial system and upper world economy. Yet a number of common transaction monitoring rules will look at these accounts and see if anything unusual is going on.

But there is also an entrepreneurial side to crime, where criminals and economic crimes can be compared to legitimate entrepreneurship across its entire spectrum. Some criminals act primarily individually, and their business can be compared to the self-employed entrepreneur; others work together in small partnerships and may even have erected legal entities to formalize their collaboration. Larger structures and even kin-based criminal organizations have much in common with a mid-size business with a hierarchical structure, executive management, and employees on the payroll. Economic or profit-driven crime is, in many ways, no different from legitimate commercial activity and entrepreneurship, with the only difference being that with the usual challenges that come with any type of business, criminal organizations have additional challenges on information management. This is because the true nature of the activity, and the fact that the law is broken by it, requires concealment, and concealment is a matter of information management. At the end of the day, who can one trust with what information? As a side note, studies around the American and Italian mafia show that a family structure provides a good starting point as a natural source of loyalty, but not all criminals have the luxury of being able to build and expand a criminal business with the help of a wider family. Another interesting detail is that where the mafia grew beyond its family structures, it often adopted a hierarchical type of self-organization that was more akin to that of the military than that of commercial organizations, with roles (and titles) like that of soldiers, captains, advisors, and heads. But however criminals organize themselves, sooner rather than later they will want to use financial services in a manner similar to that of any commercial organization. Indeed, a big part of the internal finances will be dealt with on a cash basis; one would not expect the mafia or any similar type of criminal organization to pay out its members, employees, and contractors through a payroll account with the local branch of a nationwide bank. However, assets, especially when they build up, will need to be managed and if, for example, front stores are used to give the operations and logistics a semi-legitimate appearance, then these will have to operate as much as possible as legitimate outfits and use financial facilities. These, in most cases, will be small and medium-sized business financial products and services.

A third category is formed by the money launderers. These can be either the same individuals as the criminals (DIY money laundering), or these can be professionals who sell their money laundering services to criminals and criminal organizations, either as independent professional service providers, or as employees of the criminal organization they work for. Money launderers, like lawyers and notaries (and not uncommonly that is what they actually are), will receive assets and move them around, and get involved in the layering and integration side of money laundering. Layering and integration, by definition, require the use (and abuse) of financial services and most commonly the products used are individual/retail or commercial banking products. The setting up or takeover of shell companies; opening and closing accounts, financing structures such as lease and loan-back structures; taking out commercial mortgages and redeeming them; engaging in real estate transactions, partaking in investment projects, equity fund management . . . all of these are financial instruments used by money launderers and most of them are offered in the space of retail and commercial banking.

It therefore makes sense that AML regulations, at the beginning, focused on retail and small and medium-sized business commercial banking. However, over the years the focus has widened and nowadays also incorporates other financial industry sectors.

CORRESPONDENT BANKING

Fund movement between territories often relies on correspondent banking. Investopedia defines a correspondent bank as follows: "A correspondent bank is a bank that provides services on behalf of another, equal or unequal, financial institution. It can facilitate wire transfers, conduct business transactions, accept deposits, and gather documents on behalf of another financial institution. Correspondent banks are most likely to be used by domestic banks to service transactions that either originate or are completed in foreign countries, acting as a domestic bank's agent abroad." Correspondent banking essentially is a global network of banks connecting almost any registered bank (and any branch) in the world to the global banking infrastructure. When account holders transfer money from one account into another, in its simplest form, both accounts would be held at the same bank or even the same branch. The debiting of the remitter's account and the crediting of the recipient's account can be done internally. No other bank will need to be involved. When remitter and recipient account are not with the same bank, the transfer can still be done directly from one bank to another, although these days systems are in place to pool many multiple transactions and only the surplus (for one bank) and the deficit (for the other bank) across the batch of transactions between the two banks are being registered. This is how things work domestically. For cross-border transfers multiple banks may be involved to make up the chain from remitter to recipient. The bank or banks in the chain that are not holding the remitter's account or the recipient's account only act as a conduit for the transaction and are neither the origin nor the end point of the funds.

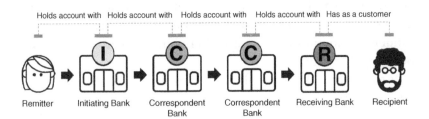

Figure 2.1 Banks along the chain in a remittance.

If the remitter and recipient do not have an account with the same bank or with a bank that has a direct working relationship (holding accounts with each other), then the initiating bank will seek a path to the receiving bank through a bank with whom they both have a working relationship. If such a bank exists, then that bank will be the sole correspondent bank in the chain, connecting the initiating bank to the receiving bank. However, if there is no direct mutual relationship the chain will have to include more correspondent banks, as in the example depicted above.

From a money laundering point of view, correspondent banking is risky because the funds may go through multiple countries, and the correspondent bank is yet another bank at which the anti-money laundering controls and measures are different and its level of compliance sometimes difficult to assess. Also, it can be difficult to identify the funds as they move from bank to bank.

AML for correspondent banking is mostly done at the initial stage of establishing a new correspondent banking relationship. Much hinges on the risk assessments conducted as part of due diligence, where the counterpart bank is vetted before creating the correspondent banking account.

Although correspondent banking can cover a wide range of banking services, it is most commonly used for international wire transfers. Transaction monitoring on correspondent banking usually focuses on two aspects.

Comparative analysis will be done from the current months against the previous months, and scenarios will pick up on significant fluctuations across a number of transactions, number of money market transactions, number of trade finance transactions, and/or number of transactions to and from high-risk countries. Here, a correspondent bank is treated like a normal customer and its account is monitored through a subset of scenarios.

Another type of specific correspondent banking scenario looks at batches, or even across batches, of wire transfers with a one-to-many or many-to-one relationship. Either the same remitter wires money to multiple parties repetitively or receives wires above expectation:

▓ Disbursing funds from a bank customer to an excessive number of external parties through wire transfer.

▓ Integrating funds into a bank customer from an excessive number of external parties through wire transfer.

▓ Disbursing funds from an external party to an excessive number of bank customers through wire transfer.

▓ Integrating fund into an external party from an excessive number of bank customers through wire transfer.

One of the biggest challenges with correspondent banking is that of data quality. When we take, for example, SWIFT messages – SWIFT being one of the most commonly utilized mechanisms for international wires and using correspondent banks — these are unstructured and contain remitter and recipient information and often also corresponding bank information in one open text string.

This string needs to be parsed by text analysis. Whilst it is one thing to break down the SWIFT messages and discern which elements in that one message pertain to the remitter, which are names, which represent addresses, which represent banks, and which pertain to the beneficiary, it is a completely different story to recognize one and the same external party across different messages, potentially generated by different banks.

Since correspondent banking transactions will always contain one (or at least one) external party and that party may be referred to differently in different SWIFT messages, they are therefore difficult to match and recognize as pertaining to one and the same entity in real life. The same goes for recognizing an external party, with an account at a bank that the financial institution has no relationship with, as actually being one and the same entity as an internal party. Customers may wire funds to themselves in offshore accounts or in the other direction, and it may not be straightforward to recognize both remitter and recipient as one and the same. Depending on the diligence the financial institution feels it needs to apply, it may include in its transaction monitoring system specific entity resolution algorithms. These algorithms are very similar to those applied for watchlist matching. They help in analyzing unstructured or structured data and to identify one entity with another, even if there are differences in spelling of the names, different addresses, or address notations. This helps in resolving multiple transactions with seemingly different parties to being executed or received by the same entity, albeit a truly external entity, i.e. non-customer, or an internal entity, i.e. a customer. The social network linkage that emerges is highly relevant for AML, as it allows for the aggregation of transactions that otherwise would be treated as involving completely separate entities.

BANKING – TRADE FINANCE

Trade finance is financing by a financial institution for a trade business of a customer with an external party. Trade financing typically includes products like letters of credit, whereby money for a payment of goods is held by the bank until it has received proof of the goods being shipped or received. Another form of trade financing is factoring, whereby the bank buys the invoices of a company (at a reduced price) thereby taking on the responsibility of collection and the risk of default . . . which it may sell again to another party. And then there are the various trade-related insurances, whereby the financial institution ensures cargo during transport or delays in goods reaching their destination at an agreed time.

Trade finance is often very bespoke, as the terms and conditions of the service, the amounts involved, and clauses in the agreement are often very specific to a particular trade. There may be some level of standardization, but usually to a much lesser degree as compared to many other banking areas. As a result, trade financing has traditionally relied very much on human processes and documents. These trades normally involve large amounts and are much less frequent than everyday retail and commercial banking transactions, like point-of-sale or card-not-present payments. Trade financing is either provided by specialist trading banks, or by specialized departments in larger, often multinational, financial institutions. Thus, trade finance business commonly doesn't have automated systems developed to support their operations, because of the lower benefit such automation would bring as compared to bulk banking sectors. As a result, trade finance transaction data are traditionally less digitized and less well formatted.

This makes it more difficult to implement reliable automatic transaction monitoring software.

Trade finance is therefore more vulnerable to abuse from money laundering, and money launderers across the globe seem to have recognized the opportunities presented by these vulnerabilities. According to the International Narcotics Control Strategy Report (INCSR), hundreds of billions of dollars are laundered through trade-based money laundering (TBML) every year.

There are a number of money laundering modus operandi involved, specifically in trade-based finance. Each of these may come with its own red flag.

Over- or Undervaluing the Goods (Mispricing)

One of the oldest money laundering techniques is to artificially inflate or deflate the value and trade prices of the goods or services. An international import or export company feigns a good profit from goods it manufactures or buys at a low price and sells at a high price, with a good profit margin. In reality the goods are either bought or manufactured for much more, sold for much less, or even just given away or destroyed – as they are merely a cover and destroying these goods is easier and cheaper than truly selling and delivering them. The criminal money to be laundered is presented as the gains from these trades, and the operation effectively becomes a transfer of value rather than a trade. Trade-based money laundering can only be detected with either a good understanding of the market and/or a solid base of reference data. From an AML perspective, one approach could be to routinely investigate trade samples and closely analyze the end-to-end chain for one trade at a time. This is law enforcement work rather than a task for a financial institution.

One way the financial institution can act against trade-based finance is through the vigilance of the account manager. In these specific industries, account managers are dedicated customer service managers with in-depth knowledge not only of trade finance, but also of the specific trades they are servicing. For example, back in the early 2000s the largest Dutch financial institution, ABN AMRO Bank, was the largest financier in the diamond sector and it had a specialized department for the sole purpose of servicing diamond manufacturers, wholesalers, and retailers. Another department of the same bank, which was later taken over by the Royal Bank of Scotland (one of the UK's Big Five and at the time the second largest bank worldwide from an asset value perspective), dealt with trade financing for sea and port cargo, i.e. anything to do with containers and container transport. Account managers in trade finance often have become industry experts and know what normal prices and profit margins pertain too. They are in the best position to sniff out unusually low or high prices or profits . . . and in most countries AML regulations or even the law requires them to report any suspicions of money laundering or other (fraudulent) misrepresentation of business. The reality, however, is that front office account managers have incentives to be lenient towards their customers, as their jobs and success depends on the volume of customers, and the value that the relationship with their customers represents to the financial institution. And despite efforts to make staff aware of their specific duties and rolling out training programs to raise awareness amongst staff, relying on the account manager's alertness and willingness to report may, in reality, not be the most effective way to detect trade-based money laundering.

Alternatively, the financial institution can rely on data. Let the numbers speak for themselves. In order to detect mispricing, one would need reference data, no matter what algorithm or analytic technology is employed. So, a database would be needed to capture historical prices, comparable market prices or competitor information, such as profit margins and other economic performance issues.

One of the challenges trade-based money laundering may face is the lack of data. The commercial customer base for certain products and services may be relatively small and the transactions limited in volume, and related data is therefore insufficient for statistically meaningful analysis. Automated monitoring of trade-based money laundering would therefore be primarily suitable for larger (specialized) financial institutions, with sufficiently large customer bases. Alternatively, financial institutions could consider collaborating and pooling their data, which would have to be either masked or aggregated so that individual customer data will not be shared with the pooling partners.

Another challenge is the availability of meaningful reference data. Reference data will allow for thresholds to be set, expectations to be established, and outliers to be detected. Reference data can come from the history of the customer on the account (for sudden spikes that cannot be explained away as, for example, expected seasonal fluctuations), but this requires sufficiently frequent use of the account over a longer period of time. Scenarios that look at the history on the account will not work if the account and/or customer are relatively new or when use of the account or certain banking products is sparse.

Alternatively, reference data can come from a peer group: other customers that operate in a similar industry, whose data allow a meaningful comparison.

Challenges may become clear when looking at a specific example, assessing the authenticity of the price of goods and, derived from that, the economic or market value of shipments. This value is determined by the specific type of goods, size of the unit, commercial terms and conditions, and quite often, the market. For retail items prices may be relatively stable or only slowly changing, but for bulk items and commodities, especially those that are traded on the exchange, price forming can be volatile, making it more difficult to assess the realistic value of goods. Retail goods will come with their own challenges, such as:

- Country of origin: manufacturing costs absorbed by the selling price).

- Country of destination: some goods are so popular in countries that importers are willing to pay a higher price to keep their market share.

- Brand: some goods are sold at higher prices simply because of their brand and associated reputation.

- Season: during certain periods of the year (or running up to these) higher trading volumes may lead to lower prices or goods are sold at discounts due to higher competition.

- Expiry date: prices will drop sharply if goods are nearing (or have exceeded) their expiry dates.

- Quality: seemingly similar products may trade for very different prices because of their quality or the extra service (e.g. guarantees) that is incorporated in their price.

All of these factors create margins where money launderers can easily explain lower prices at which goods are bought or higher prices for which they are (re)sold. As long as the ledgers reflect these prices (or no one bothers to look at these), artificial mispricing goes undetected.

> One financial institution requiring trade-based AML presented us with two years' worth of data to analyze. In these data the largest group of goods types (based on type, unit, and incoterms) only had 200 rows of data. This was just about enough to do a meaningful statistical analysis. We estimate that over 90% of commercial banking data relevant to trade-based money laundering lacks the volume of data required for data driven scenarios and does not meet the minimum requirement for reference data.

Money laundering can ride on the back of other crimes, such as smuggling of high excise goods (cigarette smuggling is a good example) and or counterfeit goods (replicas of brand products being traded as the real thing, if only on paper). Even if the entire chain, from manufacturer, through wholesaler to consumer, to a nosy bank account manager, are aware of a Louis Vuitton bag actually being a counterfeit replica, these may still be represented as the real thing. Money that needs laundering is used to bridge the gap between the actual retail price for the counterfeit and what the original product would have sold for.

Dual-Use Goods

Dual-use goods are products and technologies that are normally used for civilian purposes but may also have military applications. If a trade involves dual-use goods, the customer may be supporting terrorist or other military actions and trading in dual-use goods is a risk factor.

When dual-use goods are part of a money laundering or terrorism financing scheme these are usually not declared as such, and to identify these correctly the transaction monitoring system will have to rely on the free-text description that is provided with the transaction details. Finding dual-use goods is a text-parsing and string-matching problem, which is further exacerbated by the use of short forms, different languages, and the usual spelling and typo errors. There are some data providers that offer watchlist databases and different vendors providing screening solutions for this purpose, or, if this is an important area for a financial institution to pay extra attention to, the financial institution may create its own algorithms, although this usually requires specialized text-parsing and fuzzy search or matching logic as well. Whilst the technology may be coming from one vendor, the specific business relevant rules and list of keywords and phrases may come from a different vendor or specialized consultants.

Commodities Traded Are Inconsistent with the Customer's Primary Business

A firm registered as a fertilizer manufacturer or wholesaler is expected to trade in fertilizers, a toy company trades toys, etc. Companies can shift business either through natural growth and expansion into unchartered waters or by adapting to changing economic circumstances and focus on new areas of revenue. The fertilizer company may evolve into a broader agriculture company and the toy manufacturer may discover there is more money to be made from children's books, but it would raise suspicion if the toy company, on an occasional or regular basis, traded fertilizer. This would probably be something worth looking into and worth investigating.

From an implementation perspective this is simply a match between the industry of customer company, and the industry of the traded goods. The customer's industry is a piece of information that most, if not all, financial institutions require their entity customers to declare when opening their first account with them, leaving aside that these days regulatory frameworks demand such information to be captured as part of the know-your-customer (KYC) process. The customer can choose from more than one industry classification or can even deliberately produce false information (although a check against the Chamber of Commerce records and its authenticity is expected), but that is beside the point. The comparison here is between the self-declared applicable industry categories against those of the traded goods.

For the traded goods, some banks rely on the staff of the trade finance department to determine and input an industry code. Sometimes, the goods are misclassified, and some are hard to be judged for a suitable category. Automatic name matching may be adopted to identify the goods, and in that case the analytical challenges are the same as described above for the dual use.

High-Risk Goods Categories

The next category of trade-based money laundering detection focuses not so much on the discrepancies between self-declared intended and actual trading, but on the mere fact that some types of goods and commodities have proven to lend themselves to money laundering and thus are more prone to it.

One example is the online selling of gift cards and prepaid phone cards. These cards are characterized by the fact that monetary value can be placed on a card, and that this value can be redeemed relatively easily, either by a refund of the value of the card, or by reselling it, or by using it for high-value purchases, which can then be resold. In effect, such prepaid cards are very similar to cash withdrawal, as they work like bearer bonds, which can be freely sold on or given to someone whose identity and/or link or link to the purchaser remains unknown.

Another category is relatively high-value goods, such as domestic appliances. Some financial institutions have chosen to include certain product categories as high risk. Money laundering alerts may be generated on the back of it, or this factor contributes to a score card and will only trigger an alert in combination with other risk factors, such as card-not-present payments (very common in e-commerce) and trading in bulk.

Another, completely different, example is in the trade of carbon emissions. In the wake of international agreements on climate change and the almost global acknowledgment that man-made emission of so called greenhouse gasses (amongst which is carbon dioxide, i.e. CO_2) contributes to global warming and jeopardizes the earth's ecosystem, countries have imposed limitations on companies as to how much CO_2 they are allowed to emit as part of their industrial processes. Depending on the industry they are in and the size of the company, each of them will be given an allowance, which comes in the form of certificates. The crux is that these certificates can be exchanged. A company that produces less CO_2 than it is allowed (for example because they have reduced their CO_2 footprint by using green energy sources) can sell the surplus of their allowance to companies who have a need for more. As it happens, these carbon emission allowances (simply referred to as carbon credits) are traded on stock exchanges and have been abused for money laundering purposes. The real value of carbon credits is difficult to establish, as one company at a given time can have a higher or more urgent need for them. For example, industrial manufacturing processes, particularly in the chemical industry, ideally keep their plants operating 24-7 as it can be expensive to shut down and restart the plant. For the plant to continue operating legitimately carbon emission certificates need to be in place to demonstrate compliance. Demand may rise or fall but it is difficult to predict what the actual demand is. Although open trade on a stock exchange, especially in these days of electronic real-time information exchange, creates a fully transparent market, that transparency can still be a false transparency when the market is flooded with criminals and money launderers who artificially create demand and supply. Since there are no tangible shipments, merely invisible allowances, and a company can pile up allowances for future use, artificial price inflation can go undetected for a long time. Between 2010 and 2015, reports emerged warning of the abuse of the carbon credit trade by criminals and money launderers.

Unusual Shipment Route

Many trades involve the shipment of physical goods. The transportation may be done by vessels, which are registered, and the route can span across different countries and territorial and international waters. Routes could be directly from port of origin to port of destination, but also include stops at multiple ports along the way. Trade routes may be a cause of suspicion, or at least deemed unusual, if the path:

- deviates from normal, or
- does not make sense economically, or
- passes through high-risk waters or a country on a sanction list, or
- if the vessel used is related to a high-risk or blacklisted country, or
- if the vessel itself is on a sanction list.

To identify a route as unusual or suspicious, the actual route must be captured and compared against reference data. There are vendors that specialize in the provision of shipment route data that can be used to identify significant deviations of the shipment route from normal routes. There are also data providers that bring together the sanction lists issued by different countries worldwide, which contain both blacklisted countries and blacklisted registered vessels.

Unusual Weight

Some trade-based money laundering, much like trafficking of counterfeit goods or for the sake of excise evasion, is done by using a legitimate or legitimately declared cover load, but part of the goods is simply not there, or not the same as what was declared. One possible way of detection is to weigh the shipment and compare the result with the weight on the bill of lading or the expected weight. This modus operandum and the way of detecting it is very similar to that of over- or underpricing . . . and detection is more a duty of a public sector customs and excise department than of a private sector financial institution. However, if weight data is made available electronically then automated AML is technically possible and may analytically be meaningful.

Under-, Double, and False Invoicing

Again, very similar to mispricing is the tampering of invoices. Shipments could be deliberately (and systematically) misrepresented in the books and on the invoice. There are a few varieties that lend themselves to money laundering. First, there is the plain and simple false invoicing: invoices are created (and income justified with these) whilst there is no real-world exchange of goods or services as mentioned in the invoice. The trade is a fake trade and exists on paper only. The challenge, from a money launderer's perspective, is that it is not only the invoices that have to be fabricated but probably also a number of other documents, such as bills of lading that are expected to come along with it. If the invoice is for services (with no material goods to account for), then false invoicing becomes somewhat easier.

The main challenge for a money launderer is to produce a continuous flow of invoices that are representative and realistic as to mimic real-life business. This is not always easy. One analytical method that can help money laundering detection can be found in Benford's Law. Benford's Law, in a nutshell, acknowledges that many data sets describing (natural) phenomena will not have an equal distribution of the leading digit. In other words, when phenomena are described quantitatively, like the height of a person expressed in meters and centimeters, then most of the observations will start with the number 1 (as most adults and teenagers are between 1 meter and 2 meters tall), a lesser amount with 0 (for infants), and a relatively small number with 2 (for the Swedes, Dutch, and NBA athletes towering above all the others). The numbers 3 to 9 will not occur at all. Whilst this is an example with an understandable cause (we know there are limitations to how tall humans grow), such a logical explanation may not be there or not evident, whilst the data set still shows a skewness in terms of the first digit distribution. Something similar may be applicable to the last digit, e.g. where retail prices are concerned. In retail it is very common to have a higher frequency of 99, 95, 50, 49 and 00 as the last two digits (or decimals for those countries using cents or pennies), as somehow this seems psychologically preferable by many vendors. The idea (or myth) is that the consumer's brain will ignore the 9 and round off downward, so that a product priced at $14.95 is interpreted as a mere $14. The point here is that when a money launderer has to create an artificial flow of invoices and related transactions he may either, subconsciously, use a bias that is different from what we observe in the industry, or he may be forcing himself to have an equal distribution (to make invoices look random) as this is his perception of how real-life business looks like. In reality, however, legitimate businesses and trades may show a different pattern (whether we can explain it or not), and a statistical approach to leading and trailing digit(s) can be a very effective and easy way to find outliers and suspicious behavior, purely based on numbers.

Other variations to the false invoicing schemes, but which may avoid the above money launderer pitfalls, is double invoicing. With double invoicing a real-life trade is used twice (or multiple times), thus artificially creating the appearance of revenue. The obvious benefit is that, since the original trade and invoice are legitimate and actually exist, the invoices are lifelike. The challenge, from a money launderer's perspective, is that you will have to run an actual business or at least a front store to generate the original genuine trade. Otherwise there would be nothing to duplicate or replicate. Another challenge is that it may look odd, from a number-crunching perspective, if every payment amount is presented in the books twice or more. However, if the trade runs by a standard pricing book, then this is easily circumvented, as many amounts will be very similar. Some effort must be made to artificially create an unbroken string of invoice numbers, as required by the tax authorities in many countries.

Lastly, there is the under-invoicing practice. One may wonder how this may contribute to money laundering, as instead of generating artificial revenue, the revenue is artificially decreased . . . or so it seems. There are (at least) two money laundering use cases for under-invoicing. The first use case is where the under-invoicing is applied to the acquisition of goods, half fabricates, or source materials. If the cost is decreased on paper, then the profit margin is increased. The additional benefit is that sales prices can be kept the same as normal and are therefore realistic and will not trigger any overpricing alarms. The other use case is where the business is deliberately allowed to make a loss. This loss can be deducted from taxes and form the basis of tax refunds. These tax refunds can then serve as the legitimate source of income that money launderers are looking for.

Over- and under-invoicing are difficult to detect by automated means, as they both allow for mimicking legitimate business very well. Benford's Law, or a variation, may be applied, and possibly proper customer segmentation and peer group analysis may provide some solace.

BANKING – CREDIT CARD

From a money laundering perspective, credit card transactions are not so different from checking account transactions. In some countries, like the UK, debit cards and credit cards can be used by the consumer in the same way: both allow for online and card-not-present purchases and both are used for refunds by retailers (who only provide a refund through the same means of payment for the original purchase). There are still, however, a few additional money laundering risks associated specifically with credit cards. Payments towards the balance of the card are allowed through a variety of means, such as cash deposit, cheque, and third party payment, which are more prone to money laundering. And if a transaction is annulled and the money refunded through a different means than the original payment, this may also serve for money laundering. This is why most retailers only provide refunds via the original payment means, for example the exact same card. This limits any money laundering risk to cash payments and refunds (which is outside the scope of retailers' bank and transaction monitoring).

In a payment card scheme, both the cardholder and the merchant might be subjects for fraudulent behavior.

The high-risk areas are:

- Cash/cheque/third-party payment for credit balance. Third party or a less easily traceable source of funds is more vulnerable to facilitate placement.
- Cash advances can facilitate integration of illicit funds into the wider financial system.
- Refund after retail purchase. Money launderers may use this refund mechanism to work around cash controls, such as restrictions put on travelers to bring cash cross-border. A mule could bring a credit card on their travels and then draw cash by refund after purchase.

INSURANCE

Compared to banks, insurance companies process far fewer transactions. AML in the insurance industry is more focused on KYC and risk assessment than on transaction monitoring. Customer due diligence (CDD) procedures are done at (new) customer onboarding but often also on setup of a new insurance policy. Once a policy is created, related transactions are typical to insurance products, such as the (incoming) payment of premiums, the (outgoing) payments of successful claims against the policy, lump sum payments on surrender (when the policy is prematurely terminated or when the conditions for pay-out are met). Many insurers also issue loans, which may or may not be attached to insurance products, such as a loan based on the value of a life policy. As a result, loan repayments, which are very similar to premium payments, also need to be monitored.

Insurance transaction monitoring is in some ways different from its retail banking equivalent. Due to the lower frequency and more volatile pattern of payments on an account (read policy) a strictly analytical approach focusing on pattern detection becomes less meaningful. Outlier detection based on the history of the account or policy becomes largely meaningful when pay-out of bulk sums (following claims and events as detailed in the policy) is part of the core business model.

Where money launderers get impatient and do not want to make gradual payments over a longer period of time, money laundering in insurance may look very similar to fraud, or in fact coincides with it; the event invoking the policy is deliberately caused or brought forward so that the pay-out can be legitimated as income from insurance. Or, not necessarily fraudulent, the money launderers, after a shorter or longer while following the opening the insurance policy, can decide to step up the periodic premiums or loan repayments, therefore bringing forward the termination of the insurance and the associated pay-out. In a slightly different scheme, money launderers can be seen to prematurely terminate the insurance; this will usually come with a loss in the form of a penalty charge, but money launderers accept these as the necessary costs of money laundering – the remaining sum can be explained as legitimate income.

Therefore, things to look for in insurance transaction monitoring are:

- Overpayment of premiums
- Unusual aggregated activity at the level of insurance agents and resellers

- Large redemptions
- Termination of multiple policies
- Premiums paid from multiple accounts
- Early termination of a product resulting in loss

Since many of the techniques, such as prematurely terminating the policy, are by themselves perfectly legitimate and in fact part of the policy, insurers must take a wider view to detect suspicious behavior, either across multiple policies that either have the same policy holder or beneficiary, or are otherwise related to one another. Social network analysis becomes highly relevant. When a policyholder occasionally files a claim, prematurely ends the policy, or increases the premium (re)payment rate, that is perfectly normal, but when one and the same person or entity or a group of persons seem to have a higher frequency of any of these behaviors, then that is when suspicions may arise for a more structural misuse of insurance products and is indicative of either fraud and/or money laundering.

Evidently, pay-out to persons on regulatory watchlists or to people in high-risk countries or geographical areas is also something insurers will need to look at, although, as mentioned above, that would normally be dealt with at the customer take-on or policy opening stage, under KYC and CDD processes.

Lastly, the above is mainly applicable to the retail and (small) commercial insurance business. Where insurance meets capital markets, money laundering has only very recently become somewhat of a concern but has been largely absent until now. For example, a money launderer with a deep knowledge of derivatives and specialist products, such as the infamous Collateralized Debt Obligation (CDO), has plenty of opportunity to use the opaque nature of these products to create a seemingly legitimate stream of income. Where open markets are considered transparent by their very nature, especially with the electronic revolution that has changed the game for capital markets and brokerage, this transparency at the level of individual trade relationships disappears when buyer and seller collude and artificially engage in trades and/or do business under the counter. This brings us to the next industry that is affected by money laundering: securities.

SECURITIES

In securities trading, the number of transactions would normally be a lot more than that for insurance.

In terms of the volume of transactions, securities trading can be compared to retail and commercial banking. Even though the purpose of securities trading is very different from retail and commercial banking, at a basic level the transaction types are much the same and include money deposits (e.g. margin payments), money withdrawals, deposits of securities, withdrawing of securities, buying of securities, and selling of securities (in the case of commercial banking, securities could be replaced with merchandise, goods, or services).

The money deposits and withdrawals can be monitored in similar ways to retail and commercial banking. One type of scenario would be looking for imbalances between money deposits and withdrawals and trade volume and velocity. A high number of deposits and withdrawals against low trade activity may be indicative of money laundering, since the trades do not account for the withdrawals (but the deposits do). This can be monitored and assessed through a purely calculative (e.g. data-driven) approach.

Money launderers' primary aim is to cleanse the money through securities trading, and the trades do not necessarily have to make economic sense. Securities trading may be an attractive way of laundering money due to a relatively low risk (of being caught) against a relatively low operational cost in terms of fees and commissions to be paid for each trade. In contrast, bond trading may cost too much for money laundering purposes and is therefore less attractive.

Figure 2.2 Activities behind trading.

Money launderers operate best in a volatile market where sub-
stantial losses or gains blend in with the other trades, where there is
less risk of being caught out as an outlier. One way to detect suspicious
trades is to compare activity over a period of time against the market.
Going against the grain too often or executing trades in a very steady
rhythm regardless of market movement, at least invokes the impres-
sion that the people behind it do not much care if the market is bull
or bear.[3] In addition, money launderers may differ from legitimate
traders when it comes to frequency of the trades in combination with
volume per trade, although again, the market may be characterized
by attracting participants of many different sorts with many different
investment strategies and it may be difficult to find a pattern amongst
legitimate traders too.

In all of the above potential for money laundering detection,
market data (e.g. Market Index) may be a useful source of information on determining whether a customer is trading in an unusual or
suspicious way. This may require help from expertise on securities
trading on this design. The market itself proves how difficult money
laundering detection is, because in a way being able to sift out the
money launderers leads to finding the golden egg: one data analysis
step further and one would be able to explain and predict winning by
legitimate users!

As a by-product, transaction monitoring in securities trading can
also serve another purpose – detecting financial crimes such as market
abuse and insider trading. The following are some monitoring rules
that may (also) be indicative of market abuse:

- Matching of long and short trades (buying and selling) in particular securities, creating an illusion of trade, but with a (guaranteed) net zero result.
- The buying and selling of a stock in similar amounts (regardless of the volume).
- Trading of a stock dominated by a small group of market
  players, where trades by an individual player can push prices

---

[3]A bull market means a buyer's market where there is more demand of a certain equity
than supply; the sentiment is that of optimism (prices will further rise in the near
future). A bear market is the opposite where supply exceeds demand and the market is
driven by pessimism, meaning the expectation that prices will further fall.

(through buying erratically) up or pull them down (by dumping large batches of a stock).[4]

▨ Highly frequent trading in a particular stock.

▨ Trade volumes (of a certain stock) being large compared to the exchange market.

Money launderers navigating the seas of the stock markets must be well aware of the rules imposed by the stock exchanges they operate on. If they do not keep their commitments, then they will soon be kicked out of the exchange.[5]

Note that in some situations, transactions are recorded after netting off. Only the net offset value is stored, hiding the customer's original actions. Transaction records in a settlement account may only store the net transactions and may not be a good data source for AML transaction monitoring purposes.

On the other hand, a customer may issue one single order for securities trading, but the transactions recorded are split. This happens because stock trading in a market needs a process of matching between buyer and seller orders. One order issued by a customer may need to be executed through multiple partial orders. Therefore, on implementing transaction monitoring, some effort may be required to verify if the transaction data is truly reflecting the customer's intended actions. Enhancement to the source system may be needed.

---

[4]Many exchanges allow the trading of futures where stock does not have to be owned or be in possession at the time of being sold (this is also referred to as going short or shorting), which allows for artificial (yet legitimate) trades.

[5]A relatively good insight into how stock markets can be manipulated for fraud and money laundering can be found in the autobiographic novel *Rogue Trader* by Nick Leeson. Leeson, operating on the stock exchange in Singapore in the 1980s, brought down his employer, Barings Bank, by engaging into rogue trades to compensate for losses and internally presenting these as wins. Whilst his story is that of one of the largest internal fraud cases ever, it is easy to see how the same mechanisms and vulnerabilities to the system can be exploited by money launderers. Since the Barings Bank collapse and a number of other notorious rogue trading cases, regulations and internal policies have changed, but since taking of risk and betting on future movements of the market is inherent to this type of banking activity, fraudulent behavior or abuse by money launderers will never be fully eradicated.

STORED VALUE FACILITIES (SVFS)

Stored value facilities (SVFs) are facilities that store monetary value. A user can deposit value into this facility and use it for retail payment. Some support peer-to-peer transfer. Although the storage amount capacity and daily transfer amount are usually limited, there is a risk that SVFs could be used for laundering money.

SVFs can be seen as a hybrid between a bank account and cash. Some of these SVFs store monetary value on a physical medium (like a card) that can be used by the bearer of the medium (the person who presents the card), but the actual value on the card is linked to a (non-banking) account. One can think of retailer gift cards or plastic voucher cards with a chip. In other variations there is no underlying account and the value is actually stored on the card itself, e.g. through topping up with cash upon purchase. The chip on the card keeps track of the contents as a true electronic purse. Value can be transferred simply by handing over the card to another person, like we do with cash. No record is being kept on who owns or uses it. If the card is accepted in multiple countries, then they lend themselves to smuggling money into or out of a country.

Typical transactions for SVFs include:

- Peer-to-Peer Transfer: Money is transferred from facility of one person to another.
- Retail Purchase at a Merchant: Payment for a retail merchant purchase.
- Online Purchase: Payment for an online purchase.
- Autopay to Merchant: Automatic payment to a merchant.
- Cash Deposit: Deposit value into the facility by cash.
- Credit Card Deposit: Deposit value into the facility by credit card.
- Return of Remaining Balance: User stops using the facility and cashes out all remaining value from it.

Depending on the nature of the SVF the issuer in some countries is subject to AML/TF regulations and needs to comply with these. However, these are mostly not banking or financial institutions in the more traditional sense, and the total value that can be stored on a card or in an account or that can be spent in one purchase is limited. Commonly, the regime these companies are subjected to is less stringent than for financial institutions. SVF issuing companies usually do not have the operational apparatus for full-blown transaction monitoring. The below example may be an exception.

A start-up company in Northern Europe needed an AML transaction monitoring system. Their earning model was based on a customer loyalty scheme for multiple retailers to join their program. They had two types of customers: retailers and retailers' customers. Instead of participating in a loyalty program for each of the retailers, customers could benefit from a program and collect points from the collective of affiliated retailers, a bit like the Diners Club in the US or employee discount schemes. Making purchases with one retailer would result in points that could be spent with that retailer or any of the others. Points could even be bought or cashed in through a linked bank account (of any bank, not provided by the start-up, much like an account that one would link to a PayPal account). The Central Bank of the country in which the start-up was established considered the start-up a financial institution and subject to banking regulations. In order to obtain a banking license, it had to demonstrate the implementation of a robust AML transaction monitoring system along with a customer risk-scoring capability for the onboarding of customers. Because the points system represented value and value exchange, the transaction monitoring had to be set up for two communicating universes: that of the points and the point exchange, and that of the interactions with the real bank accounts used for deposits and withdrawals (or buying and selling) of points.

Monitoring SVFs is very similar to transaction monitoring of retail banking activity. Activity on an underlying account can be analyzed with virtually the same rules as those for retail banking accounts, albeit that data volume and statistical relevance and critical data mass may become an issue. Where physical storage facilities are involved, these can be compared to debit or credit card transactions if linked to an underlying account. If the value is stored on the card itself, then depositing (loading) value onto the card can be considered similar to an ATM withdrawal (when a physical purse is topped up rather than an electronic purse, as is the case with the prepaid value car).

Scenarios similar to those of banks include statistical outlier of each transaction type, high-risk country, sudden increase of activities, etc. Monitoring scenarios specific to SVF may include:

- Many-to-one/one-to-many peer-to-peer transfers.
- Multiple peer-to-peer transfers from/to the same originator.
- Multiple payments from the same person to the same retail merchant.
- Return of remaining balance of a newly opened SVF.

Some SVFs allow the facility to be issued without customer information but require personal information when any remaining balance is redeemed or cashed out. The suspicious behavior may then be analyzed only upon redemption.

CASINOS AND ONLINE GAMBLING

It is not difficult to understand the level of risk of money laundering that gambling houses, especially casinos, represent. Traditionally these are cash-rich operations where income is generated by gambling, either by skill or luck or a combination of both. Of old, casinos have welcomed players from abroad, advocating themselves as a tourism subsector. For a long time, the casinos were not massively regulated and, in the US, this was exacerbated by the fact that many casinos were established in Indian reservations, which had a certain degree of autonomy and therefore even less oversight. In some countries casinos are not required to perform proper KYC checks on their customers and gamblers do not have to ID themselves. Obviously, self-respecting legitimate casinos do know their core customers, especially those who represent good revenue, if only because casinos tend to extend credit to their loyal customers.

If casinos were not be regulated at all, they would provide an easy opportunity for money launderers. They would only have to pretend to have made money with gambling and no record would exist to prove that they had not really won. With regulations that include casinos, now casinos themselves become responsible and obviously they do have first-hand access to data indicating who has won what and when. Any claim of revenue from gambling, therefore, can be cross-checked against the bookkeeping of the organization that paid out.

One has to bear in mind that, for a successful money laundering scheme, the money launderers do not really want to win. Any truly gained income does not make the problem go away of finding a different seemingly legitimate source of the funds that need to be whitewashed. Money launderers would rather not win in reality but pretend that they have won and put the criminal proceeds in the place of the alleged gaming wins.

One possibility might be not to cash in the wins, but to keep the chips or tickets[6] (casino) or credits (online gambling) and pretend to have converted these. This is easier done with physical chips than with online credit. But even in the case of chips, this would, at some point raise the suspicion of the casino, although there would also be an incentive not to act on such a suspicion, because any chip not converted into cash would positively affect the casino's bottom line.

In other money laundering modi operandi, the gambling institutions are complicit in the money laundering or, in fact, are the main perpetrators of it. This would open up a number of possibilities. They could let complicit strawmen play rigged games where they would lose a lot, and the casino could declare this a legitimate income resulting from the business operation. This would give free play to malicious gambling institutions as long as there is no regulatory requirement to perform KYC on such perpetually losing customers and no question need to be raised on the origin of the monies they are gambling away.

Gambling institutions could also cook the books, thereby supporting complicit gamblers in their claim of gambling profits that in

[6]Tickets here refers to the so-called ticket-in-ticket-out (or TITO) system operated by some American casinos, whereby slot machines larger denominations are not taken in or paid out by the machine through coins, but through creating and reading thermally printed bar code tickets, where the value is stored in the barcode.

reality does not exist, or make these exist by running a rigged operation where it can be determined who wins or loses. In any of these schemes the risk of being detected shifts to the accounting side of the casino or gambling provider. Money laundering and fraud go hand in hand, but the increased risk in running such illicit operations complicates the risk mitigation that the professional criminal will need to put in place to avoid detection.

From a regulatory perspective it is key to subject casinos and online gambling firms to at least the same level of scrutiny they apply to financial institutions. Which means active customer identification (KYC) and risk assessment (CDD), and a data-driven analysis of incoming and outgoing funds in parallel of transaction monitoring of virtual currency (chips and credit) flows.

Internationally speaking, the financial network is as strong as its weakest links and this is where online gambling operations impose increased levels of risk on the entire sector. Often based in less regulated jurisdictions, but with a global reach and customer base, these firms easily become entry points for money launderers. The AML regulatory framework responds in a similar way as it has responded to similar issues with weak spots in a global network: either demonstrate compliance or become blacklisted. Whatever option the gambling operator chooses it will become less useful for money launderers either way.

Typical monitoring rules for casinos and online gambling include statistical outlier of each transaction area (amount/count on cash-in/cash-out, money movement) and international transfers. A specific scenario would be targeted transfer of funds from one person to another through games, at which one player keeps losing money while another player keeps winning.

LOTTERY AND JOCKEY CLUB

Conceptually, closely linked to money laundering through casinos and online gambling is whitewashing funds through lottery and like operations. Usually fake lottery schemes are set up to serve both the crime of loan-sharking and of providing a seemingly licit origin of the goods. Through extortion, loan-shark organizations, so-called protection rackets, force their perceived debtors into opening a lottery or betting account and making regular deposits. Whilst the debt is being paid back, the lottery set-up provides for a seemingly licit front to explain the flow of funds. In addition, the pay-out of funds to the winner, in case of a rigged lottery, also provides a cloak of legitimacy, as long as the relationship between the lucky winner and the lottery owners/organizers is being concealed.

In a case in Hong Kong, an illegal loan shark made use of a betting account to collect debts from borrowers. It forced the borrowers to open betting accounts and then kept the account cards. The borrowers then repaid the debt through these betting accounts. These betting accounts are easy to open with little regulatory requirements to be met.

Obviously, if the entire operation is a criminal set-up to facilitate criminal extortion practices and launder the proceeds, then such an organization will not be inclined to set up a robust transaction monitoring system. The onus is on the authorities to enact legislation and bring lotteries and other gambling clubs under regulation. In many countries this is currently the case, even though the primary focus may not be on abuse in terms of money laundering but to ensure the lottery, club, or operation is not a fraud.

Regulations may have implications for those financial institutions (banks and even insurance companies) having lotteries and gambling operators as their customers.

Similar to those in securities firms, the betting accounts must reflect behavior associated with betting. A monitoring scenario rule would therefore check the number of cash deposits and withdrawals in comparison with the betting transactions. An alert should be generated if the volume of cash deposit/withdrawal is large but actual betting volume is low. This is an indication the account is being used for something else than placing bets.

OTHER BUSINESSES

There are other businesses that are identified as being at higher risk for money laundering and/or where the service providers have been designated as gatekeepers. Typical examples are lawyers and solicitors, in particular criminal defense lawyers and notaries, and real estate firms and letting agencies. Most of these professions or service providers have a legal obligation to establish the identity of their customers and/or ask questions on the whereabouts of the funds used to pay legal fees (solicitors), deposits (real estate brokers, notaries), or rent. We will not discuss these in detail as commonly these are smaller companies or partnerships who have neither gained the critical mass, nor have a regulatory obligation, to put in place a data-driven AML transaction monitoring system. Their involvement in AML is usually confined to KYC with a rare extension into CDD, but without the need or ability to engage into transaction monitoring. These professions and industry sectors are therefore not relevant for our topic.

Whilst each of the above-discussed industry sectors are in some way exposed to money laundering and most of them would allow for specific approaches of transaction monitoring, we will, for the remainder of this book, focus primarily on AML transaction monitoring for retail and commercial banking. These banking sectors have not only been exposed the longest to AML regulations, but also were the first adopters of data-driven transaction monitoring software; hence, the software and analytical sophistication built into these is more advanced for retail and commercial banking than for any other sector. Retail and commercial AML constitutes the paradigm of automated anti-money laundering effort. Let us zoom in on a number of aspects of this effort, from the perspective of those who are responsible for implementing the software and delivering a practical, reliable solution, to those financial institutions in need of a robust and efficient AML alerting operation.

SUMMARY

Over the decades the regulatory framework has extended its scope across a wide range of financial services and high-value goods markets, ranging from retail banking to wealth management corporate banking, gambling facilities, and high-value goods retailing. Whereas there are common denominators across all of these industries, many of them require specifically designed scenarios and models to address specific money laundering vulnerabilities intrinsic to the type of (financial) service delivery. Different criminal modus operandi and differences in product data and volumes across these various lines of business may require a different approach in the detection and prevention of money laundering.

CHAPTER **3**

The Importance of Data

Like any automated system, transaction monitoring relies on source data: the data that is fed into the system and that need to be analyzed. Data availability and quality are decisive factors for any analytical software to produce meaningful results in terms of business intelligence. For AML transaction monitoring this is no different.

Any discussion of the data aspect of an implementation project cannot escape the more technical detail behind data structure and data transformation, and as authors we do realize that this is not everyone's cup of tea. We have tried to write and illustrate this chapter in such a way as to make it understandable and digestible, to include the reader who is still a novice in data management. Please rest assured that the following chapters do not have a heavy dependency on this chapter about data, should you be inclined to skip this part and continue straight on to the next chapter.

ETL: EXTRACT, TRANSFORM, AND LOAD

AML transaction monitoring systems, for a number of reasons, will almost never use the data directly at its original source. Execution of transactions is perhaps the most business-critical process for any financial institution and the stability of these processes are of utmost importance. Financial institutions won't jeopardize these processes by letting secondary processes, like AML transaction monitoring, directly feed off that same data. In addition to this, performance service-level agreements (SLA) for secondary processes, especially if these are very different and there is no need to use source data directly. A third reason is that most financial institutions use many different systems for executing different type of transactions, all of which may be in scope for transaction monitoring. Deploying separate transaction monitoring systems for each of these source systems separately would not be wise. Finally, the data needed for risk-based transaction monitoring is not strictly transactional data, but also other data, such as customer details, account details, and the links between these and changes to these data. Often, but not always, these different sets of data may be brought together by the financial institution in a central data repository or warehouse, which may be considered a source, but in fact is already a copy of the truly original data kept in disparate systems and sources.

Data used for AML transaction monitoring usually travels through multiple layers; by travel we mean that (partial) copies of the (relevant) data are taken and processed further to prep these for the transaction monitoring and alerting process.

This process is referred to as ETL: Extract, Transform, Load.

EXTRACT: DATA AVAILABILITY AND SOURCING

Extract stands for the extraction of the relevant data from its original source and bringing it together in one single place; a repository of some sort is often referred to as a staging or landing area. For any system to work, it will need to have the data it requires directly available. This may appear as a given: transaction monitoring assumes the existence of transactions, and therefore transaction data, to be monitored. What does not exist does not need to be monitored. But in IT things are never that simple. For the transaction monitoring to be successful, data on different object types will need to be combined. Transaction data will need to be tied to customer and account data. Different scenarios may require different data points to take into consideration and not seldom a new system is chosen for its capabilities and scenarios *before* checks have been executed on the availability of the data these scenarios assume. What data is required depends predominantly on the scenarios the financial institution wants to put in place, and, to a lesser degree, also by requirements end users may have for so-called enrichment data. Enrichment data is data that is strictly not needed to run a scenario and to decide if an alert must be generated, but information that is added to the alert after it is generated provides additional information relevant to the analyst or investigator. For example, at which branch or ATM a transaction took place may, by itself, not be of relevance to the scenario, but the analyst triaging the alert may nevertheless have a need to know this. For that information to be made available in the alert user interface, the data must be available in the first place, hence extracted from a source. A third category of required data is data that the system needs at the minimum to run. An example is relational data, linking accounts to customers. Many systems come with pre-built data constraints that seek to protect the data integrity. If, for example, alerts are rolled up at customer level, then for that part of the process not to fail, every account must have at least one account owner associated with it. If that information is somehow missing, the system may break, and the alerting process may come to a premature halt.

It is not enough to check the availability of data merely by looking at the database structure or the data model. Too often data is assumed available merely because the formal data structure is there. The fact that there is a table for customer data does not mean that it is also populated or that all customer data is in there. This may seem trivial, but years of experience in implementing software have taught us that (false) assumptions are rife, and that includes data that should be there . . . but isn't.

One must bear in mind that data repositories and warehouses are often designed and built with vision and often reflect a would-be or future projected world rather than reality. Data integration teams must check the actual fill rate of the columns that are key to the scenarios or the system at large.

So far, we have considered the financial institution's customer management system as the source of the data. In reality much of the data is actually sourced before that, by manual input into a front-end application or web form. Data can be put in by staff at the branch, but in these times also by the customer him/herself through an online banking web form or app. To ensure data availability and minimum data quality, validation checks are built into the front-end mechanism used to capture the data. Dropdowns, date selectors, address lookup widgets, radio buttons, and validation messages prevent the end user submitting incomplete forms; all of these are mechanisms to (pre) structure and (pre)format the data and contribute to data quality and availability.

Some data, however, may still come as free or unstructured text: where a specific format is not enforced and, in computer terms, it is not predictable where (i.e. at which character position) a particular piece of information will appear in the text, or whether it is included at all. Typical examples are SWIFT messages that contain multi-aspect beneficiary and remitter information in many different formats. The message may be structured from the perspective of the issuing bank, but as no standard has been agreed on by banks, there is a multitude of different variations exchanged amongst tens of thousands of financial institutions worldwide. Multi-aspect here means that one unstructured text string encompasses first name, middle name (if any), last name, address details, and more. The multi-aspect text string will need to be parsed and each component may need to undergo quality assurance transformations, such as standardization (e.g. of country and/or province and city names). Transforming the data is discussed in the next paragraph. The breaking down of a multi-aspect text string and categorizing its elements (as an individual's or entity's name, a street or house number, a country) is called (text) parsing. The parsing of data is required for the data availability checks and the more sophisticated the parsing analytics, the completer and more accurate the data in the output.

Regardless as to whether data is captured as open text or in a pre-formatted form (such as by multi-value dropdowns or checkboxes), if the data is manually selected by a customer or onboarding staff, the accuracy or correctness of the input is not guaranteed. Depending on the nature of the data point, the personal judgment, expertise, and experience of the end user may play a role and, sometimes, end users may simply not be knowledgeable enough to determine accurately. As an example, for a trade finance department, the staff might give a product classification code for each trade. There are too many different kinds of goods and services, making an accurate categorization nearly impossible.

Questions around data availability start with the selection of scenarios and alert enrichment requirements; at least those data points should be collected that will make the scenario able to run or that are of pertinent importance to the analyst or investigator when triaging or investigating an alert. When considering a scenario for inclusion in the transaction monitoring system, one should look carefully at the available data before deciding to implement it. Not carefully considering scenarios in relation to data availability may result in a scenario being useless.

As we have seen in the above example around free text and data capturing by humans, these scenario-driven checks do not stop at the mere availability of data, but also need to look at the quality of the data, both in terms of the technical quality (does it come in the right standardized format?) and the intrinsic quality of the content (are most fields reflecting the situation accurately and/or correctly?). This brings us to the second letter in the ETL acronym, the T for *Transform*.

TRANSFORM: DATA QUALITY, CONVERSION, AND REPAIR

The transform step takes care of any further transformation the data may need to undergo in order to be readily usable by the transaction monitoring system. At best, and for most of the data, it will not need reformatting and can be used as is. If it needs reformatting this can take many different forms (Figure 3.1).

Data (re)structuring is not concerned with the individual data points, but with how the data is structured. For example, a vertical table in the source system may need to be pivoted into a horizontal table, simply because that is how the system expects the data. Account details and permutations to these may be stored in a long narrow vertical table, whereby each row contains not more than the valid-from and valid-to date,[1] the account reference, an attribute identifier, and the actual value of that attribute, may need to be converted into a wide table, where one row contains all attributes and the attribute identifiers will form the column names (Figure 3.2).

Another example is that data stored in one row may need to be split into two rows, such as where the source system stores both sides (debit and credit) of the transaction in one row (treating it as one transaction), but the transaction monitoring system expects these as two separate rows, effectively distinguishing between two different transactions: one for the debit aspect and one for the credit aspect.

Where some systems may store account holder information as account attributes, the transaction monitoring system may utilize a relational database schema where customers and accounts are different dimensions with each their own table or family of tables, or vice versa. Even if both are relational schemas, then one schema may

[1]Valid-from and valid-to dates are used to delineate the time window for which the data is valid. This links into version control and the keeping of historic data and a record of change to see previous versions of a record and permutations over time. These topics will be discussed in more detail below.

EntityKey	EntityFullName	EntityType	EntityNationality
E0112213	Clark Kent	Natural Person	USA
E0112214	Bruce Banner	Natural Person	GER
E0112215	Wayne Enterprise Ltd	Legal Entity	-

FOREIGN_KEY	FIELD_NAME	FIELD_VALUE	VALID_FROM	VALID_TO
AML_0112213	FULL_NAME	Clark Kent	1974MAY22	2999DEC31
E0112213	TYPE	Natural Person	1974MAY22	2999DEC31
E0112213	NATIONALITY	United States	1974MAY22	2999DEC31
E0112214	FULL_NAME	Bruce Banner	1981JAN04	2999DEC31
E0112214	TYPE	Natural Person	1981JAN04	2999DEC31
E0112214	NATIONALITY	Germany	1981JAN04	2999DEC31
E0112215	FULL_NAME	Wayne Enterprise Ltd	1984SEP01	2999DEC31
E0112215	TYPE	Legal Entity	1984SEP01	2999DEC31
E0112215	NATIONALITY	n/a	1984SEP01	2999DEC31

Figure 3.1 An example of data transformation – vertical table pivoted into a horizontal table.

Transactionkey	Amount	RemitterAccount	Rtype	BeneficiaryAccount	Btype	ExecutionDate
T123322333	200.000,00	ES52 0182 1238 6102 0164 4701	INT	ES83 0182 1238 6202 0164 2232	INT	2018JUN28
T123322334	34.675,50	ES52 0182 1238 6102 0164 4701	EXT	ES18 0049 0190 1923 9416 4511	EXT	2018JUN28

InternalTransactions

Transactionkey	RelatedTransactionkey	Amount	Account	Ttype	ExecutionDate
T123322333	T123322334	–200.000,00	ES52 0182 1238 6102 0164 4701	DEBIT	2018JUN28
T123322334	T123322333	200.000,00	ES83 0182 1238 6202 0164 2232	CREDIT	2018JUN28
T123322335	E354454433	–34.675,50	ES52 0182 1238 6102 0164 4701	DEBIT	2018JUN28

ExternalTransactions

Transactionkey	RelatedTransactionkey	Amount	Account	Ttype	ExecutionDate
E354454433	T123322335	34.675,50	ES18 0049 0190 1923 9416 4511	CREDIT	2018JUN28

Figure 3.2 Another example of data transformation – one row is split into two rows.

link dimensions with in-between bridge tables (allowing for many-to-many) relationships, whereas the other system may be lacking bridge tables and store foreign keys (i.e. references to the related objects in other dimensions, such as an account key, or array of account keys stored as customer attributes). See Figure 3.3.

Some structural transformation may result from the database schema. For example, the SAS AML system uses a star schema for many of its data where dimension data is separated fact data. Whereas the dimension data contain descriptive, non-quantitative attributes, the measurements, or quantitative data, is stored in one or multiple separate columns. This has performance benefits as columns that contain strictly numerical data can be searched through and linked faster than alpha-numerical columns and tables. In some systems month and date are created as separate dimensions with a numeric key for the same reason. Data that may be in a large flat table in the source repository may need to be split out over a dimension and multiple fact tables.

Minus values, such as debit amounts that are stored as a negative number may have to be stored as positive values in a separate debit column, where the column indicates the negative, rather than a mathematical symbol.

Structural data transformations are of key importance to the baseline functioning of any transaction monitoring system and the transformations needed, without exception, vary from financial institution to financial institution. One must learn to understand the data structure from both sides, the source data side and the transaction monitoring side, in order to make right transformations, and it usually requires experienced data management consultants, or data stewards or data scientists to make the right decisions. Knowing "what to transform to what" is only one part of it. How to do it, is not trivial either, as different approaches may come with different processing times and performance implications and in most situations batch processing time is a scarce commodity.

Then there are transformations at data object level, such as the way addresses and names are stored. Both address and full name often have multiple different elements and they can come as separate data items (tokenized) and need concatenation, i.e. to be merged into one

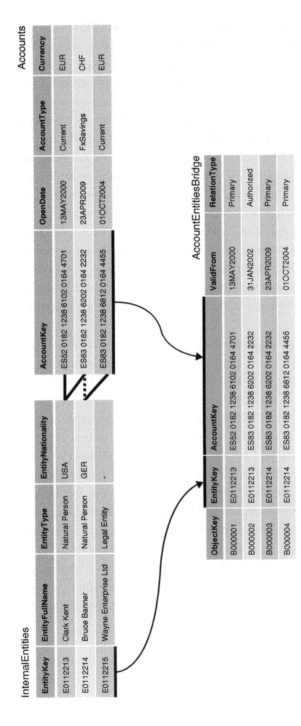

Figure 3.3 Linking dimensions with in-between bridge tables.

single value (where the elements are separated by a space, or comma- or semi-colon-separated); or the other way around, where concatenated data need to be parsed in order to store the different elements separately, such as first name, middle name, last name, prefix, suffix, or, in case of the address, house number and street name, postcode, state, and country (see Figure 3.4).

Thirdly there are data value transformations, where data must be reformatted or mapped against and replaced by codes. Typical candidates for reformatting are date and timestamp data. Some systems require date and datetime information to be stored in a specific format that may be different from the source data and a conversion needs to take place before timestamps and dates can be loaded.

Some systems will prefer storing indexed data in a predefined case, most commonly uppercase, for faster indexing and searching. Interpunctions may be removed to simplify the formats. John W.H. Smiths may be converted into JOHN W H SMITHS before loaded.

Often open text data will need to be (re)structured to codes. Country names may need to be standardized and converted into the ISO2 or ISO3 code; United States or United States of America will be converted into either US or USA. Debit and credit indicators, transaction types, customer types – even when they come as codes in sources – may need to be mapped to pre-existing codes used by the source system or, the other way around, to a set of codes used by the AML transaction monitoring system. For example, the country names captured in ISO2 codes (US, UK, NL, DE) may need to be converted into ISO3 (USA, GBR, NLD, GER) or vice versa.

Sometimes data may need to be provided with a prefix or suffix, e.g. when a key column only allows for unique values but takes a feed from a multiple source system with the possibility of duplicate keys. This is typically the case when transactions come from multiple transaction systems, which have keys unique to the source system, but not necessarily across these, and a unique reference to the system of origin may need to be added to avoid duplicity (Figure 3.5).

Also, part of the transformation step is when data is created for the sake of the transaction monitoring system. A good example may be match code creation, which is discussed in more detail in the section on Watchlists and Matching. Match codes are created to standardize

2 1/2 Premier Place
Devonshire Square
EC2 6WE
London
Greater London
United Kingdom

Egészségház út 4
Lakás 13b
Eger 3300
Heves, Magyarország

Burj Al Arab Jumeirah.
PO Box 74147, Dubai,
UAE

100 NORTH CHATHAM
STREET, CARY, 27511
NC UNITED STATES

100 N. Chatham St.,
cary, North Carolina,
27511 usa

Street	Building No	Flat No	Postcode	City	State	Country
DEVONSHIRE SQUARE	2 1/2	-	EC2M 4YE	LONDON	GREATER LONDON	UK
EGÉSZSÉGHÁZ ÚT 4	-	13B	3300	EGER	HEVES	HU
JUMEIRAH	-	-	74147	DUBAI		AE
NORTH CHATHAM STREET	100		27511	CARY	NC	US
NORTH CHATHAM STREET	100		27511	CARY	NC	US

Figure 3.4 Concatenated data is parsed to store the different elements separately.

Suffix	Description	Example Fields	Example Values
_DT	Date	DATE_OF_BIRTH_DT	02/04/1978 / 19780402 / 02-APR-2018 / 02APR1978
_DTTM	Datetime / timestamp	TRANSACTION_DTTM	02/04/2018_12:50:34:0300 / 201804021250340300 / 02-APR-18 11.46.45.287000000 AM
_NUM	Numeric / Integer	HOME_TELEPHONE_NUM	44619027783, 938178110
_CD	Code / Lookup Value	ADDRESS_COUNTRY_CD	US, NL, ZA, DE, UK / USA, NLD, ZAF, GER, GBR
_FLG	Flag / Boolean	REPORTED_FLG	Y, N / 1, 0
_KEY	Unique Key	PARENT_CASE_KEY	C2018_023322, C2018_023323 / 23322, 23323
_ID	Unique Key	TRANSACTION_KEY	233444333, 233444334, 233444335

Figure 3.5 Naming conventions for data fields.

and normalize the data with the specific purpose of supporting fuzzy logic and locale matching (Figure 3.6).

In the case of fuzzy logic both John Smiths and Jonny Smiths may be considered a match against a search for Jon Smith. All three names are converted into exactly the same code and these codes may be stored in a separate table or column for that purpose. Some of the match code algorithms may also create codes for common name variations in a certain language, such as Jan, Johan, Johannes or John, Jon, Johnny and Jonny.

Full Namecv	Match Code
James T. Kirk	PHDF8B~$$$$$87B$$$
Jim Kirk	PHDF8B~$$$$$87B$$$
JAMES KIRK	PHDF8B~$$$$$87B$$$
Dr. James Kirk	PHDF8B~$$$$$87B$$$
Jimmy Kirk	PHDF8B~$$$$$87B$$$

Full Name	Match Code
Moammar Gadafi	F&88&G7$$BY$$$$
Moammar Gadafy	F&88&G7$$BY$$$$
Moammar Gaddafi	F&88&G7$$BY$$$$
Moammar Qadhdhafi	F&88&G7$$BY$$$$
Moammar Gadafi	F&88&G7$$BY$$$$

Spelling Variations and errors	Resolves to
The Hague	
Den Haag	
's Gravenhage	
's gravenhagen	
S' Gravenhage	DEN HAAG
Haag	
Hague	
Denhaag	
DenHaag	

Figure 3.6 Match code generation.

One could argue whether the creation and adding of these match codes is strictly part of the ETL or is the actual processing based on functionality provided by the system. This is a matter of definition and the answer may change depending on when and by what tool this is done.

Another form of data augmentation is when missing data is replaced by a default value if the target system requires a value, and from a logic perspective it is better to work on the basis of an assumption rather than a null value. For example, if there is a telephone number but the field for the country code is missing or contains a value that cannot be mapped against a list of allowed values, then the base country code may need to be filled in rather than a blank. The same may be done for transaction currency or account currency. These default values can be local country and currency code or $ and +001.

Data augmentation as part of the ETL process also happens when data are created when the data is loaded into the target system: load keys and/or load timestamps and surrogate keys. The former may be required by the alerting engine (as it may have a need to know which data is new and not looked at before), the latter is typically required by the destination database, that will add its own keys to preserve its own integrity.

Finally, after all transformations are done there may still be data that does not meet the required format, but it will cause an error and break the system if the data is loaded anyway. When the data cannot be augmented as no augmentation rule seems to apply, then the data must be expelled from the records that will be loaded into the target system. Relevant rows will be removed, and the instance will be included in an exception report, which will be discussed in further detail in the next section. Examples are null values where there should not be any, such as for a transaction amount, or missing or non-existent foreign keys making an object into an orphan object, such an account without an identifiable account holder, or a transaction without an identifiable account. These can be caused by incidental glitches in any of the systems through which the data passes, to more structural errors in the configuration of the ETL logic. The exception reports will help the application admin and data steward to find out if there is something structurally wrong somewhere upstream that needs to be addressed.

DATA LOAD AND FURTHER PROCESSING

The last step in the ETL process is the *loading* of the data and then the creation of exception reports and/or other reports providing data lineage information.

Loading of the Data

Most systems will load the data in a database that is part of the system. These data are usually referred to as "Core" data and are distinguished from data generated by, or added to, the system as part of the alert generation process or the alert triage or case management handling. Systems commonly have at least one database schema where it will store (a copy of) the core data. Most systems will have a relational database or another type of schema where objects of diverse types are stored in separate tables or datasets.

Load Sequence

To preserve data and database integrity constraints will be set up, for example to avoid illegitimate references. For example, accounts cannot be "orphan" accounts and must have at least one customer (or "internal party" or "entity") associated with it in the role as primary account holder. To enforce the internal checks ("constraints") are set up that new accounts cannot be added to the schema unless the parties have been loaded. Depending on where the link is captured – as foreign (account) key to the party, foreign (party) key to the account or in a bridge table (supporting many-to-many relationships) between accounts and parties – the sequence will be different to make sure that the table holding the relationship will be loaded last.

Delta Load

Batch systems runs as per a schedule. Usually this is done either on a daily basis before or at the end of each business day excluding weekends and bank holidays. Intraday runs, where the systems run multiple times a day, are very rare and most systems and the wider ecosystems they operate in will not support them. If the ETL process is part of a daily run then it would not make sense to execute an alert generation process multiple times a day and in between two ETL runs: it would be executed on the back of the same source data and simply create a result that is an exact duplicate of the first previous run.

If the financial institution – or more accurately, the system— serves a distinct geography with a distinct time zone, then it is very common for the batch run to be executed overnight, when front office branches and most mid- and back-office departments are not open for work (quiet time). Many systems will require the alert and case management user interface to be inaccessible during the batch run, as any manual updates from end users in the case management UI may interfere with the update of the source data and the generation of alerts from a back-end batch perspective. Running the batch would disrupt the operations. Another reason for running the system during quiet times is that the ecosystem cannot support anything else. It may be that a number of ETL steps will be executed internally (collecting and aggregating the data from multiple payments systems, before it can be presented to the staging area from which the AML ETL will pick it up. Many financial institutions will opt for doing this separately, and let the various processes run in parallel. As a consequence, there may be some additional "latency": the AML system's ETL will not pick up data from the first previous business day, but from two or three days before, to give the data time travelling through the various stages of internal processing. From an AML regulatory perspective this is an accepted practice.

Systems that run and load the data on a (business) daily frequency, and the requirement to do this within quiet hours with the least impact on core business activities, may put some additional restraints on the time available to complete this process. This is called the batch window and it refers to a cut-off time where the process must be successfully completed in order to avoid any disruption to the daily, business-as-usual, activities. The actual batch window may be even shorter because some margin will be built in to allow for error investigation and response and for a go- or no-go decision in case the batch run for whatever reason fails.

As a result, quite often, the batch window imposes limitations on the volume of data that can be loaded and one way to meet these restraints is by loading only relevant data. The data needed for doing the transaction monitoring analysis consist in part of, what is called slowly changing dimension data. Things like customer data, account data, branch data will not change for every customer, account or branch every day. From the perspective of a single customer, account or branch, a change, such as a change of address opening a new account, is a relatively rare event. Therefore, it is not needed and would take up too much time to completely load the entire customer, account, and branch population during every batch run: only the delta of changed data will need to be loaded with inclusion of some data elements that capture the time of the change and a possible new version. Depending on which slowly changing dimension approach is taken — there are several numbered from I to VIII, which we will not discuss in detail here — the core database will gradually expand as every new version may be saved on top of the older one but not replacing it. However, while database size will increase, the time it takes to load data will not increase but fluctuate per batch, depending on the number of changed objects. In times of organic growth of the financial institution, where the number of (new) customers increase or when due to online banking innovations the financial institution has made it easier for customers to make changes, the change delta may increase. When planning for the computing capacity needed one must take into account near future growth expectations.

Transaction data is not subject to slowly changing dimension considerations as these are one-off events and not subject to change after these have been executed. It is important that every transaction subject to money laundering will be included in one batch and one batch only. From a regulatory perspective it is important that no transactions are missing, but for an analysis perspective it is equally important not to consider any transaction more than once as this would lead to double count and will incorrectly skew the risk assessment. One must therefore decide on a fail-safe mechanism that defines a load key to meet those requirements. One may think that the transaction date would provide for an easy and clear-cut criterion, but the reality is not that simple. First, usually more than one date is tied to transactions, such as a request date, execution date, and/or settlement date. Even in times of online real-time banking these dates may lie more than a day apart. But one could settle for any of these dates as long as these are consistently used across all transaction types and will not be subject to change. From that perspective, it would be safest to use the settlement date although this may lead to a further, and significant, increase of the latency and transactions; by the time they are included in the analysis it may be outdated even beyond a scenario's lookback period. This does not necessarily have to be a problem, as long as this latency is consistent across time and different transaction types that are considered by the same scenarios.

Data Lineage

As mentioned above, it is important to regulators that all transactions and other relevant data are accounted for. If, for data quality and integrity reasons, data is transformed, and certain data elements are rejected, then this needs to be captured in an audit trail. All data must be accounted for and the output, in terms of the staged sources data must be reconcilable with (raw) input. This ability and process of reconciliation is referred to as data lineage.

Data lineage is part and parcel of the ETL and closely connects to database restraints and other minimum data requirements built into the ETL process. For example, if there is a rule that expels "orphan" accounts from the record, the ETL job must verify the integrity of accounts and the expelled orphan account record must be logged and be retrievable for the audit trail (data lineage) and data quality analysis and optimization.

MULTIPLE ETLS

The above-described ETL process mostly refers to the main process where data is extracted from the core source data and eventually loaded into the central database for the principal purpose of the transaction monitoring system: the analysis of these data with the aim of generating alerts for unusual or suspicious behavior on the accounts of customers. However, depending on the scope of the system, other ETL processes may be set up on the side. One example is that of the ETL for Management Information (MI) reporting. Whilst the main

ETL process deals with the actual data to be processed, the MI data *describes* these data and the data generated from it, mainly and mostly for the purpose of operational management. Depending on what data these reports use at input there can be more or less challenges around sourcing the data. Commonly the MI ETL is much less challenging compared to the source data ETL. Many reports primarily ingest internal data, that is generated by the system itself, such as the number of alerts, number of cases, and alert/case status distributions and associated user data. These data are produced within and by the AML transaction monitoring system and therefore their format and accuracy are known and tested. If out-of-the-box reports are used that come prepackaged with the AML software, then the ETL will be delivered as part of the software; no further effort is required. However, financial institutions commonly have their own specific reporting requirements and reporting packages are either fully bespoke or have elements of customization. Depending on the degree of customization, the associated ETL may face any of the challenges as described above. Whilst it is only natural for the acquirers of the software to focus on the reports and the implementation effort and cost associated with designing those reports, vendor representatives should be aware that updating the ETL or building it from scratch may have further significant impact on project cost, duration, and/or risk.

SUMMARY

Like any automated system, transaction monitoring relies on source data: the data that is fed into the system and that need to be analyzed. Data availability and quality are decisive factors for any analytical software to produce meaningful results in terms of business intelligence. Data used for AML transaction monitoring usually travels through multiple layers. This process is referred to as ETL: Extract, Transform, Load. Extract stands for the extraction of the relevant data from its original source and bringing it together in one single place, a repository of some sort is often referred to as a staging or landing area. The transform step takes care of any further transformation the data may need to undergo in order to be readily usable by the transaction monitoring system. Structural data transformations are of key importance to the baseline functioning of any transaction monitoring system, and the transformations needed, without exception, vary from financial institution to financial institution. One must learn to understand the data structure from both sides, the source data side and the transaction monitoring side. The last step in the ETL process is the loading of the data and then the creation of exception reports and/or other reports providing data lineage information, as it is important to regulators that all transactions and other relevant data are accounted for. Assessing data readiness, making it fit for purpose, and loading it into the system on a regular basis, without exception is a big component of any AML software implementation, and at the heart of any system. Data and data management can make or break the system.

CHAPTER 4

Typical Scenario Elements

Many scenarios have some elements in common. All scenarios, for example, have an actionable entity as their focal point, albeit that the actionable entity can be different for certain groups of scenarios: some will focus and aggregate at account level, some at customer level, some at household level, whilst other scenarios may focus on branches, (corresponding) bank, or even aggregate at associate/employee level. From a different viewpoint, while some scenarios do not differentiate between transaction types, others may consider only transactions of a certain type, such as cash withdrawals and deposits, or wire transfers. All scenarios, in a way, utilize a lookback period. A lookback period is the time window a scenario looks back on to consider transactions and aggregate data across that period. A scenario will at least have a lookback period of the interval between two batch runs, as otherwise transactions will be skipped in the analysis and this will cause a significant regulatory problem. Most of the scenarios will use thresholds and often these are parameterized.

TRANSACTION TYPES

Every transaction can be described by its features. It can be a credit or debit transaction (seen from the perspective of the account under investigation). It is conducted through a channel and, as a result, we can distinguish between wire transactions, cash transactions, ATM transactions, credit or debit card transactions, etc. The transaction would belong to an account of some type and a business product: a loan payment, a savings deposit, etc. There may be further qualifiers describing the properties of the transaction. These parameters are relevant for AML transaction monitoring. Sometimes, very similar types of transaction may be handled by a number of different systems, each slightly different in their data properties or with varying granularity. Ideally, any discrepancies are handled in the ETL or even before as data quality issues. Sometimes, transaction data is richer than necessary; for efficiency and efficacy reasons it can be better to keep the business logic relatively simple and straightforward. This may vary from scenario to scenario, where some scenarios may be considering only subsets of the transactions, such as wire transfers only.

On consolidating data from various source systems into the AML transaction monitoring system, transactions need to be generalized to a defined set of transaction types. This facilitates scenario rules to pick the target transactions in concern. For example, a scenario rule for cash withdrawal would pick the transactions of type belonging to Cash and Debit. Another scenario for loan repayment would pick for Loan and Credit. If the transaction types are defined too granular, it would be hard to specify on setting up rules. A categorization process is needed to extract the most important characteristics, leaving aside the obsolete or redundant details. This process resembles a statistical modeling process, whereby the resulting set of transaction types describes the transactions by the representative properties that are used by the set of scenario rules.

Typical Transaction Information Useful for AML Transaction Monitoring

Basic information of a transaction

- Account
- Amount
- Currency
- Type of transaction
- Date/time
- Branch involved
- Involved bank staff
- Country where the transaction happened

Information related to wire

- Beneficiary/Remitter – name and address
- Banks involved (Ordering bank, Cover bank, Sender bank, Receiver bank)

Information related to a loan repayment

- Source of payment
- Payer

Type of transaction

- Credit/Debit/Event/Intermediary
- Media (Cash/Cheque/Internal transfer/ Wire)
- Product
- Channel (Branch/ATM/Phone banking/Mobile banking)

The scenario rules can be implemented to specify the simple criterion for the target transactions. A scenario for cash withdrawal would have a simple filter for medium being CASH and action being DEBIT.

One must keep in mind that the monitoring is about customer behavior. Anything that is out of a customer's control would be less useful for the transaction monitoring system and there is no need for such information to be stored (and take up space) in the database. The following information is probably less useful for the purpose of transaction monitoring:

- Any information that the customer cannot control or has very little control over
  - Fee and charges by the financial institute
  - Interest rate
  - Foreign exchange rate
- Any information related to the financial institute's internal operations

  - Related to institute's internal accounts
  - Internal approval process
  - Fixed deposit account roll-over
  - Corrections due to internal mistakes

For example, in a check deposit transaction, there's a deposit action and a check settlement action. They have the same amount but with different dates. The customer's direct, intended action is the deposit. The check settlement is an operation that happens behind the scenes and is not something that the customer asks for. So, the deposit action, rather than the settlement action, is useful for AML monitoring.

In general, any transaction monitoring system differentiates between data for analytical purposes and data for information

Table 4.1 Example list of transaction types.

Transaction Type Code	C/D/I/E	Primary Medium	Secondary Medium	Mechanism
2911	CREDIT	CASH	OTHERS	ATM
2912	DEBIT	CASH	OTHERS	ATM
3901	CREDIT	WIRE	OTHERS	OTHERS
3902	DEBIT	WIRE	OTHERS	OTHERS
3911	CREDIT	WIRE	OTHERS	INTERNET
3912	DEBIT	WIRE	OTHERS	INTERNET
4011	CREDIT	TRANSFER	N/A	INTERNET
4012	DEBIT	TRANSFER	N/A	INTERNET
9091	CREDIT	OTHERS	N/A	OTHERS
9092	DEBIT	OTHERS	N/A	OTHERS
etc.	...		...	...

purposes. The one does not exclude the other and many data will serve both. Data for analytical purposes is used by the scenarios to determine if an alert will need to be generated and, sometimes, also to calculate a risk score.

On implementation, the set of transaction types is defined mainly based on (i) scenario rules logic, and (ii) the need to facilitate investigative actions after an alert has been raised and/or a case been created.

Many systems may come with a transaction typology, and the fastest route to value is to map the organizations transaction types to these. Additional types may still need to be added or be split into two or more categories, especially if there is a specific requirement for certain rules or scenarios to do so. Table 4.1 is an example list of transaction types for transaction monitoring.

On extracting transactions for a scenario or rule, it specifies the few attributes of transaction types. A scenario for cash deposit may have a parameter primary medium = CASH and another parameter cdi = CREDIT.

In the database, the transactions have a transaction type code field with single numeric values like 2911, 2991. Both 2911 and 2991 would be included for CASH − CREDIT scenarios.

A typical AML scenario would, for example, look at a structured depositing of cash sums (increase in number of deposits, all of or around a certain amount more than a few hundred dollars, shortly followed by a few debit wires at approximately the same total sum of the cash deposits.

Coding to a Convention

It may be useful to use a convention to determine the unique key for each transaction type, so that the information can be implied directly from the number. Below is an example coding scheme:

- First digit: Primary medium (1–exchange, 2–cash, 3–wire, 4–transfer, 5–credit card, 6–loan, 9–other)
- Second digit: Secondary medium (0–N/A, 9–other, 1. . . 8 for different values)
- Third digit: Mechanism
- Fourth digit: C/D/I/E: 0–event, 1–credit, 2–debit, 3–intermediary

So, in the above examples, any transaction type with the first digit as 2 and last digit as 1 are cash deposits.

ACTIONABLE ENTITY

Banks organize their data according to the objects that make up their business: customers, accounts, transactions. We can call these "dimensions" and, not by coincidence, banks organize their core data often in a dimensional nature, hence, literally in dimensional databases. This allows for economic data management, and facilitates the linking of the dimensions to reflect the financial services reality, where a customer can be party to one or multiple accounts, most accounts can have multiple parties associated with them, multiple transactions, or done on any given account. Furthermore, customers can be further organized in units, such as households. Usually, accounts are organized internally as belonging to a specific branch. Events on the account (such as account opening) and transactions may be executed by a specific bank employee and that can also be a factor of interest.

Table 4.2 Transactions under a party.

Party	Account	Transaction Date	Transaction Amount
P	A001	3/1/2017	$1,000
		3/1/2017	$20,000
		17/1/2017	$40,000
		17/1/2017	$7,000
		18/1/2017	$9,000
P	A002	16/1/2017	$5,000
		17/1/2017	$20,000
		17/1/2017	$30,000

A full-fledged transaction monitoring system is capable of investigating and detecting patterns for each of these dimensions. In the world of data management, the dimensions are called BY factors, derived from the database action to group transactions or other events *by* account, *by* customer, *by* branch, etc. In the world of alerting and case investigation these dimensions are called actionable entities: it is the *account* that is being looked at and requires action, it is the *customer* who is being looked at and may require corrective action, etc.

Scenarios, therefore, will have to accommodate certain ways of looking at transactions and can be distinguished as *transaction* scenarios, *account* scenarios, *customer* or *entity* scenarios, *household* scenarios, *branch* scenarios, and *teller* or *associate* scenarios.

Party-Level Monitoring

However, it is the individual person or corporation who initiates the actions. Therefore, when it comes to AML transaction monitoring, it should monitor not only the account, but also the account holder(s). On aggregating transactions, normally they should be aggregated at the party (i.e. account holder) level. For example, a person P has two accounts A001 and A002. Each account has certain transactions, as shown in Table 4.2.

Aggregating the transactions by account would give 77,000 for A001 and 55,000 for A002. However, party P has $132,000 in total transactions if aggregated by party. This is a more holistic view of the party's activities. It could cover all actions by the individual person on the institute. Most scenario rules monitor transactions at the party level.

Naturally, such a holistic customer view is still limited to activity within the financial institution only. If the person disburses the illegal fund through different banks, monitoring from any single bank can only capture a portion of that person's activities.

Account-Level Monitoring

Sometimes patterns will be missed if taking too wide an angle, and zooming in on a single account is required to detect suspicious activity. Typical examples are velocity rules and dormant account rules (which are in fact velocity rules in their own right). Velocity rules look at a sudden increase in activity on a particular account. This is extremely visible for dormant accounts, i.e. accounts that for a long period of time do not see any activity and then are awakened. Typically the scenario will only look at certain types of accounts where this is unusual; long-term savings accounts or trust accounts for minors are exempt, as it is perfectly normal for those accounts to see no activity for a long period following which all or part of the savings are used at a significant moment in the beneficiary's life (e.g. reaching a mature age, going to college, buying a house, retiring).

Household-Level Monitoring

In some cases, the scenario may group transactions at household level, which means it aggregates the transactions of different customers belonging to the same household. This household can be any relationship across the multiple parties.

Examples are:

- Child companies under same parent company
- Shareholders and/or directors of the same company
- Employees under the same organization
- Individual persons in the same family
- People living at the same address

A number of criminals may launder money working together or even using their kin as mules. Monitoring would be effective if transactions among these multiple parties could be checked collectively. The biggest challenge is that the financial institution has to know about the relationship in the first place. Corporate structure information is normally declared to banks, but employment and family structure are not mandatory. Addresses would be available, but it would need the financial institution to dig out which parties have the same addresses, and even then, people sharing an address may not necessarily representing a household, such as students living in the same dormitory.

Transaction-Level Monitoring

In some scenarios, a single transaction is enough for producing an alert. These scenarios are often remnants from the time of the original 40 FATF recommendations, when a simpler and cruder rule-based system was adopted. An example that most will recognize is the scenario or rule whereby a single cash deposit exceeds a certain threshold, usually $10,000 or its equivalent in local currency. Another example can be found in the scenario that identifies the counterparty of a wire transfer as appearing on a watchlist, more specifically a sanctions list. One does not need to look further than the one transaction to generate an alert.

One can genuinely wonder about the efficacy of such single transaction rules, as by now, those committing money laundering know about these rules and will evade them with little effort. However, one should remember the primary objective of AML for financial institutions (as discussed in Chapter 1 of this book): AML at financial institutions is not so much geared towards catching the crooks, but to avoid abuse of the financial system and avoid making it easy for criminals and launderers to whitewash their criminal proceeds. Simple rules like the cash deposit rule must stay in place as a safety blanket, without which it would become much easier for malicious account holders to make use of it, i.e. abuse the financial system. Although these rules do not have much of a deterrent effect, at least they seem to have a preventive effect, even though one can ask what exactly it is that they prevent.

In case of the sanctions list example, one may also question the efficacy, as sanction screening at payment level will, in most countries, need to be done before executing the payment. If the AML transaction monitoring system has a real-time component, such a scenario makes sense. Many banks will have separate payment screening tooling in place to take care of real-time sanctions screening, and not so much rely on the batch (after the fact) transaction monitoring system. However, depending on the reliability of the real-time system, it is always good to have a safety net in place to catch those transactions that have, for whatever reason, not been caught by the real-time provision.

Handling of Joint Accounts

Be aware that party and account is a many-to-many relationship. In this day and age customers usually have more than one account, often with the same financial institution. And, evidently, one account can have multiple account holders or signatories, either in terms of a joint account or in terms of otherwise authorized persons on the account holding power of attorney.

In Figure 4.1, party A and party B each have their own accounts, and a joint account 002 owned by both A and B. For a party-level scenario, it aggregates for party A the transactions under account 001 and 002, and for party B the transactions under account 002 and 003.

The two wire transactions under account 002 are aggregated by A and by B. Therefore, if these two wire transactions can produce an alert, there would be an alert for A and another alert for B. Note that this would happen for all joint accounts. The number of alerts for joint accounts would be expected to be nearly doubled while the transactions involved are actually the same.

In some implementations, these duplications are avoided by reporting only the primary owner of an account, which is always one single party for each account. However, a party can be the secondary owner of multiple accounts but not primary owner of any account; this person can manipulate funds with these accounts and these transactions are never aggregated together on monitoring. In Figure 4.2, party B is not the primary owner of any account. The three wire transactions here may be initiated by B but they are never aggregated together so no alert may be generated.

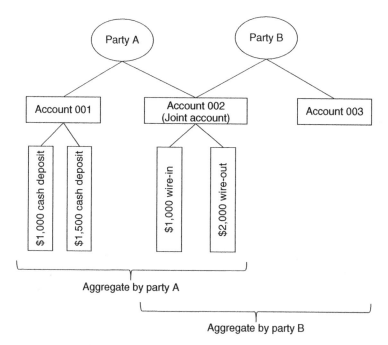

Figure 4.1 Aggregating by party with joint accounts.

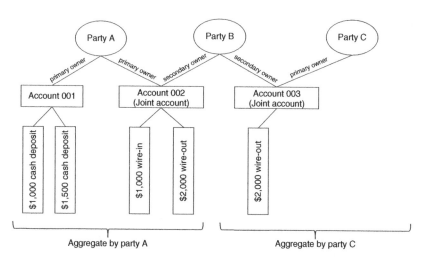

Figure 4.2 Aggregating by party with joint accounts, with a party not being primary owner of any account.

Branch-Level Monitoring

Branch-level monitoring serves the purpose of detecting money laundering hotspots amongst branches. Branches can become such hotspots because they find a concentration of money launderers nearby or because a bank employee is colluding with money launderers. It does not necessarily require branch level scenarios or aggregation as part of the AML system to detect an unusual high level of involvement of a particular branch. This can more easily be achieved by periodic analysis on the generated alerts and/or accommodated by setting up the right management information or business analysis reports.

However, a quicker identification and more alert response is to be expected when one or more scenarios aggregate by branch. Such scenarios would look very similar to account-based scenarios, although the lookback period and, in particular, aggregate threshold values would have to differ significantly and take into account the higher volume of transactions and bigger range of transaction amounts as the aggregation stretches over way more accounts.

Another type of branch-specific scenario looks at the associate party involved in transactions or performing activities that can be deemed suspicious, associate here meaning bank employee. For example, an unusual amount of account opening events at a branch or specifically by one associate can be an indicator of collusion with money launderers. A relatively weak but nevertheless legitimate indicator is the number of balance inquiries by one and the same associate.

SCENARIO PARAMETERS

As a general practice, when software is developed, the variable information is normally defined as configurable parameters (parameterized). This is done so as to conceptually separate computation logic from data, which is more fixed and subject to a lesser degree or frequency of change, and from input data, which is either changed more frequently, such as thresholds being revisited and revised periodically, or dynamic variables that are dependent on a stream of data, such as the financial transactions data to which the logic is applied (Figure 4.3).

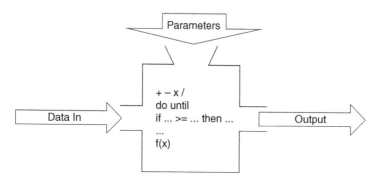

Figure 4.3 Scenario rule program input/output.

Logic operations and configurations parameters are both software pieces stored in machines. They work together to automatically process business data. Formatted configuration parameter data is designed to be easily understood and maintained by humans without technical knowledge. In contrast, computer programs are designed to be read by machines rather than humans, although modern computer languages are generally more comprehensible. No matter how many documents are provided, it takes more time for a human to trace the logic of a computer program than to understand the parameters.

That is the reason for the common industry practice to parameterize data values in programs to give flexibility. A user or administrator can adjust configuration parameters by reading the description of the parameters.

Moreover, a computer program must be well tested before it is put to real use. Once it passes the tests, it is considered to be trusted to perform as expected. If a change is required on the program, all the tests need to be done again to ensure the program change does not disrupt the original behavior besides the planned change. If the change is on a parameter, it is generally considered to be just a data change requiring less verification.

Parameters in scenarios can be classified by the following purposes:

- Describe target transactions (types of transaction that are eligible for this monitoring logic).
- Describe target customer/account/product (objects that are eligible for this monitoring logic).

▨ Threshold values defining how high or how low certain measurements should be considered suspicious.

Classifying by data type, parameters can be:

▨ Categorical, having discrete values. They are stored as text strings or a list of values. Target transactions and target objects parameters are often categorical.

▨ Numeric thresholds, having continual value that can be fine-tuned.

Categorical parameters for target transaction and target objects actually define the scenario rule. A scenario for cash deposit may have a parameter transaction medium with value CASH. If this parameter is changed to something else, the business meaning of this scenario rule would probably be changed. Therefore, categorical parameters seldom change. These parameters are not to be revised every year with the numeric thresholds. They are much less affected by market trend, economic environment, etc.

Numeric parameters define how much of a measured value is to be considered as suspicious enough for an alert. The measurement can be an amount, a count (of transaction/counterparties/countries), a ratio or proportion, or an index derived from some sophisticated formula. It can refer to a single transaction or an aggregate over a period of time. The parameter for a lookback period is also a natural number. Numeric thresholds are dependent on the population in the institution and affected by environmental factors. They need to be reviewed periodically (say 6 months or 1 year).

Use of Maximum Instead of Minimum Value Threshold

In most situations, alerts are generated if a variable exceeds a threshold minimum value. So, the threshold is the minimum value of a variable for the entity to be eligible for alert.

In some scenario rules, there is an alert condition at which the alert is eligible only if a variable does not exceed a certain threshold. That is, the threshold is the maximum value of a variable for the entity to be eligible for alert.

The following are a few common situations where a maximum threshold is applicable:

1. If the variable exceeds a threshold, it would have triggered another alert or report. For example, if $10,000 of daily aggregate cash transactions is the limit for currency transaction report (CTR), then it may not need to catch aggregate cash transactions in the past five days with a single transaction exceeding $10,000 because that should have been reported right away. Adding a maximum single cash transaction amount may eliminate duplicated reporting.

2. For scenario rules intended for small transactions aggregating to a large sum (e.g. structuring), if a customer has transacted a large amount then it means that the customer did not intend to hide away from monitoring. Having a maximum amount threshold may lower false positives.

3. On finding a large increase, while the increment and recent transaction is a minimum amount threshold, the amounts in previous periods should be small enough to indicate a contrast from a small to a large change. Then there may be a threshold-like maximum aggregate amount in the previous three months prior to the current month.

Threshold per Customer

Under some scenario rules, the variable value to be checked varies so much in the customer segment, that a few customers are always alerted. Imagine a restaurant customer segment type that includes restaurants that are cash-intensive. Two leading customers perform exceptionally well in business and have over 10 times the cash turnover than any of the other restaurants. A scenario for a statistical outlier cash transaction in this customer segment will always produce alerts for these two customers, if the thresholds are established in an ordinal way.

A rectification would be to exclude them from the customer segment and have dedicated threshold for each of these exceptional customers.

On implementation, the table per customer threshold is used, so that the customer entry with this per customer threshold will be treated differently, while those without will be used as the threshold common to the whole customer segment.

PRE-COMPUTING DATA

One way to improve batch job execution performance is to do periodic summarization so that the scenario rule program does not need to look through every transaction in the lookback period.

The below example illustrates the formation of monthly summary.

Jan

Date	Amount	Type
3/1	1000	Cash, credit
7/1	800	Wire, credit
8/1	700	Cash, debit
18/1	2000	Wire, credit
29/1	800	Wire, debit

Feb

Date	Amount	Type
1/2	900	Wire, credit
8/2	3000	Wire, credit
10/2	500	Wire, credit
11/2	800	Cash, debit
23/2	20	Cash, debit

Summary for Jan
Total cash credit = 1000
Total cash debit = 700
Total wire credit = 2800
Total wire debit = 800

Summary for Feb
Total cash credit = 0
Total cash debit = 820
Total wire credit = 4400
Total wire debit = 0

Further derived
Total deposit = 1000 + 2800 = 3800
Total withdrawal = 700 + 800 = 1500
Total turnover = 3800 + 1500 = 5300

Further derived
Total deposit = 900+3000+500 = 4400
Total withdrawal = 800 + 20 = 820
Total turnover = 4400 + 820 = 5220

In February, a scenario rule looking back over two months of aggregate wire deposit can be computed using the monthly summary:

Aggregate wire deposit for past two months

= Total wire credit in Jan + Total wire credit in Feb
= 2800 + 4400
= 7200

Without monthly summary, the calculation would be:

→ For each transaction since 1 / 1,
    If the transaction is a wire credit,
        add amount to aggregate wire deposit

→ Wire credit on 7 / 1 + Wire credit on 18 / 1 +
Wire credit on 1 / 2 + Wire credit on 8 / 2 + Wire credit on 10 / 2
= 800 + 2000 + 900 + 3000 + 500
= 7200

The calculation is executed over a period of a month. If the look-back period is longer than the execution period, then a monthly summary saves the repeated aggregation work for previous months.

However, the monthly summary is generally calculated on the basis of very generic conditions like all withdrawals, or all cash deposits. Moreover, it should not depend on any scenario threshold that may be adjusted over time. This is done so that the pre-computed summary information can be leveraged by different scenario rules and support change in scenario parameters.

Another consideration for pre-computing data is the storage volume. Both time and storage capacity may use scarce resources and a balance may need to be found between the two. Summary data is calculated from the transaction which needs to be stored or at least processed at the most granular level, which is that of individual transactions. Summary data is constructed from aggregating these transactions, e.g. at account level (all transactions on the account, regardless of the number of account holders) or at customer level (all transactions for a particular customer, regardless of the number of accounts). Pre-computing the summaries and then storing these makes sense, as it will be much quicker for each scenario or function to leverage these details. But it takes additional storage capacity and may stretch the available capacity, especially when the transactions are also stored at their granular level. Not storing the transactions, only the summary data, may provide a significant benefit from a storage perspective, but also means that these transactions will not be available in the system, e.g. for investigation as individual transactions. This could be a big disadvantage or a no-go from a business end user perspective. If the transactions are stored, then there is no absolute need to also store the summaries. Each time a summary data point is needed it can be (re)calculated on the basis of the transaction (see Figure 4.4). However, depending on the computing capacity available, this may take an unacceptably long time and duplicate the effort. This can be avoided by pre-computing and storing the summaries. Processing speed and efficiency comes at the price of storage capacity. Economizing on storage usually comes with a price in either (expensive) computing power . . . or time.

Note that a monthly summary is efficient if the transaction volume is large. If the transaction volume is very small, then the overhead of maintaining the monthly summary data outweighs the benefit gained for execution performance.

TIMELINESS OF ALERTS

An AML transaction monitoring system is usually a batch execution system instead of real-time. Alerts are normally generated after the transaction happened. Users would wish to see alerts as early as possible.

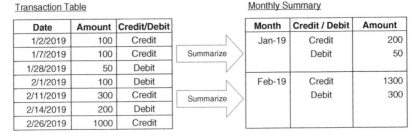

Transaction Table

Date	Amount	Credit/Debit
1/2/2019	100	Credit
1/7/2019	100	Credit
1/28/2019	50	Debit
2/1/2019	100	Debit
2/11/2019	300	Credit
2/14/2019	200	Debit
2/26/2019	1000	Credit

Monthly Summary

Month	Credit / Debit	Amount
Jan-19	Credit	200
	Debit	50
Feb-19	Credit	1300
	Debit	300

Figure 4.4 A monthly summary can be (re)generated at any time, as long as the underlying transactions are there.

	Sun	Mon	Tue	Wed	Thu	Fri	Sat
Office hour		Sat alert available	Mon (Sun) alert available	Tue alert available	Wed alert available	Thu alert available	Fri alert available
Night		Mon (Sun) data ready	Tue data ready	Wed data ready	Thu data ready	Fri data ready	Sat data ready
		Alert Generation for Mon(Sun)	Alert Generation for Tue	Alert Generation for Wed	Alert Generation for Thu	Alert Generation for Fri	Alert Generation for Sat

Figure 4.5 Alert timeliness – T+1.

For an institution with little data volume, source data is ready at day-end and alerts are available on the next day. So, the Time to alert is T+1 (Figure 4.5).

In the world of AML, "after-the-fact alerting" is widely accepted. Alerts may follow up to 3 days after the execution of the transaction. That means for a suspicious transaction happened on day T, alert is generated 2 or 3 days later. Here's why it takes that long:

1. The transaction operating system (source system) normally produces data at the end of the day.

2. At night, when the data is ready, it is already close to the office hours of the next day, so there's not enough time to run alert generation.

3. As a result, the data on day T is ready for process on T+1, scenarios are executed at T+1 night and so alerts are available on T+2 (Figure 4.6).

Some institutes do T+3 if for some reason the data can be available only at T+2 (Figure 4.7).

If the front-end operation systems are very well integrated and data are processed very quickly, it is possible to have near real-time detection and alert generation. Of course, the system architecture and hardware requirement would have to be more advanced, not only because of higher performance requirements (the transaction must be executed within seconds of or even sub-seconds since the request for it), but also because transactions are a business-critical process and the systems must be sufficiently robust to avoid any technical errors that will grind the payment, or worse, the payment system to a halt.

USE OF RATIOS

Ratios are often used to derive a second level of information from primitive data. It is a simple but useful tool to reveal underlying information. Common areas on adopting ratios are:

- Measure increments/decrements. For example, increment of aggregate transaction in current month against historical value.

	Sun	Mon	Tue	Wed	Thu	Fri	Sat
Office hours		*Fri alert available*	*Sat alert available*	*Mon (Sun) alert available*	*Tue alert available*	*Wed alert available*	*Thu alert available*
		Sat data ready	Mon (Sun) data ready	Tue data ready	Wed data ready	Thu data ready	Fri data ready
Night		Alert Generation for Sat	Alert Generation for Mon(Sun)	Alert Generation for Tue	Alert Generation for Wed	Alert Generation for Thu	Alert Generation for Fri

Figure 4.6 Alert timeliness – T+2.

	Sun	Mon	Tue	Wed	Thu	Fri	Sat
Office hour		Thu alert available	Fri alert available	Sat alert available	Mon (Sun) alert available	Tue alert available	Wed alert available
Night		Fri data ready	Sat data ready	Mon (Sun) data ready	Tue data ready	Wed data ready	Thu data ready
		Alert Generation for Fri	Alert Generation for Sat	Alert Generation for Mon(Sun)	Alert Generation for Tue	Alert Generation for Wed	Alert Generation for Thu

Figure 4.7 Alert timeliness – T+3.

▓ Determine whether two values are similar. For example, comparing credit amount and debit amount within a period.

▓ Measure proportion of subset within a full set. For example, amount of cash withdrawal transactions over all transactions in a period. Another example is the loan close period over the whole contract period.

Ratio as Degree of Change/Similarity

To measure how different a value is from some origin, the ratio of present against origin can be used. There are many variations of such ratio:

▓ Actual value vs. customers anticipated / declared value

▓ Current value vs. past history

▓ Current value vs. peer group

Sometimes, the ratio is to measure how much deviated is a value. An alert is triggered if the present value has deviated too much. The threshold would then be minimum percent value of X to Y. The alert condition is satisfied if the ratio calculated is greater than or equal to the threshold value.

There are some points to note when using ratios. Small base values are more sensitive to a value change. For an original amount of $100, adding $1 gives increment of 1%, whereas an original amount of $2 gives increment of 50% for the same $1 increment. Therefore, usually an amount threshold is present besides the threshold for the change ratio. Or else, a small amount change will contribute to a large percentage change triggering a lot of false positive alerts.

When a ratio is used to detect similarity, the threshold would be a percentage range of the ratio between two numbers for it to be easily understood. It composes of a minimum ratio and a maximum ratio of the two numbers to be tested for being similar. Example is aggregate deposit amount D1 and withdraw amount D2, where the ratio would be D1/D2. The scenario condition is satisfied when the ratio falls between these two percentage values. These two percentage values are usually a (relatively limited) distance from 100%, for example. 90–110%, 85–115%.

Note that two values are the same if the ratio between them is 100%. However, the upper and lower bound for the percentage range are not totally complementary to each other. For the downward side, the maximum decrease is 100% for any value dropping to zero. But, for the upward side, there's no limit. An increment from $20 to $200 is 1000% with the increment amount being $180, while a decrement from $20 to $2 makes 10% with a decrement amount of just $18. Therefore, on setting this pair of thresholds, take care that the range is wide enough.

The minimum and maximum percentage is a reciprocal relationship. To explain, let's assume the tolerance for "similar" is a relationship of 90 vs. 100. That is, 90 is said to be "close to 100." Then 91 must also be "close" as 91 is closer to 100 than 90, so is 92, 93, . . . , 99, and of course 100 itself. Among these numbers 90 ~ 100, the minimum ratio is "the minimum over the maximum," which is 90/100 = 90%. On the other hand, the maximum ratio is "the maximum over the minimum," which is 100/90 = 111% (not 110%). While 110% is very close to 111%, Table 4.3 shows a wider range.

A mathematic explanation can be seen from the graph of the function $f(x) = 1/x$. Note the range around 1 at y-axis: 0 ~ 1 vs 1 ~ infinity (Figure 4.8).

Table 4.3 Minimum ratio vs. maximum ratio.

Minimum ratio R	Maximum ratio as 1/R	Difference
99%	101%	+- 1%
95%	105%	+- 5%
90%	111%	+- 10%
85%	118%	Deviates from here
80%	125%	
70%	143%	
60%	167%	
50%	200%	
40%	250%	
30%	333%	
20%	500%	
10%	1000%	

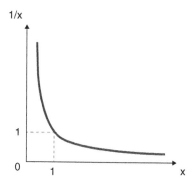

Figure 4.8 Graph of function f(x) = 1/x.

On the other hand, it can be one single percentage value to represent "similar" (e.g. 11% for 90 ~ 100), but the interpretation would be like "the largest percentage increment between the larger amount and smaller amount," which is a bit harder to explain to others than "a percentage range of ratio between two values."

Ratio as Proportion

Ratio is often used to measure the proportion of a part over the whole. Examples are:

- Proportion of transactions in amount using high-risk channel
- Proportion of repayment amount over the outstanding amount
- Proportion of loan account at closing date over the entire tenor period
- Proportion of high-risk transactions over all transactions

In the second example, the formula of the ratio is

$$\frac{\text{Aggregate amount of repayment transactions over a period}}{\text{Outstanding amount before the repayment}}$$

Note that the denominator is the amount BEFORE the repayment, which is as of the period start. If the outstanding amount at the end of the period is used, the outstanding amount can be left a very small number resulting in a huge ratio value. Therefore, think carefully about the meaning of a ratio.

For the third example, to determine if the loan payment is early, a ratio is used because the tenor period for each account may be different. See also the section in Chapter 5, "Early Termination/Quick Reciprocal Action" for further discussion.

Other Common Issues

1. Any potential division by zero must be handled on a scenario-by-scenario basis in a way that null or zero values will never cause errors that will break the process and disrupt the scenario run. If the denominator is empty, does it mean the alert condition is considered a positive? Or, does it mean the data is invalid and should not be alerted? These should be analyzed case by case.

2. If the ratio is about account balance, would a debit balance contain a negative value? If a balance is negative, should the ratio be taken absolute, converting to a positive number before comparison to the threshold?

3. Some scenarios consider account balance and a subset of these require intraday balances in order to perform optimally. However, an account balance may only exist in the source data as a per-day value. There are multiple ways to deal with this. Sometimes the post-transaction balance may be captured as part of the transaction data, and so intraday balances are available. If not, the transaction monitoring system may be configured to calculate the balance for each transaction, taking that day's start balance (or previous day-end balance) as a starting point. Either way, one also has to accommodate for exception days where no balance, intraday or start-of-day, may be available at all, such as holidays or non-business days.

CHAPTER **5**

Scenarios in Detail

This chapter describes common scenarios in detail and discusses the algorithms at a high level, common thresholds, common issues, and common false positives.

These categories and elements of monitoring can be combined and mixed. Remember to review for whether the monitoring is complete, covering well the different business aspects and different anti-money laundering risks.

LARGE AGGREGATE VALUE

Large aggregate value scenarios look for statistical outliers comparing to customer past behavior and customer-segment-specific threshold settings. For example, a scenario may aggregate all cash transactions in the past 10 business days. If, within that period, the aggregate cash amount is higher than the threshold, an alert will be generated.

The threshold is usually set dynamically, expressed as a percentage or standard deviation from transaction volume or amounts over the lookback period, which in the above example is 10 days. The scenario may in the comparison differentiate between debit and credit transactions or simply accumulate and aggregate these, and the same goes for transaction types or channels used.

Customer segmentation becomes much more important if the threshold value is not calculated dynamically on the fly, but hard-coded and absolute. Transaction amounts and volumes may differ significantly between low-, middle-, high- and extremely high-income households and the same goes for companies and business sectors: a high-end car dealership will transact very differently compared to a grocery. Applying a one-size-fits-all measure would generate heaps of false positives (over-alerting) and negatives (under-alerting). As explained in Chapter 1, whilst false negatives are not well appreciated by the regulator, false positives lead to unnecessary operational costs and may annoy customers who may be affected by it.[1]

---

[1]This is usually not the case for AML, as the alert is generated after processing the transaction and not impacted by it. In this respect AML is different from (real-time) fraud detection where customers may find occasionally their (legitimate) transactions blocked or temporarily put on hold because of a fraud alert.

This is easily avoided with dynamic thresholds, which in their simplest form are based on the account. A more complex approach would be to aggregate the accounts at customer level or household level, although different accounts may be used very differently for different purposes, and mixing and aggregating a customer's savings accounts (to which he writes larger sums on a regular basis) with his daily-use deposit account, which may see much more but smaller transactions fluctuating throughout a salary payment interval, may not be the best way of looking at things. Dynamic thresholds can also be based on the segment as a whole, rather than individual customers, households, or accounts. In that case segmentation is used to build profiles and the segment becomes a peer group.

UNEXPECTED TRANSACTION

When we find an outlier, there must be something normal to be compared against. Here are some common references:

I. Customer Segment in the Past

II. Oneself in the Past

III.Peer Group in the Present

The threshold in these scenario rules is set to be high enough for results to be considered an outlier (Figure 5.1).

Here, the y-axis is the population and the x-axis is some measurement, for instance the amount of the cash transaction. The darker

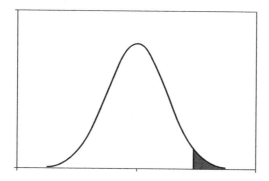

Figure 5.1 Outlier over a normal distribution.

tint shows the population above a certain threshold. Threshold tuning means to pick a point so as to declare those in the darker tint as being an outlier. (For simplicity in understanding, this diagram assumes the distribution follows normal distribution, which is not true for most of the cases.)

I. Compare against Customer Segment in the Past

This is to set a static threshold based on a group of similar entities for some historical period of time. For example, a low-risk individual person exhibits rather similar transaction behavior. We pick these customers and get their cash transactions for the whole past year (e.g. 1/1/2015–12/31/2015). For 1,000,000 there would be 1,000,000 × 12 months = 12,000,000 data points for customers' monthly aggregated cash transaction amounts. Sort them and pick the top, say 2%, as outliers. The value that cuts the top 2% would be the threshold for alert. For example, the top 2% of the population have aggregate cash transactions larger than HKD 500K. This 500K is the threshold. Then, it means 98% of the population has aggregated cash transaction amounts smaller than 500K; any customer having an aggregated cash transaction amount larger than 500K is an outlier and an alert is produced.

Here, the threshold is a fixed number until the threshold is reviewed next time, maybe 12 months later. It is easily understandable and explainable for why an alert is generated. However, note that,

1. The number is not connected to the person. Some customers may be exceptional for some legitimate reason and they always fall into the outlier zone.

2. It uses historical data. In this fast-changing world, the situation one year ago may be different from the situation now. There may also be seasonal factors.

3. There needs to be a large amount of reference data for a statistical value to be sound. If the size of the customer base

is small, then one may consider taking a longer past period to reference.

II. Compare against Oneself in the Past

This is a more dynamic way to detect an outlier. Instead of comparing to other customers, it compares against the customer's own past. This would give a personal threshold.

For example, get a customer's current month total cash transactions and compare against its past 6 month (prior to current month) average.

Cash transactions of one single customer:

Month	Aggregate cash transaction amount
Jun 2015	110,000
Jul 2015	100,000
Aug 2015	120,000
Sep 2015	170,000
Oct 2015	80,000
Nov 2015	90,000
Dec 2015	110,000
Jan 2016	400,000

Looking at Dec 2015:

The past 6-month average is (110k + 100k + 120k + 170k + 80k + 90k) / 6 = 111.67k

Transactions in Dec 2015 total 110k. Comparing to the past 6-month average, 110k/111.67k = 98.5%

Looking at Jan 2016:

The past 6-month average is (100k + 120k + 170k + 80k + 90k + 110k) / 6 = 111.67k

Transactions in Jan 2016 total 400k. Comparing to the past 6-month average, 400k/111.67k = 358%

So, obviously, in Jan 2016, the transactions are much higher than the previous 6 months. The threshold may be set to, say 200%. An alert will be produced if the current month is higher than its average for 2 times.

Some may think an average is not good enough to reflect the variations. One reference approach is to take the second largest in the 6 months and take the midpoint between it and the 6-month average. This is to somewhat incorporate a rather high point within the 6 months.

Then, in the above example:

The past 6-month average is (100k + 120k + 170k + 80k + 90k + 110k) / 6 = 111.67k

The second largest in the past 6 months is 120k

Expected monthly transactions

$= $ Past 6 months average $+ 2^{nd}$ largest among past 6 months / 2

$= (120k + 111.67k) / 2$

$= 115.84k$

Transactions in Jan 2016 total 400k. Comparing to the expected monthly transaction, 400k / 115.84k = 345%. There is no absolute truth about how to derive this expected value. One can adjust this calculation based on the situation.

One drawback is that some customers show seasonal behavior. For example, some factories may have more customer orders near Christmas so the transactions in certain months would be high in every year. Consequently, every year when it comes to a certain month, the transaction volume naturally rises and there would be a lot of false positive alerts.

Another source of false positives is that some transactions are affected by the market. In some circumstances, transactions are impacted by some one-off events like the issuing of bonds, or a big rise/drop in the security market, at which a large proportion of the population acts similarly at the same time. The approaches discussed above will not accommodate these changes and will produce a lot of false positive alerts.

A money launderer could use the tactic of a gradual increase in the transaction amount in order to create a higher historical reference. Thus, the comparison period must be long enough, so this tactic is harder to achieve. The threshold for the increment should not be set too high as well.

What if a customer does not have enough historical data?

If a customer does not have enough historical data, then taking an average of multiple months will result in a smaller number. In the below example, if a customer has been created since September, then the average of 3 months would include less than 3 months' worth of transactions. In an extreme case where a customer is created on September 30, only 2 months of transactions is divided by 3, giving 67% of full transactions. Therefore, the customer should be earlier than the whole historical period prior to current month in order to compute the average of 3 months (see Table 5.1).

If a customer has less than the desired months of history (say just 2 months), should it take only 2 months to compute the average of 2 months? One consideration is that the 3-month average aims to level out the fluctuations between months so that a more stable value can be used for comparison. If a shorter period is taken, there would be more false positives. However, users may tend to include more false positives, rather than missing the true cases as false negatives.

If customer was created just last month, then it should simply be excluded from this monitoring, as there is no reference data to compare against.

III Compare against Peer Group in the Present

The previous two approaches compare against past history. Another approach is to compare with peers in the present. This approach would then be free from seasonal factors and market influence.

Table 5.1 Insufficient transaction table at customer level.

	3 months history			Current month
	Sep-16	Oct-16	Nov-16	Dec-16
Customer has long enough history	full month txn	full month txn	full month txn	Current month txn
		Average of 3 months		← vs ↑

	3 months history			Current month
	Sep-16	Oct-16	Nov-16	Dec-16
Customer don't have enough history	less than one month txn	full month txn	full month txn	Current month txn
		Average of less than 3 months worth of txn		← vs ↑

Take the same cash transactions as an example. On a month-end day, compute the statistical distribution of aggregate 1-month cash transactions of the 1,000,000 customers for the same month. Then, the top, say 2% again, produce alerts.

Here, the predefined threshold is the 2% portion, rather than the monetary amount, which changes every day.

The trade-off is that the values for comparison need to be computed on the run day; they cannot be pre-computed. This would require more computation power of the rule-executing machine.

Threshold Tuning in a Statistical Outlier

In any of the three approaches for catching a statistical outlier, threshold tuning is important. Since the eligible transactions and customers are all legitimate and normal, it is easy to fall into an alert unless the thresholds are high enough to be considered an outlier. This detection is very sensitive to the threshold because it captures a large portion of the population. Care must be taken in setting an appropriate threshold in order to maintain accuracy and efficiency.

Common false positives are due to seasonal effects and market factors causing an increase in volume for a large portion of customers.

Besides a comparison with its own actual history, another approach is to compare against the customer's declared value in the KYC profile when the customer was first registered in the institution.

Usually, this declared value comes in the form of a selection of value ranges, rather than an exact value.

For example:

Question in KYC form: What is your expected number of transactions in a month?

1. *0–25*
2. *26–50*
3. *51–100*
4. *101–200*
5. *201 or above*

Answer: 3 (51–100)

In the scenario alert condition, the actual number of transactions in the current month should be compared against the declared value. An alert is generated, say, because 190 transactions in the month is greater than the declared value × 180%.

A customer's answer in the KYC form is a range of values, so each selection is a pair of lower value and upper values. Exactly which value should be picked for comparison? If the lower value is picked, then the lowest band (0–25) would be 0. That means the condition comparing against 0 x 180% = 0 would always give a true. If the upper value is picked, then what is the value for the highest band (201 or above)?

There are a few approaches to this problem:

1. Use the middle value between the lower and upper value in a band (lower + upper / 2). For the top band, take upper value (e.g. 101–200 ➔ 151, 201 or above ➔ 201)

2. Use the upper value. For the top band, there's no value to use. Then, use the average in history. (e.g. average of past 3 months)

3. Use the upper value. For the top band, use lower value and multiply by, say, × 2. (e.g. For 201 or above, use 201 × 2 = 402)

HIGH VELOCITY/TURNOVER

In financial terms, the account can be used to track assets or keep money. There would be fund flow from and to any account. If the amount of fund flow is exceptionally high, then an account might have been used as a transient point for laundering money.

We refer to this situation as high velocity. This high volume of fund flow can be detected in a number of ways.

Compare between Aggregate In and Aggregate Out Amount

The most basic way is to check the aggregate incoming amount and aggregate outgoing amount over a lookback period. If these two aggregate amount values are large enough and are similar, then it means the account is used solely for transferring money. Here, the lookback period and percentage range is important. If the lookback period is too long, then it will capture other transactions making the resulting similarity check fail. The incoming and outgoing transactions may come in multiple small chunks. If the period is too short, then it may only cover part of the whole transfer and the similarity check again fails.

Ratio of Turnover over Balance

A large corporation has larger transactions volume by nature, and at the same time the account balance should also be large. If the aggregate turnover (all deposits plus all withdrawals in a period) is large while the end balance is small, then it is rather suspicious. Here, the threshold is a ratio: Aggregate transactions amount/End balance.

Change of Account Balance

Another way is to measure the time period where the account balance is close to the lowest level. Figure 5.2 shows a change of account balance value over time. If the account is credited and then debited gradually, the graph would be something like this. The average balance over the whole period is somehow at the middle between highest and lowest watermark.

If the account is often debited soon after credit, the graph would be something like this. The average balance would be close to the lowest watermark. This indicates money has been staying in the account for just a short time (Figure 5.3).

If the account balance is to be monitored, it would be good to trace the account balance movement as accurately as possible. However, an account balance is normally available from the bank system only once

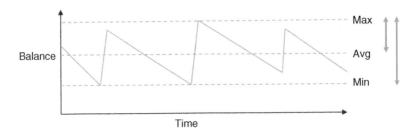

Figure 5.2 Change of account balance over time.

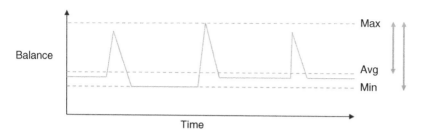

Figure 5.3 Account balance change over time, with high velocity.

every day-end. If money comes in the morning and then goes in the afternoon, the balance captured would stay the same as previous day and get unnoticed by this scenario detection.

Common False Positives

However, in certain payment actions, high velocity is popular. Many mortgage repayment accounts are credited right before the debit day. These false positive cases can be blocked by a minimum aggregate transaction amount threshold. Some customers will have large transaction volume by nature of their business, accompanied by a relatively high and stable account balance. So, monitoring both aggregate amount and balance level would be necessary.

However, some customers may use one bank for transactional banking (i.e. receipts of client payments) but use another bank for cash management because of higher interest rates. Such customers will remit most of the funds from one bank to another (same name account) for higher interest before day-end and thus this could lead to the scenario where the aggregate turnover is large while the end balance is small.

TURNAROUND/ROUND-TRIPPING

A debit transaction to a party in a relatively short time followed by a credit transaction from the same party can indicate money laundering. However, common explanations for this can be found, such as individuals lending money to family or a friend who later pay back, retailers who process refunds for returned goods, or parents who use their children's accounts as mule accounts around the end of the

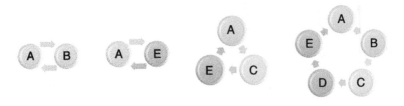

2 accounts I same FI   2 accounts I multiple FI's   3 accounts I multiple FI's   multiple accounts I multiple FI's

Figure 5.4 Circular payment schemes (nodes represent accounts or account holders).

year to lower the balance on their account for tax purposes (and in January getting the money back). With so many legitimate explanations, would it still make sense to look for a pattern where similar debit transactions are followed in a relatively short period of time by debit transactions? The answer is yes. First of all, money laundering, to be of any significance must generate some turnover. Neither money launderers nor regulators have a huge interest in small fry. So, the occasional loan to a friend or relative will probably not meet the threshold. Retail business accounts may be exempted from the rule or the rule may be tweaked to filter out legitimate business use. For example, a normal retailer will still have way more credit transactions than debit transactions within the range of prices for the type of goods or services they sell. For a money launderer who uses round-tripping as his modus operandi it will probably be difficult to sustain the level of asymmetry between credit and debit. This may open up a means to distinguish the good from the bad. True, a not so successful retailer on the brim of foreclosure may also face an equal amount of debit versus credit transactions, so it is more likely to be alerted as a false positive . . . unless the foreclosure too is part of the money laundering modus operandi.

Round-tripping is even more difficult to detect when the loop does not merely comprise two stations, but multiple. However, the true positive rate will increase, since legitimate use usually does not include a multi-tier loop, let alone a repetitive one. For example, none of the above-mentioned use cases would fit the multi-tier loop. Friends and family do not usually relend borrowed money whereby the last borrower repays the first lender . . . that would be unusual indeed, if not outright suspicious. In the retailer example, too, a closed multi-tier loop does not fit well in our large society with open economies.

One can only imagine such a loop to be legitimate in a very tight-knit and closed community, where, for example, the farmer buys with the grocer, the grocery with the baker, the baker with the butcher and the butcher with the farmer. In this day and age, even with small villages having thousands of inhabitants, things usually do not work that way.

The round-tripping scenario with a multi-tier loop reveals one of the biggest limitations of a financial institution-driven approach to transaction monitoring: as soon as the links in the loop are spread across multiple financial institutions, no single institution will have full visibility of the loop, hence will not be able to recognize it as a closed loop. Despite numerous interbank cooperation initiatives, banks (still) do not see, let alone monitor, each other's accounts beyond those payments in which the external account is the counterpart of a payment to or from a customer account. If only two banks are involved in the loop this is not an issue, but as soon as a third or even a fourth or fifth bank is involved, the loop spreads too wide and will not be recognized as such, unless someone deliberately follows the trail. Such loops can be found following an investigation, not by automated bank-driven transaction monitoring.

This is different in the case of blockchain when, for example, related to a cryptocurrency. The blockchain will contain all transactions ever performed with that currency. Apart from the simple fact that banks do not necessarily play a role in these transactions, the fact that the entire cryptocurrency history is in the blockchain means that, no matter how many links a loop comprises, it will always be recognizable. Modern-day network analysis software will not only visualize the loop but will also detect it. However, this does not mean that cryptocurrency transaction monitoring does not come with limitations. It does. The currency itself is the limit. As soon as it is an open or semi-open system, meaning that the currency can be bought by and sold for other currency (crypto- or conventional alike), loops can and will be created that include more than only the one cryptocurrency and loops will no longer be visible from an automated systems perspective, unless the other currencies are all also cryptocurrencies and their blockchain is monitored together with the initial blockchain.

External parties, being counterparties to a transaction who do not bank with the financial institution (but with another bank) create additional challenges. The good news is that financial institutions still have some information about the counterparties, though no KYC or CDD is done with these external parties.

Information on these may not always be standardized or complete and external parties may not be recognized as one and the same over multiple transactions. This is especially the case for SWIFT transactions where the party information does not (always) come in a strictly defined format and may contain open text. Text can be automatically parsed and analyzed, and fuzzy matching can be applied, but none of these will fully mitigate the risk of non- or misidentification. We discuss the limitations of entity resolution and fuzzy matching in more detail in Chapter 7.

Even when all data is visible and network analysis or graph analysis software is capable of detecting loops, larger loops will come at a price and its currency is computation power. With lesser computation, power time may become a bottle neck and putting in place more computing power will drive up hardware and maintenance cost.

For example, one algorithm to find out these loops is

- ▦ Get all the transactions within the desired period, say, 1 month. Each has a Sender, a Recipient, and of course the date/time, amount, transaction type, etc. (A ➜ B)
- ▦ For each transaction, find out any other transaction with Sender matching its Recipient. This effectively finds the first layer of the relationship (A ➜ B ➜ C). Check if the first sender and last recipient are the same (A = C?); if yes, then a loop is found.
- ▦ Do it again to find another layer (A ➜ B ➜ C ➜ D) and check again (A = D?).
- ▦ Do it again and again for more layers (A ➜ B ➜ C ➜ D ➜ E ➜ . . .).

With each additional layer the computing needed to identify and resolve the parties involved exponentially increases. The computation order here is $O(n^l)$, where n is the number of transactions (e.g. number of transactions of all customers in the bank in the past one month), and l is the number of layers to check. That is, the time to find out a loop, with whatever machine is used, is proportional to the number of transactions to the power of number of layers to check. You can imagine for a reasonable number of transactions, adding one more layer to check is a huge increase of computation time.

So, in order to minimize the computation resource to do this monitoring,

- Limit the transactions (the n)
- Limit the number of loops to check (the l).

To limit the transactions, a minimum single transaction amount can be set. The main reason for doing this is that from a money laundering perspective, structuring the funds in small transactions is simply not cost efficient and therefore unlikely to be a modus operandi for money launderers. In addition, some type of transactions can be excluded. For loop finding, only traceable transactions are useful. Cash deposits and withdrawals are not traceable (although they may be suspicious by themselves). Only the transfers between accounts and remittances may contribute to loop finding, as the involved accounts and therefore account holders are registered at least somewhere.

Of course, the covered time period directly impacts the number of transactions to check. This would be the normal duration within which a money launderer will do this round-tripping. It may be a week to a few months.

On checking the transactions between entities, group all the transactions between entities. The alert criteria include the in/out ratio across a party. That is, for a A ➔ B ➔ A relationship, the total money at A➔ B and the money at B ➔ A should be both large enough and in similar amount. If not, even if a loop is found it is just a single-way transfer with little return, which happens in some commodities trading. Another alert criterion is, of course, the total amount transferred out from an entity. If the amount is too small, then it is not worth investigating.

To detect for a similar amount, we may use a percentage difference between two adjacent lines in a triangle. There is another complication. What if a customer has multiple loops of fund transfers at the same time, while all loops go through a common path in between?

Figure 5.5 illustrates an example. There are three loops, all involving A and B. Let's say all three loops circulate $10. Then, the arrow A➔ B is carrying 3 x $10 = $30.

Then, looking at single loop (e.g. A ➔ B ➔ C ➔ A), the arrows A ➔ B vs B ➔ C would be a $30 vs. $10, which doesn't seem to be similar. So, the similar detection cannot be too strict (Figure 5.6).

The thresholds of this scenario can be

- Minimum aggregate amount between two parties (each of x, y, z).
- Or a minimum loop amount x + y + z. Beware that if the loop involves more parties, then the same money passes multiple times resulting in a larger loop amount.
- Similarity between links:

Maximum percentage difference $\geq \dfrac{x}{y} \geq$ Minimum percentage difference.

$$\text{The same applies to } \frac{y}{z} \text{ and } \frac{z}{x}$$

STRUCTURING

Structuring means to break down a large bulk of money into smaller chunks. It can occur at all three stages of money laundering

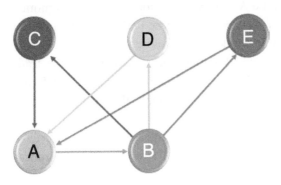

Figure 5.5 Multiple loops with a common link.

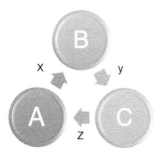

Figure 5.6 Triangular loop.

(placement, layering, or integration). From a money launderer's perspective, structuring serves multiple purposes. First, it is an easy way to avoid breaching thresholds. Even when money launderers are not aware of the exact thresholds, they know that smaller chunks of money are less likely to attract attention. Another reason is to avoid placement of money in the same or similar amounts as income from crime. Should it ever come to a criminal or financial investigation, then it is harder to explain money is not the proceeds of a crime when balances are matching. This is a matter of criminal accounting where slightly different rules apply than for normal legitimate accounting (even though the objective is always to make it appear as such). A third reason for structuring is because it is a preparatory step for layering: obfuscating the origin of the funds by breaking it apart and generating separate money trails, so that following the money becomes more difficult, but also so that, where possible, the money can no longer be tied to the criminal (or his hoodlum money launderers).

A Well-Known Structuring Example

Albeit not proven as money laundering, a well-known and widely publicized structuring example can be found in the case of US President Trump's payments to his longtime lawyer and self-declared problem fixer Michael Cohen. To cover up an affair that the then primary/ presidential candidate Trump allegedly had with a former porn star (as made public by the latter person), Cohen, acting in his capacity as

Trump's personal lawyer, paid $130,000 to the lady as part of a non-disclosure agreement. Apart from any personal reasons Trump may have had to distance himself from this payment (thereby distancing himself from the affair – which he denied), there was the possible issue of abuse of campaign funds, since the timing of the cover up (years after the alleged affair) was so that it was likely to aid Trump in his campaign. Trump, further, denied any knowledge of the non-disclosure agreement or any payments. Cohen therefore claimed to have paid out of his own pocket as a matter of loyalty to his long-term principal. However, it later transpired that regular payments had been made to Cohen on a retainer basis, the total of which exceeded the $130K. If the payments had been made as compensation to Cohen for his efforts and expenses in relation to this non-disclosure agreement, then indeed this could have constituted a breach of the campaign financing rules under federal law. The breaking down of the money into smaller regular payments for services unspecified, indeed would amount to structuring, as it would facilitate that version of the truth where Cohen acted on his own initiative and without Trump's specific knowledge, yet still on his behalf and with the obvious intent to allow Trump to deny any involvement. This would have been much more difficult if Cohen was paid the exact amount of $130K, as it would have become more difficult to convincingly argue that this amount was not paid specifically to reimburse Cohen for this particular expense. This is an example of structuring, albeit not money laundering: not so much the *origin* of the money was illicit, but its *use*. However, similar means are applied to achieve a very similar end: disassociating one money stream from another, obfuscating the real reason behind payments, and separating certain money flows and related events from their beneficiaries, so that malversations by that person cannot be proven.

Transactions Count

The simplest way to look for structuring is to check the transactions count and aggregate amount over a period. However, there may be fees and interests or something that must not be part of a structuring. Therefore, you should add a minimum single transaction amount to filter out those transactions that are too small. For example, an alert may be generated if there are 10 transactions, each over $50,000, with a total of at least $600,000; they contain deposits and withdrawals; and some are in cash, and some in wire, etc.

Similar Amounts

When you chop something, you would usually cut it into equal pieces. So, one way is to find transactions with relatively similar amounts. To tell whether two numbers are relatively similar, one way is to look at the percentage difference between them. Here, a threshold would be the maximum percentage difference between two amounts to be considered similar, say, 5%.

You can imagine this monitoring is to look at each transaction in the pool and look at the other transactions to see if this other transaction is similar or not. So, 10 transactions involves 9 comparisons for each, totaling 9 x 10 comparisons. In terms of computation order it is of $O(n^2)$. The computation time is proportional to the square of number of transactions. Please be aware of this performance issue and take care of the eligible transactions by limiting the single transaction amount or transaction types (Figure 5.7).

One possible false positive would be a corporation's payroll. If there is a way to identify payroll from transactions, then it is good to filter them out.

Round Amounts

Another interesting monitoring method is to look at the transaction monetary number. People tend to give round numbers on an initial offering of a price or quotation. However, this world has a lot

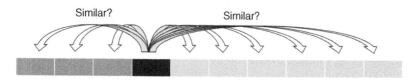

Figure 5.7 Comparing each transaction with all other transactions under the same customer throughout a period.

of complicated calculations. With fees, tax, inflation rate, salary rise, valuation calculations, etc., transaction amounts we normally come across are not in round amounts. If a customer has a lot of round amount transactions, then the person may be intentionally chopping money into chunks.

> More experienced launderers are aware that too many round number transactions would flag an alert, so they avoid too many round numbers, or apply a generator to come up with random amount decimals. However, what they usually don't do is take into account Benford's Law or even simple statistics. We have discussed Benford's Law in Chapter 2: the law is based on the premise that certain number series are not completely random and that there is not an equal occurrence of 0 to 9 in a large population of amounts.

Be aware that this monitoring method looks at the number from the person's intention. So, while all other scenarios look at a base currency amount converting all amounts into the same currency for comparisons and common threshold checking, round amount checking must be done against the transaction currency and before any fee or service charge. This reflects the amount that the person intended, without foreign currency conversion and any distortion.

A threshold would be number of trailing zeros in an amount number. For example, the number $123,000.00 satisfies for the condition of 5 trailing zeroes. Currency may be a concern, in which for some currencies the number of trailing zeros may be more common than others. Another threshold could be the portion of round amount transactions over all transactions. It can be expressed as a percentage, say, alert is generated if 50% of a customer's transactions are with 5 trailing zeros, totaling over $500,000.

False positives can happen in situations where a customer wants to move money around, but due to some foreign exchange control policy or limits on the account imposed by the bank, the amount is split.

EARLY TERMINATION/QUICK RECIPROCAL ACTION

With long-term contracts, such as security-backed loans and private and commercial loans or insurance schemes that have a nominal duration of multiple years, early termination may be an indicator of money laundering. Frequent use of the early repayment option by the same customer is even more indicative of suspicious behavior.

Long-term credit is useful for money launderers, as this allows them to refer to the credit as a means of income, the source of their funds, without the need of also providing a legitimate source for the weekly, monthly, quarterly, or annual capital and interest payments, as these are comparatively small in comparison to the loan amount and too small to warrant such justification. However, money launderers do not want to "sit" on their dirty money for the entire duration of the credit agreement, as it would take years to launder the funds. Instead they expedite the process by using the early repayment option and clear the credit in one or more excess repayments. When anyone asks for the source of the funds, they refer to the loan, without mentioning the expedited repayment.

The thresholds would be how early is the customer terminating the contract. It can be expressed as (account close date – contract set-up date) / tenor period. For example, if a loan is set up for 20 months and the customer repaid it all in 2 months, then 2/20 = 10%. An alert is generated if this percentage is smaller than a threshold.

False positives would be generated for those plans that are paid off early through legitimate means, such as someone who obtained a mortgage but soon after received an inheritance, which might or might not have been anticipated when applying for the mortgage. Or in the case of a successful entrepreneurial endeavor, the success and associated revenue stream may be used for early repayments. Those legitimate events of early repayment are easily identified during analysis or investigation of the alert, and the alert will subsequently be discarded as a false positive.

WATCHLIST

Watchlist screening is normally done during the KYC process at customer onboarding. For a new customer, the customer's name is screened against regulatory and commercial watchlists before, or sometimes shortly after, the creation of the account. These watchlists can be from global data providers and also the local regulator and from within the institute. Some AML solution providers also include watchlist services as part of their commercial offering.

So, watchlist checking is already done at customer record creation. However, it is also related to transaction monitoring. The watchlist is a "living" list with constant updates: new entries are added to the list, other entities are removed, or their data is replaced with more accurate details. On the other hand, the customer's information may also be subject to change. So, it is actually a matching between two data sets, both of which are subject to varying degrees of change.

Transaction monitoring is normally done once a day. So, the checking would be a delta versus full, and full versus delta.

■ Get all new and updated customer records, compare against complete watchlist.

■ Get all new and updated watchlist records, compare against complete customer list.

There are other watchlists besides customer name. The concept of matching is similar to that for names.

■ Countries – high-risk countries, low tax rate countries, countries associated with drugs, etc.

■ Suspicious address – address related to previous criminal cases (or suspected).

■ Registered agents for company – companies using a registered agent as authorized signatory may be more suspicious.

■ Dual-use goods in trade finance – there are types of goods that can be used for terrorist activities. This watchlist stores lists of names for dual-use goods.

Chapter 7 discusses watchlists in more detail.

COMMON SPECIFICATIONS ACROSS UNRELATED ENTITIES

Criminals committing fraud usually make use of different persons, or make others think there are different persons. This is done so that each falsified entity takes up part of the illicit activities, so that these actions get unnoticed when monitored in an overview.

While the customer records exist in separate entities, there may be something shared in common:

- Name
- Identification document ID
- Telephone number
- Address
- E-mail address

This checking should also be done during creation of customer records. And yes, if the criminal is smart and diligent enough and has enough resources then there can be no common specification found.

In this approach, common false positives are family members in the same household sharing the same address and telephone number. One threshold is the number of entities sharing the same information. Say a customer is alerted only if that customer's address is shared with at least four other customers. Moreover, the data value must be long enough for a comparison to be done. Data value like NA, Empty, Unknown, must be excluded for checking or else there would be a huge number of false positives.

The above checking is about the customer's status; nothing related to the account activities. The monitoring system can be implemented so that an alert is produced only if the customer has this information updated or has certain fund flow in the month.

Consecutive Numbers

Besides identical information, which is an indication of fraudulent activity, numbers that are close to each other may also be suspicious. For example, on structuring, a money launderer may issue a series of cheques for broken-down amounts. While these amounts are not similar in amount nor in round numbers, they come with consecutive cheque numbers. Checking these reference numbers may uncover this behavior.

INVOLVING UNRELATED THIRD PARTY

Money transfer to a third party is very common. Many payments are transfers to an unrelated third party. For some business, these transfer counterparties are recurrent. If it is found that the counterparty has not been encountered in, say, the past twelve months, then it may be considered a new counterparty and may need special attention. Another approach is requiring the customer to specify common counterparties during KYC profiling. If a new transaction involves a counterparty not in the KYC profile then an alert may be generated if it reaches a certain amount.

This is not particularly suspicious behavior. It is a rather half-way to a statistical outlier. An alert should be generated only if the amount is large enough.

ONE-TO-MANY

Structuring means to disburse money into chunks, and then this money can be placed as different transactions with the same channel of fund flow. Another dimension of looking at it is how many counterparties a customer has disbursed money to. There are mainly two types of transactions that involves a counterparty: (i) internal transfer within the financial institute, and (ii) remittances.

The main logic here is to spot distinct counterparties if the counterparty is not well identified. For a remittance, the counterparty has no account in the local institute. What is available is the name and address. Therefore, matching different names is also important. See Chapter 7, Entity Resolution and Watchlist Matching, for more discussion.

The threshold would be number of counterparties. It should also be checked if an organization is disbursing money to individuals for payroll. Here, with just a name, identification of whether an external counterparty is an individual is also a challenge. A list of organization name keywords may be used to match (Ltd, Corp, Co., etc.).

One major false hit is again the payroll from an organization. If payroll can be identified, then they can be excluded from checking.

TRANSACTING JUST BELOW REPORTING THRESHOLD

There are limits imposed by regulators to control some activities. In the US, transaction in currency of more than $10,000 would require filing a currency transaction report (CTR) with FinCEN. In Hong Kong, a remittance over HKD 8,000 requires the customer to produce the identity document to the remittance agent or money changer for identification. So, anyone who wants to escape from these reports or verification would do business under these known limits.

If someone is found to often transact under these well-known threshold limits, then it would appear he is deliberately escaping. One way to define just below a threshold is to measure the percentage of transacted value against the limit value. The scenario parameter would be the percentage, say 95%. So for CTR limit of $10,000, transactions between $10,000 × 95% = $9,500 to $9,999 would be considered just below CTR threshold.

A scenario rule for this pattern should probably have a threshold for the number of times and aggregate amount of these below-threshold transactions.

Be aware that this checking can operate on well-known threshold limits. Thresholds in transaction monitoring scenarios are supposed to be confidential within the financial institution and should not need such checking. One may think that monitoring should be done for catching people transacting below the internal monitoring scenario threshold, who obtained this information by bribing the insiders. However, if this is to be done, then it would jump into an endless loop:

A first level check with monitoring threshold $10,000 × 0.95 = $9,500

Now, there is a new threshold of $9,500.

Then a second level check against this new monitoring threshold $9,500: $9,500 × 0.95 = $9,025.

Now, there is another new threshold of $9,025.

Then, a third level check for this $9,025 × 0.95, and so on.

Alerts That Should Appear Only Once in a Lifetime

In certain situations, an alert is valid only once for an entity. For one of my clients, the following scenario rule was implemented:

For a new customer, if its first 10 transactions within a year sum up to $100,000 then an alert is generated.

They intend to catch those customers opening an account and do large transactions. When this rule is put to software implementation, a daily scenario rule may be implemented, checking each customer. An alert is generated when a customer has a "customer since" date if within one year, and its aggregate transaction count is within 10 and the aggregate amount equals or exceeds $100,000. If a customer has already been alerted at its fifth transaction, then the user might not want to see an alert at its sixth to tenth transactions. A storage of alert records might be needed, and the alert generation process would need to reference this storage to determine whether an alert should be produced.

CHAPTER **6**

The Selection
of Scenarios

SELECTING SCENARIOS

The question of which scenarios to adopt will come back a number of times during the lifespan of a financial institution. When the financial institution is a new start-up, or when it has only just entered the realm of anti-money laundering (AML) – e.g. following an extension of the scope of the regulation, such as we saw when luxury good wholesalers and retailers were brought under scope of AML – then it will probably have to establish an AML monitoring system from scratch. Many AML software systems come with pre-designed rules and scenarios, but these are commonly regarded as a starting point, not a finished, prêt-à-porter end product. And since scenario bundles cover a range of different types of business and may address a range of specific risks, at the very least a sub-selection should be made. The recommendation in the field is, for starters, to keep it simple but robust at the beginning with between 10 and 20 separate rules, to be later expanded and refined. From a software vending perspective, the starting-from-scratch situation is relatively rare. In most situations, the financial institution is an established organization with a transaction monitoring system and AML operations already in place, with experienced specialized staff to manage related business processes. A new system is procured because the existing system has outlived itself or no longer meets the requirements of the financial institution. In such situations, there may be scenarios that must be replicated by the new system, with or without improvements suggested by transaction monitoring staff and/or new scenarios that may be adopted to extend the system to products and customer segments that were not covered by the legacy system. Whatever the situation is, it is never as straightforward as unpacking the transaction monitoring software and switching it on; there are always decisions to make about which scenarios and how. So, what are the drivers for these decisions?

REGULATORY REQUIREMENTS

Since regulatory requirements are the main, if not sole, incentive for a financial institution to engage in AML transaction monitoring in the first place, it is not surprising that any regulatory directions regarding how to do that are of great importance to the selection of scenarios. At the core, most AML transaction monitoring systems are still based on the Financial Action Task Force's (FATF) 40 recommendations for AML and counter-terrorist financing (CTF). The FATF is an intergovernmental organization with no legislative or regulatory authority, but it has been a source of recommendations to OECD (Organisation of Economic Co-operation and Development) member states and, in that capacity, has been so successful that it convinced virtually every country and territory in the world to comply with its recommendations. Many scenarios in AML transaction monitoring software suites can be directly traced back to these recommendations. Some are either transformed into legislation, others are included in bylaws and other legally authoritative documents, such as the EU's 1st, 2nd, 3rd, 4th, and 5th Money Laundering Directives. These texts either provide or suggest straightforward rules or describe the requirements for the transaction monitoring system in more general terms and leave it to the financial institution's discretion to find a way to meet these. The move from a rule-based to a risk-based system, as discussed in Chapters 1 and 2, is essentially a move from more specific rules prescribed by legislative bodies to an approach where legislator and regulator describe end results and leave more discretion to the financial institutions to find the means to achieve this result. Freedom comes with responsibility and this puts the onus on the financial institution for selecting (and implementing) the right scenarios and adopting the right models. The financial institution must be able to explain to the regulator how the scenarios and models meet the regulatory requirements and protect the financial system from being abused by money launderers. One criterion for the selection and/or design of scenarios and models is that the people responsible for AML operations must be able to understand what these do, and feel comfortable at the prospect of explaining this to a regulatory audit committee. These days the preference, therefore, is for white-box systems, which provide full transparency of every aspect of the alert generation. From experience, we have seen customers rejecting certain logic or parts of the system, because of the sheer complexity of certain calculations and their (or the vendor's) inability to explain or replicate its results.

They opted instead for more understandable, transparent and, hence, defendable approaches to AML.

BUSINESS DRIVERS

Compliance is no longer a novel domain and all financial institutions implementing a new system will do so from the perspective of a *change* in the existing business operations. Quite often this means that rules or a system with scenarios are already in place, many of which will need to be carried over into the new system. Most software vendors, as mentioned, come with out-of-the-box rule sets, some of which cover generic retail banking transaction monitoring whilst other rule sets may cover more specific operations, such as insurance, merchant banking, correspondent banking, etc. Either way the customer would want to have value for money and use at least part of the rules and scenarios as delivered with a solution. A third factor that comes into play is that quite often there is a specific business reason for the financial institution to implement a new system or, at least, this is seen as an opportunity to improve the level of monitoring. Subject matter experts, and not seldom the MLRO, may come forth with specific ideas about which type of rules and scenarios are needed going forward. From a business perspective these three sources for rule selection will need to be consolidated: existing rules that will need to be carried over, rules that come with the software, and new rules on the wish list of the domain experts. A mapping exercise will need to be done to see to what extent the pre-built rules in the new system covers the to-be-a-carried-over rules and scenarios and those new wishlist rules and scenarios. This is not always an easy exercise, as often we find in the field that customers who make the change to a system of a new software vendor, expect that all rules can be mapped, migrated, or rebuilt on a one-to-one basis. The reality, however, can be very different where different systems can take a widely differing approach as to how to organize and prep the data and how to design the combined set of rules and scenarios. Even between different generations of AML transaction monitoring software from the same vendor we have seen significant shifts in the approach and overall design of the body of scenarios. Rule selection, therefore, can vary from project to project, but will almost always be a dialogue between the financial institution and the vendor/implementation team through multiple exchanges over time, where the initial exchange usually takes place early during the pre-sales cycle and will continue throughout the first phase of the implementation project.

Financial institutions sometimes buy a business advisory service as a package with the software, and during implementation, will engage the vendor to help them out with scenario selection. A common approach from a business advisory perspective is to assess the areas of greatest regulatory risk and exposure, either by looking at the nature and/or composition of the financial institution in terms of its business operations, or by looking at historic data, productive alert and reporting levels, and/or regulatory scrutiny or reprimand. Identifying the most important vulnerabilities or "pain points" will further guide the process of scenario selection.

Often, a phased approach will be suggested where the first go-live will include a smaller set of more impactful scenarios, followed by a further roll-out of the system to other scenario types that may address more specific areas of exposure. A phased approach, also from a scenario selection and deployment perspective, may have many benefits. It may shorten the time-to-value as starting with a limited set may bring forward the initial go-live date. Also, the first phase, when it includes more basic, straightforward scenarios, may serve to educate the team and reduce project risk when the more complicated scenarios are covered by a later phase, reaping the benefits of the learning curve from the previous phase(s).

Implementing a new monitoring system brings changes to operations. If there are existing measures that can satisfy the regulatory requirement, the institution can choose to keep away from adding new systems. Some banks have existing reports and operations and policies for, say, credit card systems, so that they choose to exclude credit card business from the AML transaction monitoring system. Of course, some institutes would need to consider the unified workflow and central control, so it is a business decision to balance between the pros and cons.

DATA QUALITY AND AVAILABILITY OF REFERENCE DATA

The factors described in the Business Drivers section above are behind the idea for having a scenario for monitoring certain aspects. When it comes to the real technical design, sometimes the desired monitoring is found to be impossible when looking at the required data.

In some situations, the data required by the scenario rule is not available in a database. An example is some "customers anticipated value" from the KYC process. Customers who have been with the institution longer than a certain number of years may not have gone through the relevant KYC process that was established some time later. Then, a scenario, say, comparing aggregate transaction amount against anticipated monthly income, may not be possible.

Even when the required data is available, sometimes it does not meet minimum data quality standards or it comes as insufficiently structured. A column with validated data that contains an overly large proportion of values like "other" or blanks may render that data point unusable for analysis. A monitoring scenario depending on such a data field may give very few valid alerts.

Another example is trade finance price data per each type of goods, as discussed in Chapter 2. The monitoring is effective only if the relevant reference data is available from inside or outside the institute.

MAINTENANCE OF THE SCENARIO REPOSITORY

Banks may be challenged by the regulator through annual reviews, saying that certain criminal activities are not monitored. The institution then responds by adding more and more monitoring scenario rules. After a period of time, the list of scenarios may become huge and very hard to manage.

Therefore, it is important that the repository is maintained. It is a common issue in knowledge management that appears in many IT systems as people rely more and more on computers. Both system end users and IT support staff will leave and new people will join; therefore, the rationale behind the software designed may easily be lost.

There should be a centralized documentation overseeing all scenarios. The implementation project team should try as much as possible to document the requirements and the reasons for the business require-ments and technical design. It is good to have the scenarios catego-rized. At one of our customer sites, we gave the scenario names some coding (e.g. 0 for all transactions, 1 for cash, 2 for wire, 3 for trade, 9 for others, etc.), so that the relevant personnel could easily tell what a sce-nario is about. Having a good documentation and repository also helps when you need to find out whether the existing scenarios are enough or need to be enhanced when facing new requirements.

Using a table is very useful for overseeing things when pieces are arranged in dimensions. Table 6.1 summarizes the scenarios appearing in a bank. It is simplified for illustration purposes. The rows represent different monitoring methods, and the columns are different busi-ness aspects. Some monitoring methods may be applicable to certain businesses only, while many of them can be transformed or adapted to cover possible deficiencies. At the same time, one may find some scenario too specific to a certain business and can be generalized to better cover the suspicious pattern over different business products.

HOW SPECIFIC SHOULD A SCENARIO RULE BE?

When you create a new scenario rule, you may base it on one real criminal case and try to build a rule to mimic that particular pattern. One of the pitfalls is that it can be easy to over-generalize a rule, which then results in too many false positives. You may turn out thousands of false alerts and find that there are many normal cases satisfying the rule as defined, which you hadn't taken into account during the initial design. Sometimes this is found only after the rules are implemented and under testing with real data. After studying the false alerts, addi-tional alert conditions may be added to minimize the false positives, thereby increasing the accuracy.

At the other extreme, if the rule is describing too much detail on a particular situation, the rule may be too specific to a case and it can hardly produce an alert. It will miss similar but different suspi-cious transaction patterns. The situation is like overtraining a statisti-cal model. The designer must step back and try to define the rationale behind the rule and give a general statement as to the kind of situation in which a pattern would be deemed suspicious.

Table 6.1 Table of scenario coverage.

| Scenario Categories | (Any) | Banking Business | | | Securities |
		Cash	Wire	ATM/Internet Banking	
Large Aggregate Value	Large aggregate transactions	Large aggregate cash transactions	Large incoming wire High tax rate to low tax rate country Wire with tax heaven		Frequent trading
Unexpected Transaction	Deposits in excess of expectations Withdrawals in excess of expectations Transactions in similar amount Transaction in round amount			High ratio of high-risk transactions	
High Velocity / Turnover	Velocity factor		High velocity funds - wires in High velocity funds - wires out	High Velocity Funds - ATM Withdrawals	
Structuring	Structured withdrawals	Structured cash deposits			
Early Termination					
Watchlist	Address in watchlist		External party on watchlist Wire with GPO box		
Common Specification in Unrelated Entities	Use of common address				
Involve Unrelated Third Party				Third Party Payment through Internet Banking	
Turnaround / U-turn	Turnaround transaction				

For example, for a scenario rule looking at internet banking, should mobile and phone banking be included as well? For cash activities, should money exchange transactions be covered?

Designing computer systems to model the important points, to the right extent, is a complex undertaking. An advantage of computer systems is that components can be added easily, and complexity increased with nearly no limit. However, a more complex system is not necessarily a better system. Sometimes usability in the short term needs to be sacrificed for flexibility and room for expansion in the long term. If a program concentrates too much on a specific situation, it would be hard to modify it later to accommodate other situations.

OVERLAPPING SCENARIO RULES

Some institutions may want to have scenarios with the same logic but covering a different scope of transaction types. In this case, an alert generated from scenario A would mean the same set of transactions may trigger scenario B. The two alerts will effectively be a duplication, which is not desired (Figure 6.1).

While two scenarios generate an alert on the same set of transactions,

- the scenario looking at a specific transaction type may be more focused, but
- the generic scenario may cover more transactions, giving a holistic view.

The institution may need to choose one of the two scenarios if the problem is that of too many alerts. It would put additional complexity on the system if both were needed to be kept, while reducing the number of alerts.

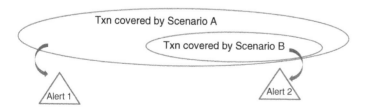

Figure 6.1   Scenario A covering transactions of scenario B.

Keeping Scenario Rules Confidential

Today, I read a news article about a person being killed in an airport by some type of poison getting onto his face. Before the murder took place, one of the killers asked an airport staff member whether the CCTV was working. According to policy, the staff member lied to him, saying that the CCTV was not working. This led to decreased caution on their part, and they finally committed the murder in front of the cameras.

A similar scenario applies to anti-money laundering. Any surveillance measures – including the transaction monitoring rules as well as the scenario rules and their thresholds – should be kept confidential. Otherwise, criminals can study and find out better ways to escape the monitoring, like further breaking down the fund into smaller chunks. This is different from those preventive measures that must be made well known to deter illegal actions (which, in the above case, is notifying people that the CCTV is switched on and "you are being watched"). Both approaches are equally important.

SUMMARY

The initial selection of scenarios to implement is an important step of any implementation. Even though scenarios can always be augmented or modified, the initial go-live event of any new software is a precarious moment where the level of customer satisfaction becomes truly transparent. The challenge is to get the balance right, and to start off with a basic scenario set that meets all immediate requirements and addresses all immediate "pains," but that does not overcomplicate the project and introduce additional project risk and dependencies that may become bottlenecks, such as data (un)availability. There are multiple factors coming into play in getting this balance right: pre-existing methods of transaction monitoring, customer requirements ("For what reason did we opt for the new system and software to begin with?"), regulatory pressure, project readiness, and more.

CHAPTER 7

Entity Resolution and Watchlist Matching

Entity resolution and watchlist matching are closely related topics in AML automation. Whilst entity resolution refers to the data analysis side of things, watchlist matching, in the context of anti-money laundering (AML) is one of the main aims of entity resolution.

ENTITY RESOLUTION

Entity resolution is the activity of identifying data records as pertaining to one and the same real-word entity. The best way to explain this is to think in terms of *documents* and *entities*. Documents, in this context refers to the data records on file that describe an entity. Entities are the (perceived) real-world objects or persons that exist outside of the record.

In AML, typical examples of entities are individuals, legal entities, addresses, and registered objects such as real estate or registered vehicles. Although blurring the lines between record and real-world, accounts and transactions could also be considered entities, even though strictly speaking one may argue these exist solely by the virtue of their record (and are not as tangible as a real person or a real building).

A typical example of a document is the customer application form, or insurance claim form, or the customer record(s) in the customer relationship management repository. One important thing to understand is that forms do not always have a one-to-one relation with an entity. For example, an application form for a new joint account can include data of multiple users of the account, multiple addresses, and multiple accounts or products, such as a credit card or a savings account linked to the deposit account that are applied for at the same time and with the same application process or form.

The *need* for entity resolution arises from the circumstances where multiple separate records pertain to one and the same entity and need to be acknowledged as such. If this is not recognized, then as far as the computer system is concerned, these separate records pertain to different entities and related data will not be reconciled or aggregated. The *challenge* faced by entity resolution is that records may contain inconsistent data, making it harder to determine whether the real-world object or person they describe indeed is one and the same, or perhaps multiple different objects or persons. For example, names may be spelled slightly differently in the two different records but refer to one and the same real-world person. The discrepancy in the record may be the result of human error or may in fact be intentional, such as a fraudster applying for multiple loans deliberately under different name variations.

But the opposite can also be the case: two objects or individuals that, looking at the record, may look like one and the same but in fact pertain to separate real-world objects or subjects. For example, two individuals may share the same name and even the same date of birth, but are not the same person.

Entity resolution is first and foremost a data management activity seeking to improve the quality of the data. Whilst this can be a purpose in itself, there are a few key aims associated with it:

■ Often, but not always, entity resolution includes the activity of merging the multiple records into one master record. One may argue this is the true meaning of *resolution,* in entity resolution as it seeks to *resolve* the situation of disparate and/or discrepant data. This golden record may replace the contributing records that are merged, or it can be added as a new additional record, clearly identifying it is the prevailing record. Whether one method is used above the other is a matter of data management concern. Database economy (size and related performance) are balanced against the need. The golden record that replaces the contributing records will reduce the number of overall records and, unless all contributing data is captured, consist of a smaller set of data than the contributing records combined. This is not always possible, e.g. when the contributing records are records of source. The actual merging of records brings its own challenges. Do we accumulate differentiating data, or do we let one version survive? But then, which version? Accumulation is, for example, the preferred method for aliases (different names for the same persons) but cannot be done for dates of birth or national insurance or tax identification numbers: at least one of the variations is incorrect. There needs to be a mechanism to let one prevail over the other(s), but a simple rule is not always a given.

▪ Another main objective of entity resolution is to, at least, capture awareness that disparate records pertain to the same entity, in other words, to establish a *holistic view* of customers. A typical example in the world of banking is that one customer may hold multiple accounts and uses different products and, as a result, banks with multiple branches, multiple lines of business, or in multiple countries. As we have discussed earlier, from a regulatory perspective, it has become increasingly important for financial institutions to be able to map all relationships they may have with one and the same real-world person or legal entity, across all of its branches, lines of business, or countries of operation. Improving data quality, in this case, is aimed at reducing regulatory risk and exposure.

▪ Entity resolution, as a data cleansing activity, becomes more pertinent in the case of denormalized source data. Most financial institutions aim to capture normalized source data on customers, accounts, transactions, etc. Their data warehouse is already designed for reconciling data from multiple channels into one master record for each entity. We call this normalization of data. But theoretical analysis for the purpose of AML and/or fraud detection can also be done on the basis of denormalized data. A typical example would be the analysis and parsing of SWIFT messages. SWIFT messages are not heavily structured. Rather than using the term *unstructured* data we prefer to call this a *loosely structured* data format. A SWIFT message will most often contain a remitter's account details (IBAN, BIC, or other format), his/her/its name (which can be in any format or character set) and the same for the recipient. It will further contain an originating bank, a recipient bank, and any number of intermediary banks. These are commonly identified by their BIC number, but not always. If the SWIFT messages are the source data, it will, in terms of entity resolution, be a *document*, containing references to multiple *entities*. The data, as such, presents itself as denormalized, and entity resolution must be applied, before meaningful transaction monitoring can take place.

▪ A fourth application of entity resolution is *social network analysis*: identifying single real-world persons and objects, but also in terms of their *relations*. This is particularly relevant in the prevention and detection of financial crime, both in terms of anti-fraud and anti-money laundering. In detecting suspicious activity, it helps knowing that multiple individuals use the same address or the same ID document, even when they seek to hide that fact by building in small variations. Before a network can be built and scored, entity resolution must be applied.

▪ The fifth purpose of entity resolution, in the context of AML, is watchlist screening.

WATCHLISTS

Watchlists are an intrinsic part of any AML effort. Watchlists, in general, are lists of individuals and entities that for some reason need to be highlighted, mostly because there is a regulatory ban on providing any or certain services to these entities and individuals.

Looking from the perspective of AML there are three types of watchlists: regulatory watchlists, subscriptions lists, and internal or association lists. Let's have a look at each of these and explain their difference.

Regulatory Lists

These are the most important lists, as the stakes of (non-)compliance with these lists are very high. Numerous financial institutions have been imposed huge fines in the range of hundreds of millions or even billions of US dollars for repetitively not adhering to these lists. Regulatory lists contain names of individuals, entities, and quite often also registered vessels, that financial institutions are not allowed to do business with or execute transactions for. These lists are issued by public regulatory bodies and are binding. Examples are:

Geo Scope	Authority	List name
Australia	Foreign Affairs and Trade	Consolidated List
United Kingdom	HM Treasury	Consolidated to Financial Sanctions
European Union	Common Foreign and Security Policy	Consolidated List to Financial Sanctions
United States	OFAC	Specially Designated Nationals List
United Nations	United Nations Security Council	The Consolidated List

For an internationally operating bank the watchlists form a matrix. Every country or group of countries (like the United Nations or the European Union) can issue its own list or even multiple lists . . . and they all need to be adhered to if the transactions and business operations are relevant to the scope of that list. For example, if the US OFAC list bars financial institutions from executing US dollar transactions with Iran, and e.g. an EU list does not have Iran as a listed country, then the restriction only applies to *US dollar* transactions to *Iran* and only to the extent that the financial institution depends on a banking license in the US.

Punitive and/or restorative action can only be taken against the financial institution if it violates the sanction provision of a jurisdiction that they have operations in and for which the financial institution has a license. The ultimate penalty is a revocation of that license, issued by each country separately. Depending on how important any given license is for the financial institution, this could put the financial institution out of business. Less drastic measures, therefore, can be applied, such as a temporary or conditional revocation of the banking license, also known as a *Cease and Desist* order, whereby the license is only revoked until the financial institution can demonstrate to have implemented a sufficiently robust business process, or a conditional revocation, whereby the financial institution is given a defined time window to get their house in order, but in the meantime the license will continue to exist. We have already mentioned fines as another measure imposed by the regulators, which often are combined with the conditional revocation of the license.

Subscription Lists

As there are many active regulatory lists globally and each of these is periodically updated, there are commercial players on the market who sell aggregate lists, making it their specialty to maintain an overall list incorporating all the regulatory lists and keeping track of changes to these. The most commonly known are *World-Check* and *Dow Jones Factiva*. Most financial institutions use a subscription list to support their watchlist screening processes.

Internal Lists

Most, if not all, financial institutions keep their own internal lists of individuals and entities, or categories of these, with which they have decided not to do any new business with. These lists are known under informal names like blacklists, bad guy lists, or do-not-bank lists. On these lists are customers who are barred from the financial institution's services because of incidents in the past or because they do not represent the values the financial institution adheres to. An example of the former is an individual or entity who has defrauded the financial institution in the past, behaved in an unacceptable way towards the financial institution employees, or have been found guilty of money laundering. An example of the latter is that some financial institutions refuse any enterprises that are (solely) operating in the sex industry, either because they believe this to be derogatory to women, or because the assumed inherent crime and, therefore, money-laundering risk of that particular industry is deemed unacceptably high. This is a real possibility, for example, in countries where prostitution is legalized but where under the surface of an upperworld industry sector human trafficking is still rife.

One is right to infer from these examples that the internal list does not only contain entities that are on the list for the risk they represent in terms of money laundering. It is up to each financial institution to maintain an overall do-not-bank list or separate lists for each purpose, with the ability to separate out parties that are unwanted in relation to money-laundering risk specifically.

Whilst internal lists are common, and were originally strictly internal to a particular financial institution, there is an increasing number of examples where financial institutions share lists bilaterally or more often multilaterally and all adhere to the same aggregated list held by the consortium of participating financial institutions. In many Western European countries, the five or six largest banks in that country work together on the exchange of intelligence in the context of fighting and preventing financial crimes, and that may include collaboration in terms of a joint do-not-bank list. Financial institutions work together with their commercial competitors when it comes to AML and the fight against financial crime in general. In some cases, such initiatives are executed at the level of the industry association where a body representing the industry maintains a collective internal list.

In the world of AML, watchlist matching is applied in the context of transaction monitoring, to see if the parties related to a transaction might appear on any of the relevant lists. It also is done outside the narrow context of transaction monitoring as an intrinsic part of customer due diligence (CDD): each customer will need to be checked against the watchlists.

As watchlists are actively managed lists they frequently change. New entities are added, existing entities removed, or their details updated. It is important that financial institutions keep aligned with these changes and do their checks against the updated lists, or at least against the updates, within reasonable time. A mechanism should be in place to keep track of updates and (re)check against the newest versions of the list.

From a transaction monitoring perspective, the parties to a payment are checked against the internal list. This process is largely automated but requires human involvement to filter out the false positives. This section drills deeper into various transaction monitoring techniques that can be applied and the concepts behind these.

Name Matching and Watchlist Matching

In its simplest explanation, watchlist matching is looking to see if a certain entity, which can be an individual person, a legal entity, or a registered vessel, appears on a list or not. As with so many things, what is relatively easy for a human being to do, gets complicated when computer algorithms take over.

At its core the challenges with automated watchlist matching is threefold:

1. Separate individuals and entities may have the same name or share attributes and one must avoid confusing the listed entity

with others. How many people share a first and last name, some may also have the same birthdate. How to tell one from the other?

2. Humans are inconsistent when it comes to the spelling of their names, either out of error, through carelessness, or even deliberately to avoid identification. Data such as address details may come unstructured or only loosely structured.

3. Watchlists may be incomplete or incorrect, either because all the information is not always available or because errors are made in the conversion, such as when names originally put in a non-Latin character set, such as a Japanese, Thai, Arabic, or Cyrillic character set, are converted into a Latin character set (or the other way around).

Let us have a look at a number of text transformations that a name or address must go through in order to predict if a seemingly different entity is actually the same, or where seemingly identical data refer to different entities. This is called entity resolution. Some of the transformations are easy and quickly done, whilst others are more complicated. Going through some examples will demonstrate the complexities, which are exacerbated by the fact that we live (and financial institutions operate) in a multicultural and multilingual world.

True and False Positives and Negatives and the Two Sides of Entity Resolution

Also, in terms of name screening and watchlist matching one can make a distinction between true and false positives and negatives. The following schema serves to illustrate this.

	True	False
Positive	A customer on record is **correctly** identified as the person or entity on the watchlist, and risk-mitigating action was justified and/or required.	A customer on record is **incorrectly** identified as the person or entity on the watchlist, and risk-mitigating action should not have been taken.
Negative	A customer on record is **correctly** identified as **not** on the list, and not taking further action was justified.	A customer on record is **incorrectly** identified as **not** on the list and **should** have been identified and action should have been taken.

Further, there are two sides to entity resolution that tie in with the notions of true and false positives. Entity resolution is all about a deeper understanding of which record pertains to which real-life entities. This is most commonly understood as resolving two or more data records that describe real-world natural persons or entities as actually referring to one and the same real-life entities: the customer on file is the same as the person or entity included in the watchlist. But the opposite scenario is equally, if not more, common: despite strong similarities in the description (i.e. name, date of birth, address, social security number), the customer on record is **not** the person or entity mentioned on the list. Separating true from false positives and negatives is difficult as it is. This is made even more difficult by the deliberate attempts of perpetrators of fraud and money laundering to steal the identity of others and commit crimes under such a stolen identity. The automation of watchlist checking, and therefore entity resolution, becomes a paradoxical task. Differences that are the result of human error or malicious intent need to be recognized, as they could indicate that a person on a record is one and the same as on the watchlist. A person with malicious intent attempts to create an appearance of multiple real-world persons or entities, whilst in reality they are one and the same. Paradoxically, in the case of identity theft, a near perfect match can also indicate the exact opposite: someone is trying very hard to establish identification as another, invoking the appearance that there is only one real-life person or entity, whilst in reality there are two or more.

Documents, Entities, Elements, and Compounds

One form of entity resolution is specifically useful for denormalized data sets. In a denormalized data set a record may contain data on multiple entities, either of the same or different entity types, and the same entity may be occurring in multiple records.

Let's illustrate this with an example from the automotive insurance industry. AML in insurance is typically different from traditional banking, as transaction monitoring is not aimed at a high volume of transactions, such as card purchases, online transfers, etc., but at insurance claims. And the focus is often not so much the actual

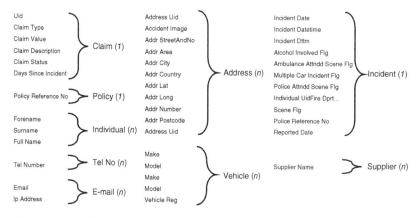

Figure 7.1 Details involved in an automotive insurance claim.

payout details of the claim, but rather the claim in its entirety, including repetitive involvement of the same subjects, an excessive number of insurance policies and high claim per policy ratio, full advance payment of the premium when spread payment is the norm, etc.

Rather than having full access to the data warehouse where data may be processed and normalized through conversion into a dimensional or relational model, the AML system may work on the basis of the original documents: the policy application forms, the claims forms, and the ledger of premium payments.

Entities may be directly extracted from the application and claim form and other documents. A typical policy application form will include a number of entities such as a policy holder; a policy beneficiary; a registered vehicle covered by the policy; and policy data, such as start date, end date, policy type, annual premium amount, coverage definitions, etc. A typical claim form will include the claimant, a reference to the policy, and a claimed amount. In case of a two-vehicle collision, the claim will also have a third party (who may or may not be insured with the same company), a second vehicle (not the object of the policy), addresses of the claimant, the injured party, the third party, and the supplier (for example the tow service and garage who did the repairs or the hospital where any injuries were treated).

All of these details are filled in by the claimant and when the claim form is sent to the insurance company, the claim form is converted into an electronic data capture format. An analytical process can be run against all (new, incoming) claims and the entities extracted and resolved against each other. The entity record is created as part of this process, and each and every time a new claim is submitted, all claims (including the older ones) are analyzed. Or, if only the new claims undergo this process, the entities that are identified will be mapped against the historic list of entities and a new entity record is created only when there is a new entity that cannot be mapped. At the same time, the claim folder also contains the relations. And based on that, a social network analysis can be executed against both pre-existing and new entities, and existing networks expanded with the new entities, and relations or new networks created if none of the entities are related to any pre-existing entity. How to build these networks, and how to make sure that they do not become a supercluster linking every entity in the database to another entity, is a science by itself and exceeds the scope of what we want to discuss here.

What is important here is to understand how entities are matched. This approach uses the concepts of elements and compounds. The fields in the claims form, the most basic information units such as street name, house number, postcode, last name, and telephone number, are called *elements*. Any entity is made up of a number of possible elements. An individual will have a first name, a last name, and possibly one or more middle names. But also, a date of birth, a social security or tax identification number, a passport or ID document number, a customer number perhaps, could all serve to identify this individual. An address has a street name, a building number, possibly a floor or flat number, a post code, a latitude and longitude (although unlikely that these are in the claims document). All of these address elements may serve to identify this address and literally tie it to the same spot on the surface of the earth, or the same real estate build on that spot (and this goes even for a postbox address).

However, not every element by itself will be capable of identifying an entity. For example, a first name is not a strong identifier as many people may have the same first name. But some elements are strong identifiers by themselves, such as social security number (SSN) or tax identification number (TIN). Before these are issued as a unique number to a person, the issuing authority already has done the appropriate due diligence (or so you may expect). Therefore, it is relatively safe to say that a match on SSN or TIN indicates you are dealing with one and the same person.

But a combination of less strong indicators may also result in a (sufficiently) high level of confidence that two records or documents pertain to the same real-world entity. A first name by itself not nearly sufficient as an identifier and neither may middle names, last name, or date of birth, but the combination of these may actually make up a pretty strong identifier with a high level of confidence.

We call these combination elements as identifiers a *compound*. To be strictly correct, a compound can also have one element, as a compound can be defined as a unit of (combined) data that by itself serves to identify and match entities as one and the same.

Let's list a number of compounds:

Natural Person

- SSN
- TIN
- First name + middle names + last name + date of birth
- Customer number (if any)

Legal Entity

- Entity Tax Number (EIN)
- VAT number
- Chamber of Commerce ID
- Full Corporate Name + Chamber of Commerce of Registration
- Full Corporate Name + Country of Registration

Address

- Postcode + House number + Floor and/or door number (if any)
- City name + State/Province name + Street name + House number + Floor and/or door number (if any)
- Latitude + Longitude

For each of the *entity types* (in bold), natural person, legal entity, and address, a match is constituted by a matching compound. A match on *all* the elements in *only one* compound for that entity type suffices to resolve two records as referring to one real-world entity (unless identity theft is established, but we ignore this complicating case for now). In the above list the plusses (+) act as an AND operand and the bullet point act as an OR operand.

This brings us to another aspect that goes to the heart of the matter of entity resolution and watchlist checking, and that is this – some of these elements are binary: they are either an *exact* match or not, but some of them could be a *near exact* match but still infer identification of two or more entities. And to make it even more complicated: the delta between the two records, in theory, can be at three different levels:

- At compound level, where elements may swap places or where *x* out of *n* elements need to match, for example
  - First name + middle name + last name + DoB
  - Middle name + first name + last name + DoB
  - 1 out of (First name + middle name) + last name + DoB
- At element-character level, for example
  - Maarten van Dijck = Maarten van Dijk = Marten van Dijck = Marten van Dick
- At element-convention level, for example
  - Captain James Tiberius Kirk = Capt. Jim Kirk

This non-exact matching poses a great number of challenges to any entity resolution effort, and particularly in the field of watchlist matching. Let's have a closer look at these challenges and how an analytical system can work around these.

Casing

Casing is the distinction between uppercase and lowercase. The name *Maarten van Dijck* in its correct (Germanic) spelling, the first letter of Maarten and Dijck are capitalized. Whilst for a computer *Maarten van Dijck* would be different from *maarten van dijck* or *Maarten Van Dijck*, for a human it would not be uncommon to look past the casing and think of this name as the same. A common transformation to overcome this problem in the context of automation, is to convert everything to uppercase. *Maarten van Dijck* then becomes MAARTEN VAN DIJCK. However, this may invoke new interpretation issues. Let me ask you this question: If you have to apply the labels first name, middle name, and last name to the name Maarten van DIjck or *MAARTEN VAN DIJCK,* how would you do it? If you are not very familiar with Germanic names, there is a big chance you would interpret it like this:

First Name	Middle Name	Last Name
Maarten	Van	Dijck

The correct way, however, is . . .

First Name	Middle Name	Last Name
Maarten		van Dijck

. . . where the last name includes the van that in its correct casing starts with a lower case.

In simplifying the name to accommodate identification that (most of the times) correctly ignores case, the risk of mislabeling name parts may increase.

Spacing and Special Characters

Another common transformation is the removal of spaces (and other special characters). Maarten van Dijck then becomes *MaartenvanDijck* or *MAARTENVANDIJCK.* As mentioned, the name is a common one not only in the Netherlands but also in Northern Belgium. Whilst in Dutch the name would much more often be written with a space between VAN and DIJCK, in Belgium it is commonplace to pull these together *Maarten Vandijck* is a different name of a different (Belgian) person than his Dutch namesake *Maarten van Dijck.* When spaces are removed and everything is put in uppercase that (for humans) distinction gets lost, as both would become *MAARTENVANDIJCK.*

Something similar happens with another typical Dutch last name *in t veld.* Neither *Mart in t Veld* and *Martin T. Veld* are uncommon names, but usually refer to different individuals. Removing special characters and applying uppercase would remove any way to distinguish between these names: *MARTINTVELD.* Conversion and interpretation problems increase when the names come in a loosely structured format, such as is the case with SWIFT payments.

Known Acronyms

Names and streets often use acronyms and abbreviations for elements. These elements need to be preserved, at least to a certain point, because they help us with text parsing and indicate the type of information we are dealing with. Take a look at the following list:

Variations	Language	Position	Standardization	Type
Street Str. Str street	EN	Prefix	STREET	Address Street Name
Avenue Aven. Ave. Ave	EN	Prefix	AVENUE	
Boulevard Blvd. Blvd	EN	Suffix	BOULEVARD	
Carrrer C. Calle Cal	ES	Prefix	CARRER	
Drive Dr Dr.	EN	Suffix	DRIVE	
Doctor Dr Dr.	multiple	Prefix	DR	Professional / Academic Title
M.Sc. Msc. Msc DCM	multiple	Suffix	MSC	
Mrs. Mrs Ms. Ms	EN	Prefix	MRS	Title (Feminine)
Mister Mr. Mr	EN	Prefix	MR	Title (Masculine)
Señor Senor Sr Sr.	ES	Prefix	SR	
Senior Sr Sr.	EN	Suffix	SR	Title
Limited Ltd. Ltd	EN	Suffix	LTD	Legal Entity Type
Incorporated. Inc. Inc	EN	Incorporated	INC	

Looking at this table, immediately the complexity of language and naming conventions become clear. Take for example the following address:

45 Dr. Martin Luther King Jr Dr.

which we would standardize as

45 DR MARTIN LUTHER KING JR DRIVE

We recognize this as a building number and street name mainly based on the relative order of the elements (e.g. Dr. as a prefix and Dr. as a suffix), but also because we know that Doctor Martin Luther King Junior was a very famous person and is revered with street names in many countries. There are Martin Luther King drives, streets, lanes, avenues, and places everywhere across the US and beyond.

Also try to count how many different words you know in your native language only to indicate a street name. In English the following are all more or less common: Street, Lane, Alley, Avenue, Boulevard, Place, Square, Gate, Market, Circle, Circus, Crescent, Drive, Park, Promenade, Dock, Mills. To make it even harder for a system to recognize an address these days, no street type indication whatsoever has also become very common, although the ones containing the name of a person as a street name usually do have an indicator like street or Square in their names. And how should a machine interpret the very common name Market Square? Market here has to be considered the Street name and Square the street indication. It does not really matter because both elements would be recognized as address indicators, but most systems would also include the address indicator in the full address name.

As we can see above, the locale or language also plays a role. Sr. in Spanish is a prefix meaning Mr. but a suffix in English meaning Senior (as opposed to Junior), however Mr. in Dutch (as a prefix) stands for *Meester* and is a professional title (very similar to esq. or J.D.) for those with a degree in law. Knowing the locale and local usage of your data files does matter.

Locale or specific county, more than language, also matters for legal entity types. Countries across the world have the same entity types, but the names and abbreviations and acronyms are language specific. Even if in the same language, different countries can have variations in the types and names that are available. So ideally, a list is being kept for all countries that the financial institution operates in or has organizational customers, and the list must contain at least three columns: one for country, one for the value domain (indicating the specific entity types available for that country) and one for all possible variations, acronyms, and abbreviations.

Exact versus Substring Matching

Exact match is the most trivial way of matching, which gives a match if all characters are matched with exact positions. Sometimes text string will not be matched for whole string, and a "contains" or substring match (a text string appears inside another longer text string) would be appropriate. That is, whether a target text string is *contained* in the given text. For example, it may be needed to match a country from a free text address, using a list of country and city names. In the address 123 DOWNING STREET, <u>LONDON</u>, U.K., the text string LONDON gives a match.

There is a problem with this substring match. In the above example, it seems obvious that LONDON is a city in United Kingdom. However, there is a state in Nigeria called ONDO, and it will give a match too: 123 DOWNING STREET, L<u>ONDO</u>N, U.K.

A similar example is CUBA contained in SCUBA.

One solution is to split the text string into individual words before matching. After splitting, the one text string becomes an array of words. The words are then exact matched with target strings.

For the above example,

123 DOWNING STREET, LONDON, U.K.

↓

123 DOWNING STREET LONDON UK

↓

123

DOWNING

STREET

LONDON

UK

Then, LONDON is matched, and ONDO is not, because each word is done exact match.

If the text string cannot be split, another possible way is to pick the longest match. In the above example, both LONDON and ONDO are matched. LONDON has six characters match while ONDO has four characters, so LONDON should be a more accurate match.

There is another problem. There can be more than one match. Take the address matching of a country as example again; a country name can appear in company name, building name, and street name, besides the real address part as country:

Room 1234, Bank of <u>Argentina</u> Tower, 123 <u>Brazil</u> Road, <u>Chile</u>

This address contains three country names. Although we know Chile is the country name, could a rule be set to take only the last match? In some places, addresses are written in exactly the opposite way, at which the country is written first.

Multi-Element Matching

Name order also have different conventions. In the Western world, names are normally in order of a given name, followed by a middle name (if any), and then family name. In China, Japan, and Korea, the family name comes first, followed by the given name. In Hong Kong, if a person has a Western given name in addition to a Chinese one, then the Western convention will be used. For example, Donny Yen has his Chinese name as Yen Ji-dan, where Yen is his family name. Sometimes, people may write his name as Ji-dan Yen.

It is not easy to be sure which convention is used when a name is encountered. At the same time, if someone intends not to be easily traced, they may deliberately use a name in a legitimate, but uncommon, way.

Therefore, when name matching for surveillance purposes, a name should be matched in different orders. For a name with two words, there are two different possible forms: (1) Donny Yen, and (2) Yen Donny. For a name with three words, there would be six different possible forms (use permutation function with all words chosen, $3! = 3 \times 2 = 6$). That is, a name with N words would be expanded to N! and each of them are matched against the target name. A permutation function of array is needed to produce the variations.

One could build in additional tolerance to allow the first and middle name to swap places, but not the last name.

Target	Source	Match
Donald John Trump	John Donald Trump	Y
	John Trump Donald	N
	Trump Donald John	N
	Trump John Donald	N
	Donald John Trump	Y
	Donald Trump John	N

Character Sets and Transliteration

Language and locale bring another issue: character sets and alphabets. Across the globe multiple different character sets are used and, less problematic, using the same character-set languages may use different characters. Also, some countries are multilingual and may contain language specific characters or even can be written in a different character set. Let's again look at a list which illustrates the range of characters. This list is by no means exhaustive in any way, but it serves to illustrate the level of variation.

Language	Countries	Region	Character Set	Special Characters
English	UK, US, Hong Kong, Australia, ++ Financial institutions in many other countries use English	Multiple	Latin	None
German	Germany, Austria, Switzerland, France	Europe	Latin	ß, ü, ö
French	France, Belgium, Switzerland, Angola, ++	Europe, Africa	Latin	á, é, ê, ô, ç
Spanish	Spain, Mexico, Argentina, Bolivia	Europe, Latin America	Latin	ñ, á, í, ó
Hungarian	Hungary	Europe	Latin	å, ó, ö, ő, ű, á. ú, ü
Turkish	Turkey			
Russian	Russia, Belarus, Kyrgyzstan, Kazakhstan, Ukraine, Georgia, Estonia	Europe, Eurasia	Cyrillic	
Greek	Greece		Greek	
Hebrew	Israel	Middle East	Hebrew	
Arabic	Multiple Arab speaking countries	Middle East	Arabic	
Chinese	Taiwan, Hong Kong		Traditional Chinese	
Chinese	China, Singapore		Simplified Chinese	
Japanese	Japan		Japanese	
Korean	North Korea, South Korea		Korean	
Vietnamese	Vietnam		Vietnamese	
Thai	Thailand		Thai	

There are a few considerations that come into play when doing entity resolution. First, every language or every locale has its own conventions around names and name variations and even spelling variations. For example, in German the *Ringel-S* (*ß*) can also be spelled as a double-*s*.

Since the s is a character in the alphabet used by virtually all countries that use the Latin alphabet, it makes sense to convert every instance of *ß* to a double-*s*, and every *ü*, to *ue* and every *ö* to *oe*, as is often done. At name level, in English, James and Jim are two variations of the same name and people who have James as their official first name, are often formally allowed to provide Jim as their official name too. And the name Mohammed can be written in many different ways. Entity resolution technology takes into account these language-specific conventions, to make sure entities are identified even when there are discrepancies between their names in the financial institution's records and the watchlist. However, one would have to know the locale or language to apply the list of common alternatives and conventions, as applying each of the lists for each locale to each element would either take too long or require too much additional computing power. For the same reason it is very difficult for a system to deal with multiple character sets at the same time. Best practice is to reduce all elements to the same character set. This is called *transliteration*. Names that are spelled in one character set are converted into another character set, usually on the basis of phonetic resemblance. The most common variation is where any non-Latin spelled name is converted into a Latin character set based on the phonetic features of English.

Name Variations

Transliteration creates its own margin for error. For example, the family name Chow is originally spelled in Chinese as 周, and the following variations are all accepted as correct transliterations: Chow, Chau, Chou, Jau, Jao, Zhou.

But also, within one and the same alphabet or locale, name variations are very common. And whilst most of the times these variations actually refer to different individuals, sometimes they are accepted alternatives for one and the same.

The name *Maarten van Dijck* is a good example. This is a common name in the Netherlands. Literally translated it means Martin from (the) Dyke.

As most of the Netherlands is below sea level, dykes have always played an important role in Dutch life and, therefore Dutch culture, so the names *van Dijck* and *van Dijk* are very common. For historic reasons, however, the name *van Dijk* is much more common in the Netherlands, whilst in Belgium the *van Dijcks* outnumber the *van Dijks*.

The name Maarten is a common Dutch name. It comes from the Latin name *Martinus*[1] and in Christian culture is associated with Saint Martin. Going back a bit further in history Martin (and Maarten) are associated with Mars, the name for the Roman god of war and the nearest planet to Earth in our solar system. In English, French, and German Martin is a common name; in Nordic countries there is Morton, Márton in Hungarian, Marcin in Polish. So, let's walk through a number of challenges based on this relatively common name.

Apart from namesakes across different languages, most of these countries also have multiple variations to the names. In the Netherlands all of these are common names: *Maarten, Marten, Martin, Martijn, Mart, Mar, Tijn, Thijn, Mathijs, Thijs, Mathias, Mart, Martinus, Marius, Maurice, Maurits, Marcel, Marcello, Marcella, Marc, Mark, Martina, Marina, Marian, Marianne, Maria, Mario.*

Evidently, most of these are not variations of the name *Maarten*. However, it serves to illustrate how easily individuals are being mistaken for someone else if one allows for a certain tolerance. And some of these names are informal versions of the formal birthname *Martinus*, so they could in effect be referring to one and the same person.

A more sophisticated entity resolution system would take into account common aliases. And not only for names, but also for cities. Take, for example, the city where the International Court of Justice resides: the Hague. The Hague, like most large cities has names in the language of the city's country but also a different name in foreign languages, which could well be the language of the bank. In addition, The Hague, in Dutch, has different names, which are both formally correct. On top of this, even Dutch native speakers sometimes have difficulty spelling the name correctly, depending on which version they choose: *The Hague, Den Haag, 's-Gravenhage.*

Levenstein Distance

To filter out minor name variations and typos, one could create algorithms that allow for some level of deviation. A tolerance margin to

---

[1] In European countries up until one generation ago it was very common to give people Latin birth names. My father is known by the name *Harry*; however, his passport says *Henricus Antionius Johannes Josephus van Dijck*.

make sure that *Chow* and *Chau* are considered a match. There is some debate about what approach would give the optimum result.

One approach is the Levenstein distance, called after its creator Vladimir Levenstein. The Levenstein distance is a string metric for measuring the difference between two sequences. Informally, it is the distance between two words – the minimum number of single-character edits (insertions, deletions, or substitutions) required to change one word into the other. Let us illustrate with a few examples.

Source	Target	Distance	Explanation
Chow	Chou	1	Replace *w* with *u*
Chow	Chau	2	Replace *w* with *u*, *o* with *a*
Derrick Jao	Derek Chau	5	Removing *r* and *c*, replacing *i* with *e*, *j* with *c*, adding h, replace *o* with *u*
Vandijck	Van Dijck	1	adding space (capitalization counts only when converting to uppercase is not a generic transformation)

The idea is that the greater the edit distance, the less similarity there is, so the bigger the chance that a name or name pair refers to someone else. The drawback of Levenstein distance as a measurement is that the count is the same for long and short names, but the distance has a different relevance. Ask yourself of the name variations below, which ones have a higher likelihood of referring to a different person.

Source	Target	Distance
Mik Dal	Mika Dal	1
Kornelus Schimmelpennink	Cornelius Schimmelpenninck	6

Alternatively, there are distance measures that take into account the relative distance, which is the distance as a ratio to the length of the string.

Source	Target	Levenstein	Relative Distance
Mik Dal	Mika Dal	1	14%
Kornelus Schimmelpennink	Cornelius Schimmelpenninck	3	12%

But any of these approaches fail to capture the fact that both *Cornelius* and *Schimmelpenninck* are much rarer names than Mik/Mika and Dal, and that Mika has a higher likelihood of referring to a woman and Mik to a man. The latter would even be stronger in names like *René* and *Renee* or *Michel* and *Michelle*. So, the chances that the name *Kornelus Schimmelpennink* refers to the same person as *Cornelius Schimmelpenninck* is higher when compared to *Mik* and *Mika Dal*.

Levenstein or any other edit distance, at best, should be a part of a wider comparison and using math codes is very powerful. Rules, of which the edit distance is but one, are reapplied in a sequence but result in a similar match when, all taken into account, we believe there is a high(er) likelihood for names to pertain to the same person.

Match codes can take into account all of the following considerations:

■ Common transliteration variations

■ Conversion into uppercase (simplification)

■ Removing special characters

■ Removing or harmonizing noise elements (titles, salutations, etc.)

■ Converting name variations to a root name (Jim, James, Jaime)

■ Recognizing element types (first name, last name, street name)

■ Restructuring multielement data (address, composite names)

■ Edit distance and tolerance setting

Take a look at the following examples of name variation resulting in a similar match code:

Full Name	Match Code
James Tiberius Kirk	PHDF8B~$$$$$87B$$$
Jim Kirk	PHDF8B~$$$$$87B$$$
JAMES KIRK	PHDF8B~$$$$$87B$$$
Captain James T. Kirk	PHDF8B~$$$$$87B$$$
Tiberius Kirk	PHDF8B~$$$$$87B$$$

Full Name	Match Code
Moammar Gadafi	F&88&G7$$BY$$$$
Moammar Gadafy	F&88&G7$$BY$$$$
Moammar Gaddafi	F&88&G7$$BY$$$$
Moammar Qadhdhafi	F&88&G7$$BY$$$$
Moammar Gadafi	F&88&G7$$BY$$$$

Address	Match Code
100 NORTH CHATHAM STREET, CARY, NC, 27511 UNITED STATES	#B~4~4$$&42942BW3Y$$$$$$$Z00PY ~2J$$$$$$$$
100 N. Chatham St., cary, North Carolina, 27511 usa	#B~4~4$$&42942BW3Y$$$$$$$Z00PY ~2J$$$$$$$$

Delta Comparison

An institution has a customer database. The compliance department may want to check if any of its customers has a match to any entry on a watchlist. So, each customer should be checked to see if it is in the watchlist. If there are 100,000 customers and the watchlist has 100 entries, then it is a 100,000 × 100 = 10M comparisons (not including the variations of each name).

However, when the customer database changes, so does the watchlist. For a new customer (or an existing customer with a name change), this name has to be checked against the watchlist. This is a delta customer and must undergo a whole watchlist check. In the above example, 1 new customer is compared against 100 entries in the watchlist (100 comparisons).

On the other hand, for a new watchlist entry, the whole customer database has to be checked to see if any existing customer has been placed in the watchlist. This is a whole customer to delta watchlist check. In the above example, say there are 3 new watchlist entries, all customers are compared against 3 entries in the watchlist (100,000 × 3 = 300,000 comparisons).

Generalizing the numbers,

- A customer database has C entries
- A watchlist has W entries

- ◾ c is number of new customer names since last check
- ◾ w is number of new watchlist entries since last check

Then,
Initial check takes $C \times W$ comparisons
On every check, it takes
$c \times W$ comparisons is needed for new customer names
$C \times w$ comparisons is needed for new watch list entries

Text Analysis

To avoid false positives, it helps if the system can recognize the type of a text element. Is a name a first name or a last name? Is it a name of an individual or an organization? And which element in the address makes up the street name? Which is the state or province name (if any)? What is the postcode and which number represents the house or building number? And which one is the floor or flat number? This is not so much an issue with properly structured text, but with unstructured or loosely structured text, such as that which comes within the SWIFT messages accompanying international wire transfers with multiple banks involved as either remitting, intermediary, or recipient financial institutions.

Let's have a look at these very different ways of addressing annotation.

SAS Software Ltd. Wittington House Henley Rd Medmenham Marlow SL7 2EB Buckinghamshire UK	SAS Instituut B.V Flevolaan 69 1272 PC Huizen Netherlands	SAS SA Barcelona C/ Josep Plà, 2. Torres Diagonal Litoral Edifici B3 - Pl. 5 08019 Barcelona	SAS Software Co., Ltd 388 Exchange Tower 38th Floor Unit 3803-4, Sukhumvit Rd. Khlongtoey Bangkok 10110 Thailand	香港, 鰂魚 涌,太古城道12號, 太古城中心四期, 14樓, 賽仕軟件 研究所

Let's try and break each of the addresses down into their components.

Name	SAS	SAS	SAS	SAS	賽仕
Common Element	Software	Instituut		Software, Company	軟件
Entity Type	Ltd	BV	SA	Lyd	研究所
Building	Wittington House		Edifici B3	Exchange Tower	太古城中心四期
Building No		69	2	338	
Floor	Pl		5	38	14
Flat/Unit No				3803-4	
Street		Flevo	Josep Plà	Sukhumvit	太古城道12號
Common Element		Laan	C/	Rd.	
Suburb/Area	Medmenham		Diagonal Litoral	Khlongtoey	鰂魚涌
Place	Marlow	Huizen	Barcelona	Bangkok	香港
Postcode	SL7 2EB	1271 PC	08019	10110	
State/ Province	Buckinghamshire				
Country	United Kingdom	Nederland		Thailand	

With addresses and other multielement components a decision needs to be made whether matching is done at element level, at entity level, or at interim level. In other words, which of the elements can be concatenated before match code creation? None, whereby each element is separately matched? All, whereby the entire address is concatenated (after standardizing the sequence of the elements)? Or a hybrid, where some elements such as street and state may be pulled together before match codes are created? Also, will one and the same tolerance apply to all elements or differentiated per element? Additionally, second-pass rules could be applied to set generic minimum criteria, such as 3 out of 6 elements must match.

A compound-based approach is an easy way to accommodate the interim approach. Multiple compounds can be created that by themselves will create a match.

Another consideration is to what extent different entities are used to support the resolution of the target entity type. For example, is a match on name and date of birth for an individual further strengthened by a match on address linked to that individual? Or, perhaps more important, can a match on a linked address compensate for a hiatus in a partial match on name and date of birth? Doing so would introduce an element of (social) network analysis into the matching arena.

SUMMARY

Watchlist matching is an intrinsic part of AML compliance and the regulatory requirements for customer due diligence and transaction screening. In addition, entity resolution can significantly increase the true positive rate and increase the number of productive alerts, with only a small cost in terms of additional false positives. The following techniques are available:

- Transliteration
- Conversion into uppercase
- Removing special characters
- Removing or harmonizing noise elements (titles, salutations)
- Converting name variations to a root name
- Recognizing element types (first name, last name, street name, entity type)
- Restructuring multielement data (address, composite names)
- Applying match codes (or calculating Levenstein distance)
- Apply compound analysis or enhanced matching rules

These can be applied in isolation or, more commonly, in combination, to successfully resolve entities and match against the regulatory lists.

CHAPTER 8

Customer Segmentation

THE NEED FOR SEGMENTING CUSTOMERS

Customer segmentation is grouping your customers and either applying different rules and scenarios specifically for each group or applying the same rules and scenarios differently, specific to the group. Customer segmentation, in AML transaction monitoring, is a logical consequence of taking a risk-based approach. This can best be illustrated by looking at the opposite situation: no customer segmentation under a rule-based approach.

Let's imagine a heterogenous customer base with a lot of low- and middle-income households and a few more affluent households and the occasional super-rich. Let's take a rule that puts a simple threshold on single-value online purchases and let's imagine a threshold of $4999. Would this rule ever trigger for the low or even middle-income households? Probably not often, if at all. Would it trigger for the higher or very high incomes? Probably occasionally and possibly even regularly for the super-rich. In the former case there would probably be a number of false negatives (no alerts where there should have been) and for the higher and extra-high incomes there would be a number of false positives (alerts that are unnecessary).

Another example: Where transaction amount, volume, and velocity would be lower for the average individual customer, this could be perfectly normal for corporate customers.

The issue is evident: AML transaction monitoring professionals mostly do not agree with a one-size-fits-all approach. There may be a few exceptions, especially with the safety blanket rules such as the $10,000 cash deposit rule and where there might be a regulatory obligation to report, but these are few and far in between.

Customer segmentation is one means available to the AML scenario author to decrease the number of false positives and negatives, just by looking at transaction parameters and customer attributes in context. This typically fits in a risk-based approach where the effort to optimize efficiency and reduce false positives and negatives is built on the approach to look at things in their context. Is this behavior abnormal or unexpected for *this* particular customer? How do we know? One way is to compare against other customers of the same type or in the same income bracket. At the highest level of abstraction, we call this customer segmentation. If we further break down the segment into subclasses, we talk about peer groups and peer group analysis.

Applying altogether different rules to different customer segments would still be considered customer segmentation, but usually the term is reserved for the practice of tweaking the thresholds of a given rule; whereas the rule or scenario is applied to all customer segments, its threshold parameters may be set differently for each of the segments.

The risk-based approach does not only manifest itself in tailoring the thresholds to the segments, but also by a widespread practice to define the segments partially based on the risk the customer represents. The customer segments can be defined and delineated on the basis of any factor, any dimension, and in fact any number of dimensions.

One widespread approach is to divvy up the customers along the lines of:

1. Individual vs. organization
2. Size (income, turnover, or asset value)
3. Risk category
4. Nature of business

Risk category stands for the regulatory mandatory assessment of the AML risk a customer represents to the bank. At (or even before) the beginning of a customer relation the financial institution will perform a risk assessment on that customer. This is usually referred to as customer due diligence (CDD). Although not strictly required by legislation in most countries, this risk assessment is reviewed periodically and the frequency (or length of the intervals between two) of reviews is determined by the last time the risk was assessed. High-risk customers will be up for re-review sooner and have a higher level of scrutiny, and low-risk customers need not be looked at so often or be as intensively monitored.

A similar mechanism is applied when setting the thresholds for each customer: thresholds will be lower (not higher!) if the customer is assessed as higher risk. As a result, a scenario will fire an alert sooner, which means that the customer is being looked at more and monitoring is more stringent than for a low-risk customer with elevated thresholds.

Theoretically, the grouping scheme can be different across different scenario rules. However, unless it is found to be really necessary, it is not desirable to do so as it will make the system too complicated to maintain.

APPROACHES TO SEGMENTATION

There are two main approaches to segmentation: expert- or domain-driven, and data-driven. The domain-driven approach is based on business experience and expertise of professionals who have knowledge of the domain of AML in their type of business. The data-driven method takes a statistical approach and calculates optimum segmentation on the basis of analysis of (historic) customer and transaction data. Both methods have pros and cons and many financial institutions take a hybrid approach.

A data-driven approach using statistical methods uses objective verifiable data and so it should be more accurate. It takes out any bias of the AML domain expert(s) as the data speaks for itself. Another benefit is that it can utilize techniques to optimize the cut-off values, determining which customer goes into which bucket, thereby reducing the number of false positives. This requires calculation effort and power that is beyond the capability of human beings.

One apparent benefit of a data-driven approach is that it allows for the automated processing of hundreds of thousands or millions of customer records, where this would be impossible for a team of humans to do in the same time. This is a red herring though, as the human involvement only concerns the use of criteria to delineate the segments, not the actual analysis of the data to assign each customer record to any of the segments . . . that is computer work, if only on the back of an Excel with formulas and fed back into the system as a CSV list (but more commonly it is made part of the ETL process that was discussed in Chapter 3).

Amongst the drawbacks of a data-driven approach is that one has to have data. This is less obvious than one might think. Often at the start of implementing a new system the relevant data is not there (yet). If it is a supervised model where the result data of the alert triaging and disposition of alerts, and final conclusion from case investigations, may not be there because the system has not been taken into production yet. Data availability is a problem. Often at the start of the process and at initial implementation stage, the domain expertise of the financial institution's AML experts may be all one has to go with.

But there is another reason why sometimes domain expertise either takes precedence over data or at least functions as a counterbalance: whilst the data crunchers may not trust *anything but* data, the domain experts may not trust the *data*, or for that matter, the data crunchers. Not that they would believe the latter do a bad job or have their own agenda (let's not go into the intra-corporate micro-politics one often finds at play on a software implementation site), but that domain experts tend to find examples where a data cruncher misses cases of evident misappropriation resulting from a strictly data-driven approach. However, this counterargument against a strictly data-driven approach is perhaps more relevant to other decisions (like what parameters should make up a scenario) and not so much customer segmentation, which is an area of lesser regulatory exposure.

Domain experts may have a point in mistrusting the data. If the data were of high quality and all data were available, then yes, almost any computer would outmatch any human team in terms of performance. But, as implementers operating in the real world know, this is not often the case right from the start, and endless (human) effort may be put into fetching the data, analyzing and profiling, performing a data quality assessment, repairing; endless hours are put in prepping the data before an automated system can even run without errors and produce trustworthy results. Without full-fledged artificial intelligence, building a statistical model is hard work too! And even then, the outcome could be more or less the same as what the domain experts would have indicated upfront (but with much less effort and cost!).

Then there is the element of human bias that comes with (working) knowledge. On the one hand, personnel in the financial institution working with their customers may know their customers best . . . but may not always work with a strict AML perspective or may have commercial incentives that conflict with regulatory interests. Commonly, the higher risk a customer ends up being classified as, the more difficult it is for an account manager or revenue-generating department to make money from that customer. There is an intrinsic tension, most tangibly at the front office, between commercial and regulatory objectives. But this is only an argument in the case that the experts are front-office staff whose remuneration depends primarily on the turnover each of their customers generates for them (which is usually the case). But the argument falls apart when considering mid- and back-office staff, whose compensation depends on their performance as an internal watch dog: the auditors, compliance staffers, and AMLROs in the organization.

Especially for the MLRO, often the head of compliance or chief (regulatory) risk officer, who is accountable for all aspects of the AML operation, mistrusting a data crunching approach can be a big problem. At the end of the day it is the officers and their teams who will have to explain to the regulatory auditors how the system works and why it produced the results it did. As these individuals know they will be held accountable for any mishaps, it is very difficult to trust a system that goes against their expert opinion and gut feeling.

All of the above explains why most financial institutions will adopt a hybrid approach where in the initial stage there is a heavy reliance on domain experts simply because of the lack of data (because the data emanates from the system that has not yet been implemented).

Later on, a data-driven statistical analysis may serve to validate or fine-tune the segmentation that was initially suggested by the domain experts. From that moment on, domain expertise and a data-driven approach will continue to work in an equilibrium of checks and balances, where one acts as a counterbalance to the other. The accuracy and objectivity of the data crunching is supplemented with a domain expertise check that helps set the initial outline for the analysis and may highlight any evident misses.

Segmentation, most often, is not a one-off activity during the initial implementation of the system, but an activity that is repeated every 6 or 12 months. It can play an important role in transaction monitoring optimization efforts that will be discussed in Chapter 9. Segmentation and segments may be tweaked to rectify a scenario's accuracy and efficiency issues.

At the end of the day, evolving from a domain-driven to an increasingly data-driven approach is a matter of organizational maturity. This term "maturity" must not be misinterpreted in a pejorative sense. It may well be a deliberate choice not to pursue a fully automated, machine-learning approach to transaction monitoring optimization and, as a part of this, customer segmentation. It may not be economically viable or make sense, as the cost will outweigh the benefits, e.g. for smaller sized financial institutions. The application of analytics and the further automation thereof is often a matter of economy of scale, where a critical mass is required for the value added to break even with the investment and associated price tag.

Since we are discussing the use of analytical software as a means to anti-money laundering ends, and doing so from a perspective of implementation, we assume the situation where there is a slighter heavier reliance on domain expertise at time of initial implementation and an increasing utilization of data and data analytics as (production) data builds up over time. We will not consider a fully automated approach, as this would take us too far into machine- and deep-learning and artificial intelligence. Although such techniques are being applied in the domain of analytics and now gradually starting to find their way to applied analytics in the field of AML transaction monitoring, the majority of our customers are not utilizing such techniques yet or at least not to their full extent.

OVERVIEW OF SEGMENTATION STEPS

Figure 8.1 shows a typical cyclic process in terms of segmentation. This cycle is not unique to customer segmentation and, in fact, not even unique to compliance analytics. Within the field of compliance, however, and as we will see later, it can also be applied to scenario optimization, with exception of initial threshold setting.

From an implementation and software vendor perspective, the organization's implementing a new data-driven system can be placed on a scale in terms of organizational readiness. On the one end of the spectrum, there are financial institutions who have never been exposed to an automated data-driven approach and who don't have in-house expertise, either in terms of domain knowledge nor in terms of analytics. Whilst such customers, in reality, are rare, there are quite a few who pretend, at least initially, to lack any expertise and expect the vendor to bring such expertise. Market leading software vendors are well staffed to deliver against a wide spectrum of needs. Some financial institutions may even completely outsource the optimization

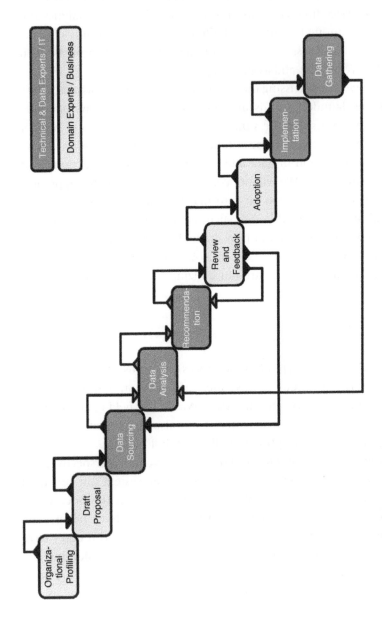

Figure 8.1 Steps in segmentation.

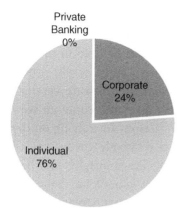

Figure 8.2   Distribution of customers by type.

tasks and even the running of a system to a vendor who supports cloud-based software as a service. On the other end of the spectrum are the highly mature, often bigger financial institutions, who have all the required expertise in-house (or through contracting entire teams of third-party consultants). Such financial institutions will more or less dictate their highly detailed requirements and expect the software to simply accommodate these, and for the technical implementers to translate these requirements in a system that works in line with expectations as stipulated. These financial institutions have done their homework well and know their stuff, with obvious implications of the level of involvement of the vendor. In extreme cases, the vendor sells the license(s) of the required software stack, and at most is only involved in installation, and the financial institution takes it from there. Needless to say, successful examples of this are equally rare.

Regardless of the maturity of the financial institution and the expectations of the vendor, the process followed to get to a meaningful customer segmentation are, conceptually, the same. The steps can be described as follows.

ORGANIZATIONAL PROFILING

Segmentation often begins with a high-level charting of the business and its customer base. Whilst theoretically this could be driven by data, it is more common to take available expertise and knowledge of the composition of the financial institution's customer base as a starting point. Sufficiently mature organizations will be able to provide their initial thoughts (or decisions) on segmentation, whilst others will be looking at a consultancy firm or even the software vendor's domain specialists to describe the customer base and come up with the high-level segments. One of the main reasons for relying on the software vendor for support is that it is a relatively cheap way (if already included in the agreed pricing) to leverage insights into best practices; the assumption is that the software vendor has done this before and knows how other customers have done it. Organizational profiling is largely considered a first step, an initial stab to get things started. At some point it is expected to be followed by a (more) in-depth and fully or partially data-driven analysis that yields more accurate results and allows further fine-tuning of the system. In a strictly domain-driven approach, business users, which could either be the compliance domain experts or account managers who are closest to their customers, are suggesting the segmentation scheme based on their knowledge and understanding of their customers and accounts and domain experience. The rules should be based on money-laundering risk and targeting for the transaction monitoring scenario rules and their thresholds.

Technical-analytical resources, with the help of domain experts and/or business analysts then translates the suggested segmentation scheme into technical terms, specifying the data fields required and logic and conditions. One of their tasks is to ensure the data is sufficient for segmentation rules. If the data does not meet the requirements, then one needs to go back to the previous step, removing this condition.

The segmentation scheme has to be verified with actual data to see if the scheme is valid and if the splitting method is useful for transaction monitoring and finding anomalies. It may be found that some segments need to be merged, and a segment may need to be further split. If this is the case, one may need to retrace one's steps even further and (re)study, perhaps reinterpret, the business objectives and guidelines, and translate these again verifying the required source data.

After a suitable segmentation scheme is defined, thresholds can be established for each scenario and for each customer segment. This process is discussed in Chapter 9.

A segmentation model should be constantly monitored to ensure it is stable. If for any reason the segmentation model is not performing well, it must be reviewed and go through the segmentation process again.

COMMON SEGMENTATION DIMENSIONS

The below list sets out some common dimensions for segmenting customers:

- Individual persons / Corporate
- Risk Factor / Risk classification from know-your-customer assessment
- Government / Public / Financial institution / Embassy
- Within corporates:
  - Sole proprietorship or partnership / Limited company / Listed company
  - Wire intensive / Cash intensive business
- Within individual persons:
  - Asset Size
  - Nationality
- Transactional behavior (e.g. in past 6 months):
  - Aggregate amount / number of all transactions
  - Aggregate amount / number of wire transactions
  - Aggregate amount / number of cash transactions
  - Aggregate amount / number of transactions with high-risk instruments

From a threshold setting and scenario tuning perspective the segmentation serves multiple purposes. On the one hand it will avoid false positives by allowing for differentiating thresholds that are relevant to that particular customer group. On the other hand, since risk classification will always make up part of the segments, it allows for more stringent monitoring of those customers who are perceived as higher risk in terms of money laundering. Loosening the thresholds for higher risk customers will reduce false negatives, at least that is the expectation. It also serves to demonstrate to the regulator that once there is a perception of high risk, closer monitoring is put in place to mitigate the higher risk. The segmentation based on risk classification is a logical consequence of the CDD process and a good example of where CDD ties into AML.

A corporate customer's transaction amount and/or count is proportional to its size. Thus, scenario thresholds of, say, transaction amount, should be larger for larger corporations. If the same threshold is applied to corporations of different sizes, there is a chance where a small corporation doing unusually large transactions will not be alerted because it is still below threshold. In contrast, there is a chance that the threshold could catch the large transactions of small corporations but yield a lot of false positives for large corporations.

Similar to corporation size, individual customers with a large asset size tend to transact in larger amounts and so should be monitored with larger thresholds. If the bank has customer schemes like VIP accounts by asset size, these can be used directly for segmentation purposes. Private banking accounts should also be considered together with asset size, as these may be one of the asset size categories.

Some corporations, like those in the money service business, by nature do more cash transactions than others. For those scenarios specific to cash, these customers should be monitored with higher amount thresholds; a similar situation as for wire-intensive business on wire-specific scenarios.

There are types of corporations that by their very nature represent a lower money-laundering risk and require a lesser degree of monitoring, with loose thresholds. Examples are financial institutions and government organizations.

The KYC/CDD risk classification introduces a whole new dimension into the segmentation, as by itself the risk classification is the result of a composite indexing taking into account a number of aspects, including geography (nationality, country of registration, country of economic activity), occupation or industry, and the financial instruments/banking products being used.

For transactional behavior, the aggregate amount and number of transactions may need to be derived from the (transaction) data and computed from within the AML transactional monitoring system, as they are often not readily available in the data warehouse. Often the transaction monitoring system is configured to keep a summarized history of the transactions on an account or the customer (across multiple accounts), enabling lookback and comparison over longer stretches of time. Again, this may serve a dual purpose, as thresholds specifically for a segment could be derived from such a historic profiling and when set will also influence the profile going forward.

CONSIDERATIONS IN DEFINING SEGMENTS

Finer segmentation, in theory, will improve the monitoring accuracy. But it may also come at a cost. There is, as always, the operational cost: validating each segment and maintaining (relevant) thresholds for each segment will add to the effort and bring additional costs in terms of the resources making this possible. But also, statistically and from a data analysis perspective, there may be a cost. Analytical factors need to be considered when designing the customer segmentation model.

However, while all of the dimensions mentioned above are valid, not all of the known segmentation criteria should be implemented. More need to be considered.

Each segment identified should have a justifiable number of entities. If the segment is too small, characteristics of the distribution cannot be well formed, and it would be hard to define a dedicated set of thresholds. The segment will probably be unstable, as a small change in the entities may alter the group's overall behavior. Usually segments that are too small are merged to other segments that are similar. This is only a problem for the data-driven approach and would have less impact on an approach solely based on domain expertise. In a similar vein, if you know clearly the behavior of the entities in a small segment (e.g. let's say, because of some policy, customers under a certain age of certain nationality cannot wire more than a certain amount so the transactions committed are limited for this group of people), then it may still be worth defining a dedicated segment even though the size is very small.

Another reason not to create a new segment is when there can be no business justification found other than the fact that the data points that way. A data-driven approach may lead to over-training; correlations are found strong enough for the model to suggest a separate segment, but an understanding of how this is relevant to the purpose of anti-money laundering may be lacking. If too many parameters are considered in the data modeling exercise, then these may lead to seemingly strong dividers that statistically may make sense but not from an overall business perspective. Best practice is to ignore and find an alternative segmentation that can be understood and explained from a domain expertise perspective. From a regulatory viewpoint there may be an additional argument: do not adhere to a model that one finds difficult to defend in the face of regulatory auditing. Obviously, this is a grey area where, in reality, much depends on the ability of the data crunchers to explain their findings in domain terms or the data-savviness of the domain experts and their understanding of and belief in a data-driven approach.

Although segments could be subject to change, especially when driven by data analysis, the intent must be to come up with customer clusters that are both stable and homogeneous over time, although strictly not a prerequisite. The segments structure should remain stable over time. It is preferred that each segment has a steady distribution of customers so that each month the outliers, and thus quantities of alerts produced, are also stable. If a big number of customers shift from one segment to another then a sudden increase or decrease in alerts may be witnessed, but without correlation to an actual increase in risk.

The more data there is available, and the more customers or accounts are in the overall population, the more bandwidth there is for a more granular, more refined clustering. And these should have more accurate results as well, as the population per segment is likely to be more homogeneous as a result. However, besides statistical relevance there are other considerations to keep the segments limited in number. The first is maintenance: (re)validating many segments is more work and may take longer and therefore bring more cost. Also, the added value can be disputed when differences between two clusters are relatively minor. And although homogeneity of a cluster's population is always a good thing in terms of predictive analysis, outliers may still need to be accommodated by a segment. Furthermore, and as explained above, it is also a good thing if a statistically and mathematically driven segmentation can still be explained in business terms; and that there is a natural, easily conceivable element that binds the customers in the same segment as well as a purely mathematical one. In the ideal situation the mathematical segmentation reflects the naturally distinct groups in a population. Such as when a divide in high, medium, and low incomes that are mathematically derived align with pre-existing conceptions of what high, medium, and low incomes are in a specific country or region. Those financial institutions that adopt a hybrid solution to begin with will already be automatically built in by the approach; if the financial institution distinguishes commercial from private customers and do the segmentation and data analysis within these two high-level customer categories (and not across), then obviously there is no overspill from one to another and customers will naturally reside in any of the (sub) segments within their overall group. Customer type as a primary division mechanism is not and will never be impacted by a data-driven approach. This is different for income level or asset value, as one of the lines along which clusters are expected to be defined or, in a data-driven approach, emerge.

CHECK SOURCE DATA FOR SEGMENTATION

In a domain-driven approach, where business users suggest a segmentation, the segmentation has to be interpreted and translated into technical terms. The respective IT system owner who maintains the systems should be able to tell whether the required data points for the delineation are available in the system and are of sufficient quality to reliably serve as a demarcation line. The translation would be from the business requirement of the segmentation to a rule, to technical design of database column, and then into logical operations. For example, compliance experts may think of occupation (as the primary source of income) as a good differentiator and suitable for segmentation. However, if in the current system 80% of the customer records are left blank or have a less meaningful value like Other for occupation, then this segmentation rule becomes meaningless, unless accompanied by an organizational (process) change whereby, for example, front staff are put to work to collect more accurate occupation information.

Another potential issue with occupation as a dimension for segmentation is that there are too many values and no easily available grouping, so that by default one ends up with too many segments. If thresholds have to be defined and inserted (and checked) for every single segment, this will quickly add to the administrative workload. Scenario tuning, of which threshold optimization is an important element, may become a huge task, as all steps need to be repeated for each segment. This is not specific to occupation and can even be the result of a data-driven approach, although in the latter there is the option to limit the number of segments that the system can suggest. In the occupation example, this can easily be avoided by rolling up the occupation to industry (as many systems and forms allow these days), but the upstream hierarchy must then be captured and available in the system . . . which is often not the case. This brings us back to the prerequisites of data availability.

VERIFY WITH STATISTICAL ANALYSIS

In a data-driven approach segments can be verified with data. One statistical method is referred to as supervised training. Supervised here means that the data that is used for the analysis is associated with alerts that have already gone through an assessment to determine the productivity of the alert: was it a true or a false positive? This target outcome can be used to calculate which data points, whether or not in combination, are strong indicators of a specific target outcome. If the target outcome is expressed as binary, such as true or false (positive), as in our case, then strong indicators for the one being true are automatically a strong indicator for the opposite being not true.

For example, if after 1 year of alert generation I have had a productive alert on 25% of my newly opened foreign exchange accounts where over $10 million, in a period of a year, with an average transaction value between $3500 and $6500 equivalent, and 90% of the involved transactions were to or from a foreign account, then these 3 factors combined make for a strong ML indicator.

The same mechanism can be applied to cluster the data. Essentially, what I am looking for in the soup of customers and accounts are groupings that, seen from a certain perspective, are more homogeneous than the other groups in a way that is relevant to my assessment or perception of ML risk. In supervised training what makes a segmentation a strong one is that the clusters either have a distinctively high or distinctively low number of alerts (relative to the size of the population in the cluster).

The following example is from a bank that applies a true positive rate to one other parameter: a split based on the line of business – retail banking (individuals), commercial banking, and private banking (high-net-worth individuals using asset management products and services). During a scenario review exercise, money laundering risk level is also considered. This is determined for each customer at initial onboarding and periodically reviewed. The analysis considers the current risk level.

Firstly, break down the customers among the current segments and against different risk levels:

Risk Level	Line of Business			Total	%
	Retail	Corporate	Private		
High	511	821	11	*1,333*	*0.5*
Medium	30	401	2	*433*	*0.1*
Low	267,765	33,262	660	*300,877*	**99.4**
Total	*267,396*	*34,695*	*674*	*302,674*	*100*
%	**88.3**	*11.5*	*0.2*		

First of all, what do these data tell us and what do they not tell us? The percentage in the far-right column and in the bottom row gives us the relative distribution of all alerts across the three lines of businesses and across the three customer risk classifications.

What it tells us is that the majority of productive alerts have occurred within Retail amongst low-risk customers.

It is also good to understand what this table does *not* tell us. It doesn't tell us the ratio between false and true positives; hence, it does not say anything on the effectiveness of the scenario in combination with these 9 segments. Neither does it tell us anything on the ratio between transaction volume and the number of productive alerts, nor about the number of customers or accounts in each line of business. It may well be that the vast majority of customers are Retail customers, which for this financial institution is by far the most important and biggest line of business. From these data, seen in isolation, we would not be able to tell, but in the real world this would all be known and part of the business profiling phase, as depicted in step one in Figure 8.1.

Customer Segment	TP	Alert	TP Rate
Individual	5,423	16,454	33.0%
Corporate	845	28,912	2.9%
Private Banking	46	941	4.9%
Total	6,347	46,932	13.5%

As we can see, for this data set, most alerts were generated for low-risk, individual customers, which is the largest portion among all. Medium-risk customers represent only a small portion of the alerts, just 0.14%, or 30 in count. Based on these data, to use risk level as a segmentation dimension, it is recommended to merge medium- and high-risk, as the low number of alerts do not warrant a separate segment. This allows for more stringent monitoring, which will likely

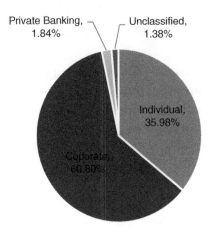

Figure 8.3 Distribution of alerts by customer type.

push up the number of alerts, and perhaps the thresholds for the low-risk category could be lowered to decrease the risk level. Again, this also depends on the ratio of alerts to the size of the population for each segment and, more importantly, to the ratio between productive alerts (true positives) and non-productive alerts (false positives).

In this bank, three quarters of the customers are individuals, and (almost) one quarter are corporate customers, with only a very small portion of private banking customers.

However, alerts are not distributed equally, as 60% of all alerts are on corporate customers, which represent only 24% of our over-all customer population. Moreover, the true positive rate for corporations is just 3%, much lower than that of individuals of 33%. It appears that corporate customers have a stronger need for segmentation review, to improve the true/false positive alert ratio.

As mentioned before, a very important factor to take into consideration is the productive alert ratio, i.e. the number of true positive alerts as compared to the total number of alerts, which also includes false negatives. Let's look at the true positive rates breakdown. This table analyzes the scenarios S0006I, S0007I, and S0008I, which are for individual customers. Here, we analyze per each scenario because segments may work well for one scenario but not necessary for another.

Alert Productivity per Scenario and Risk	Ratio of True Positive Alerts among all Alerts of this Scenario
Scenario (High Risk %)	%
S0006I	
High Risk	89
S0007I	
High Risk	-
Low Risk	-
S0008I	
High Risk	67
Low Risk	33
Medium Risk	0

Just 0.4% of customers are classified as high risk. However, they contribute to a significantly high portion of true positives (productive alerts). This reveals that this risk level is a good indicator for money laundering. These groups of customers should be monitored separately from other customers. The thresholds on lower-risk customers could be raised to decrease number of false positive alerts.

For corporations, these three scenarios are analyzed for distribution among account types and risk level. Here, a type of "proxy account for securities trading" is considered.

Account Type		Population in Corporates	%
Non-Proxy		34,611	99.76%
Proxy		84	0.24%
	Total	34,695	100%

Account Type - Risk Level	Alert Distribution	
S0003C		
Normal Account	1.53%	
Low Risk	100.00%	
Proxy Account	98.47%	← Most alerts are from proxy account
High Risk	15.16%	← High risk has large portion of alerts compared to its portion in whole population
Low Risk	84.84%	
S0006C		
Normal Account	99.87%	
High Risk	27.57%	← High risk customer has large portion of alerts compared to its portion over whole population
Low Risk	72.43%	
Proxy Account	0.13%	
High Risk	100.00%	
S0007C		
Normal Account	96.76%	
High Risk	1.12%	
Low Risk	98.32%	
Medium Risk	0.56%	
Proxy Account	3.24%	← 0.24% are proxy account but they took up over 3% of alerts
Low Risk	100.00%	

The situation concerning risk level is similar to that of individual customers. On the other hand, securities proxy accounts takes only 0.24% of all corporate customers but they produced a much higher portion of alerts for some scenarios. This may mean these accounts have different transaction behavior from the rest of corporate customers and should be split as a separate segment for monitoring.

ONGOING MONITORING

If the segments are refined enough and if the segmentation involves numeric values, it is important to monitor the segments periodically. This is done so that it can be detected early if the segments deteriorate. This report could be a monthly report showing the number of entities per segment, and for each segment, the mean, standard deviation, skewness, and kurtosis of common transaction figures, which describes the distribution. These should be displayed to compare against the past period (e.g. rolling 12 months). Scenario analysts should then be able to observe the trend and determine if the segmentation needs to be revised.

Example of population over time:

Customer Segment	2016			2017
	Jun	Sep	Dec	Mar
High-Risk Indiv	1.2%	1.2%	1.2%	1.1%
Low-Risk Indiv	73.8%	73.8%	73.7%	73.9%
High-Risk Corp	0.4%	0.4%	0.4%	0.4%
Low-Risk Corp	24.6%	24.6%	24.7%	24.5%

CHANGE OF SEGMENTATION

When the segmentation scheme changes, the composition of the various segments is changed. There may be more segments or fewer segments and the thresholds of scenario rules for the relevant segments would need to be set up again according to the latest segmentation scheme.

The segmentation scheme is implemented as the data population logic for the customer segment data field. Upon putting this logic into practice, a lot of customers will have their customer segment information suddenly changed.

In Figure 8.4, a change in the segmentation scheme occurs for individuals, which splits "individual" into "high risk" individual and "normal risk" individual. On executing a scenario rule, the latest snapshot of segment information is considered for determining which set of thresholds is to be used.

Sometimes, the segmentation scheme does not change, but a customer's information changes over time. This may lead to a switch from one segment to another. The monitoring thresholds for this customer will then be suddenly changed in the everyday monitoring by scenarios. See Figure 8.5.

So, when a scenario rule looks back at a period of time, the customer was in one segment for a period, but another segment for the rest. Which segment, thus the set of thresholds, is to be considered? Either the old one or the latest one is rational. When drilling deeper into the data, one may be able to associate velocity to the segments; some segments may have a higher average number of transactions over a given period than others. In-depth and over-time analysis is not always needed, especially when customer segmentation is introduced

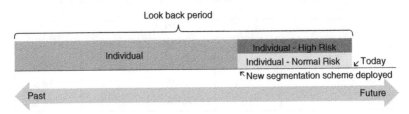

Figure 8.4 Scenario looking back period with customer segment scheme changed.

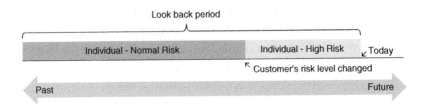

Figure 8.5 Scenario looking back at a period of time with customer segment changed due to customer information change.

for the first time. Velocity and other more advanced levels of analysis typically come into play at segmentation refinement when the transaction monitoring system and the financial institution using it are mature in terms of the AML risk-based approach.

SUMMARY

Customer segmentation means grouping your customers and either applying different rules and scenarios specifically for each group, or applying the same rules and scenarios differently, specific to the group. Customer segmentation, in AML transaction monitoring, is a logical consequence of taking a risk-based approach. Defining the segments is preferably done on the basis of automated statistical data analysis through clustering, but when this is not possible, the (initial) segments can be defined by experts. Customer segmentation can be done during the implementation or introduced later in time, when the system is already in production and actual production data has been collected to be analyzed for this purpose. Customer segmentation can be, and in many cases, is, a periodically reoccurring activity, at least until artificial intelligence has made it a fully automated data-driven process. And even then, a periodic supervision (by humans) check-up process is warranted. As such, segmentation and segmentation review becomes part of a wider scenario optimization and tuning activity, which we will discuss in the following chapter.

CHAPTER 9

Scenario Threshold Tuning

THE NEED FOR TUNING

We have already mentioned throughout the previous chapters that producing productive alerts and minimizing the number of non-productive alerts is a key objective of any money laundering system. Any time a new system is implemented, or, in fact, any time a net-new scenario is introduced, there is the challenge of initial threshold setting: the allocation of values to the numeric parameters that form the threshold to generate an alert. As we explained, under the risk-based approach these parameters are to be determined by the financial institution running the AML transaction monitoring operation (with exception of the cash deposit rule, where the reportable cash deposit amount is commonly set by the regulatory authority of a country). For any new scenario, these initial thresholds are a best guess, based on experience and expertise or test data. These initial thresholds are, ideally, to be replaced by thresholds based on the analysis of production data fed into and *produced* by the *very same* system and scenario. This is called scenario tuning, or more specifically, threshold tuning. Unless the system has an auto-tuning in place (machine learning), the first tuning exercise is typically scheduled 6 months after go-live of the (new) system, but this is subject to the strategy adopted by the financial institution. In the field we have also seen 3 months, 12 months, or 24 months for the first tuning effort and 6 or 12 months as the regular interval.

Tuning serves the compliance paradox (see Chapter 1) of the financial institution's need to be compliant and avoid regulatory repercussions on the one hand, and the incentive to keep operational cost down on the other hand. In simple terms, productive alerts are worth spending time and money on, as properly investigating these adds to the financial institution being compliant, whilst non-productive alerts are, in hindsight, a waste.

Parameters and Thresholds

The variables that can be set for the rules are referred to as parameters. A parameter is a variable that can be *set* and *adjusted* and as such is a variable that, together with the other parameters, defines the rule or scenario. In the software industry parameters specifically refer to those variables that can be set by authorized users and *commonly* refers to the fact that the system provides a user-friendly way to set them. Since the rules and the entire software system, in the end, consists of code, parameters distinguish themselves from other code by their very purpose of being adjustable, almost like the volume dial or channel selector on a radio. In terms of software design and coding one refers to parameter values as opposed to *hardcoded* or hardwired values. The latter requires access to the source code, which is usually not accessible by the user of the system (not even the technical support department and system or database administrators). One can also speak of hardcoded variables even when technical staff (at the user site) do have access to the code, but it is a higher-level access, requiring in-depth knowledge of the system and often specific coding expertise. For example, for SAS software one would need to at least understand SAS base code in order to change a hardwired code, and changing it may impact the support service level agreement, or guarantee, the same as it would when you unscrew the back of your transistor radio or any electronic device and tamper with it. Parameter variables are meant to be changeable and therefore usually a user interface is provided, like dedicated screens for authorized staff to make changes. We speak of the parameterization of rules or scenarios by allowing flexibility and expecting certain variables to be adjusted or, indeed, created, without technically impacting ("breaking") the scenario code. We speak of tunable parameters when the parameter does not change the nature of the scenario, but thresholds, telling the system *when* it should fire an alert, not changing *what* type of behavior it looks at (although one has to accept a gray area in the middle of the spectrum where these are not always so distinguishable). Sometimes only numerical parameters are referred to as parameters, but this is not necessarily the case.

For example, a scenario will trigger an alert if over the past **5** days at least **3** cash deposits have been made of at least **$2500** and with an aggregate value of at least **$10,000**.

Here, 5, 3, 2500 and 10,000 are the parameters. One could tweak the scenario by changing these number without changing the nature of the scenario and instead have a scenario that triggers if over the past 3 days at least one cash deposit has been made with a value of at least $2000 but with aggregate value of at least $9500.

One can argue that cash deposit can also be a parameter and could be expanded to cash deposit and wire credit payments (if the source or scenario code allows for multiple transaction types) or even replace cash deposits with wire credit payments. If one looks at merely the ability to make that change by a user of the system without hacking it, then yes, this would qualify as a parameter, but one could equally argue that such a change is no longer a matter of *tuning* a scenario, but changing the nature of the scenario and converting it into a completely different scenario.

Often the numerical parameters are also referred to as *thresholds*. A parameter becomes a threshold when the related operator is a *greater than* or *less than*, optionally combined with an *or equal to*. In other words, when the parameter defines a range it can be referred to as a threshold. Even though the full etymology of the word threshold is uncertain, we use it in its most basic meaning as an elevated bar, like a doorsill, that is meant to keep something out (e.g. water from pouring in) or in (wheat chaff from getting out). When the water or wheat chaff on the floor reaches a certain level, the threshold will lose its barrier function and the water will flow or the chaff may more easily blow out. It is easy to see the analogy with scenario variables in the above-mentioned examples of *at least 3* deposits of *at least* $2500 each, etc.

True versus False, Positive versus Negative

Let us briefly revisit these notions of productive and non-productive alerts through the vocabulary of the closely related terms of true and false positives and negatives.

In any predictive rule or evaluation process, a result is guessed from some input data. The result from the rule or process is an implied value from some defined conditions or mechanism. Being different from clearly defined definitions, there are always mistakes in the result. In statistics hypothesis testing, this is called type I (false positive) and type II (false negative) error.

In terms of transaction monitoring scenario rules we can summarize as follows:

		True	False
Positive	1. Alert was generated	Y	Y
	2. Warrants further investigation or would have	Y	N
	3. Likelihood of reportability	High	Low
	4. Error Type	-	Type I
Negative	1. Alert was generated	N	N
	2. Warrants further investigation or would have	N	Y
	3. Likelihood of reportability	Low	High
	4. Error Type	-	Type II
Objective		# To be increased	# To be reduced

To increase productivity and accuracy of alerts, we want more true positives to be preserved and try to avoid false positives and false negatives. There is always a trade-off between these type I and type II errors. The results from statistical analysis provides statistical information to assist in handling this trade-off in a systematic way.

Cost

Any AML transaction monitoring system produces more alerts than are strictly needed. Each alert produced must be analyzed in order to determine its meaningfulness, i.e. whether it is indicative of reportable behavior. And if discarded as a false positive, a reason must be provided before it can be closed. Many financial institutions require a second person to review the closed alerts, to make sure no true alerts are overlooked (or deliberately ignored). So, one can imagine the operational cost associated with each alert. The more alerts, the more effort and resources are required, and for each false positive, i.e. nonproductive alert, this cost can be considered a waste.

In transaction monitoring nowadays it is not uncommon to find a false positive rate that reaches over 90%. That is, for 100 alerts, more than 90 of them are finally considered to be okay and closed. If each false positive alert takes 10 minutes to process and every day 200 alerts are generated, then, 200 x 90% x 10min = 1800 minutes = 30 hours of effort (over 3 full-time equivalent) is spent each day on something that is finally found to be safe. Normally during month-end, even more alerts will be generated because of some monthly executed scenario rules. The more customers there are, the more alerts are generated and more investigators need to be hired. So, there is a need for cost control to mitigate false positive alerts.

Adapting to the Environment

Transaction monitoring scenario rules seek to identify suspicious or unusual activities. But not everything that is unusual, or even suspicious, on closer look, continues to be so. For example, households with a middle-class income, occasionally, may buy a car or a home. The transactions associated with these lifetime expenditures are most likely to show up as outliers, especially when (part of) the transaction comes from their own accounts and, for example, depletes a savings account that had gradually been built up over the past years.

In recognizing outliers, the nature of the business, market, or economy the customer operates in must also be considered. In countries or industry sectors with a cash-based economy one is bound to find more and higher amounts of cash deposits and withdrawals than in countries and business segments that have fully embraced electronic payment mechanisms, such as contactless payments. As we discussed in Chapter 8, the thresholds in the scenarios should adapt accordingly.

While the above example simplifies and takes it to the extreme, it aims to illustrate that the scenario thresholds very much depend on the environment with a given position of epoch and location. In a financial institution, the environment would mean the distribution of customers, the financial products it offers, and the economic climate (e.g. interest rate). All these directly or indirectly lead to the type and number and amount of financial transactions that happens.

Therefore, scenario thresholds must be established from within the financial institution, using the latest data. This is the only means for the transaction monitoring system to produce accurate alerts.

Other Reasons

As discussed in Chapter 4, scenarios are designed based on the behavior that we know. There is always new criminal transaction behavior, which may be outside of our knowledge. When there is a new judgment from a court of law, a new suspicious activity pattern may be discovered, which the originally designed scenarios may have missed the thresholds in use. Thresholds may then need to be adjusted to include these new known cases, or, a new scenario rule needs to be developed if lowering the threshold of the existing scenario produces too many false positives.

On the other hand, regulators nowadays require institutes to have solid support for all scenario thresholds, with proper documentation stating how the thresholds are established. As a result, a decent threshold tuning exercise needs to be conducted.

Relatively Simple Ways to Tune Thresholds

Some financial institutions review their scenario thresholds by relatively simple means and achieve a decent result. Some of these methods, when well applied, strike a good balance between available budget and benefit achieved.

Trial Runs of Different Threshold Values

Trial runs of threshold values are made simply using human judgment. This can be quick and almost effortless and may be sufficient for the purpose of improving accuracy and adjusting to the environment. However, it is also prone to human error and psychological bias and any rationale may not sufficiently support the resulting parameter settings and not necessarily convince the regulator in terms of false negative avoidance.

*Compute Statistical Distribution and Set Threshold as Mean + 2
Standard Deviations*

For each threshold variable, compute the statistical distribution over
the population, and take threshold as mean + 2 standard deviations.
Whilst this takes out the human bias, inherent to the previous method
described above, it should be noted that the population might not
exhibit normal distribution, where use of standard deviation would
not be statistically appropriate.

*Set the Threshold to Cover the Alerts on Customers Issued
a Regulatory Report*

This method is to set the thresholds so that the scenario covers all
customers for which a regulatory report, like a Suspicious Transaction Report (STR), or Suspicious Activity Report (SAR), has been
issued in the past. Whilst this seems a valid supervised training-of-
the-model approach, there are still a number of issues with it. It may
focus too much on "known" breaches and past behavior. It can only
run on the basis of historic (production) data so it needs a history of
productive alerts (for which reports have been submitted) that ideally also includes non-productive alerts (for which no reports have
been issued). However, since those historic alerts emanate from scenarios for which the thresholds have been set initially, this approach
is likely to inherit any bias in the initial thresholds that were set at
the start. Unless combined with below-the-threshold testing it would
fall short of identifying false negatives. Factors like percentage of
eligible population and volume of false positives should be taken
into account.

OBJECTIVE OF SCENARIO THRESHOLD TUNING

Increasing Alert Productivity

The primary objective of scenario tuning is to improve the true versus
false positive/negative ratio, or simpler the ratio of productive alerts.
Scenario tuning is a best estimation for scenario *tunable* parameter
thresholds.

However, this best estimation is based on the analysis on recent historical data. Whatever rule is established and no matter how much data is referenced, there will always be false positives and false negatives, because there are many moving elements and an inherent notion of unpredictability at the side of both illegitimate behavior (by money launderers) and legitimate behavior (law abiding customers). In addition, the money launderers will try to mimic the behavior of the legitimate customers to stay under the AML radar and obscure money flow generated by their laundering schemes, by designing multilayered and multifaceted schemes to pump money and assets around. Whilst our legal notion of money laundering may stay the same, our understanding of the modus operandi may change over time and so does our belief of what constitutes suspicious or unusual behavior for a specific customer segment or "peer group".

Taking a statistical approach to analyzing data sets with known outcome (in terms of productive versus unproductive) alerts that may grow over time, patterns can be discerned and indicators fine-tuned to increase the number of true positives (productive alerts), whilst at the same time reducing the number of false positives (unproductive alerts) and false negatives (overlooked suspicious behavior). One must keep in mind that this is still a best estimate, based on data from the past, applied to scenarios that will run in the future.

The objective of threshold tuning is to balance between alert volume and productivity. We want most true positives to be caught, while still being able to stem the (over)flow of (non-productive) alerts requiring human investigation effort. The aim is to strike the optimum balance between alert volume (which must stay within the boundaries of what is operationally feasible and affordable) and alert hit rate or accuracy (where the number of false negatives stay within the risk tolerance levels of both the financial institution and the relevant regulatory bodies performing oversight). As mentioned before, from an automation perspective it is easy to eradicate all false negatives, but only at the cost of unacceptable high rates of false positives, for which there is no capacity to handle, and at the point where alerting truly becomes counterproductive. On the other hand, it is easy to significantly increase the ratio of productive alerts, but this will lead to unacceptable high levels of false negatives, invoking regulatory repercussion. Productive alert rate and hit rate are like communicating vessels:

Less Alerts → Fewer False Positives

vs

More True Positives → More Alerts

Not all scenario parameters are tunable. Numeric parameters lend themselves mostly to tuning, such as lowering or increasing numerical thresholds, e.g. for minimum or maximum transaction amounts, aggregate transaction amounts, or the factor of deviation from a mean or median value. The latter can be expressed in absolute numbers, a percentage or, more commonly n times the standard deviation, which is a statistically common way of measuring the delta between an *in casu* variable against the mean or median of the same value across the measured population. As discussed in the chapter on segmentation, parameters can be tuned separately for each segment. Another numerical variable that lends itself to tuning is the number of lookback days a scenario considers when aggregating transactions over a number of days.

Also, non-numerical parameters can be subject to tuning, but the changing of these qualitative parameters is not always considered tuning, especially when they change the nature of the scenario altogether. For example the range of transaction codes that a scenario considers can be considered tuning if the range of closely related transaction types is increased, decreased, or changed, but if the scope of the scenario is significantly changed by radically extending the range of transaction types that the scenario considers, then this is no longer tuning. Arguably, including ATM cash deposits in a scenario that before only considered branch cash deposits may be considered tuning, as it acknowledges the further automation of financial services that were previously typically performed at branches only. But when the scope is extended to include incoming wire transfers then this changes the nature of the scenario to the extent it is no longer considered tuning but a repurposing of the scenario.

Definition of a Productive Alert

The most common way of tuning is what in statistics is called supervised training of the model. This means that an analysis of a large sample of (historic) production data is used, with the outcome of a previous analysis and/or investigation as a "check" value. To put it simply, the outcome of previous cases is fed into the tuning algorithm along with a number of other scenario parameters to see which parameters and which value ranges have a high correlation with any of the two outcomes (productive or unproductive alert). The threshold values that are deemed to accurately predict that outcome are applied to another sample of the same production data and then compared with the known outcome, to test the predictive value.

It is up to the financial institution and the compliance department to define what constitutes a true positive, i.e. a productive alert. In some cases, the actual submission of a regulatory report on the back of the alert makes the alert a true positive. But this approach is rare because the subset of alerts that lead to the actual submission of a report may be so small that it becomes statistically irrelevant. Most organizations make a distinction between an alert and a case, and alerts are considered for further investigation (in the context of a case) as a first pass triaging effort. An alert is considered a productive alert if it is not discarded as a false positive by the analyst but deemed to warrant additional scrutiny in the context of a case. Many organizations have different roles in place emphasizing this distinction. For example, the role of an analyst is to review incoming alerts and make that first pass decision; the role of investigators or senior analysts is to further investigate if the analyst does not disposition the alert as a false positive.

The notion of a productive alert adopted by the organization drives the scenario tuning analysis. From a system-technical perspective it means that at alert level the final dispositioning needs to be captured as well, to allow the system to use this as the validation variable and, evidently, the user interface needs to be able to support these different options on closing alerts.

In an ideal world a true positive is defined by what happens with the regulatory report further down the road. What does the Financial Intelligence Unit (FIU) receiving the report do with it: will a financial criminal investigation be launched? Or even further downstream: is the case prosecuted (or has a plea deal been reached)? And in case of prosecution: has a verdict been reached by the judiciary? Was it a conviction? Obviously, a conviction with no further possibility of appeal would represent the "truest" positive imaginable. However, this is highly impractical as a measuring rod for the productivity of an alert. For one, it may take years or even more than a decade to reach a final verdict. Moreover, many cases do not make it to a court handling and conviction, as along the path there are many alternative ways of dealing with the case (e.g. plea deal, dismissal on legal technical grounds). In many legal systems the money laundering aspects are accessory to the investigation and legal proceedings around the predicate crime, and money laundering is assumed to have taken place (and burden of proof reversed) if the suspects or convicted person cannot attest the legitimate origin of his, her, or its wealth. It does not make sense to tune your system on the basis of alerts that were generated several years ago. Lastly, it is often impossible to link alerts to the final outcome of the handling by the authorities. There is no common practice for the FIU, which receives the initial regulatory reports, to consistently report back to the financial institution as to what they have done with the report. Even more so further downstream: the link between the alert at the financial institution and any investigation into money laundering or the proceeds of crime is almost always lost.

USE OF THRESHOLDS IN DIFFERENT KINDS OF SCENARIO RULES

Different rule types require a different approach in terms of tuning. And some of these cannot or should not be tuned at all.

Regulation-Driven Rules

Some of the rules are not eligible for tuning, simply because their threshold is prescribed by the legislation or regulatory authority. Most countries have one such a rule with regard to cash deposits and the Cash Transaction Reports. Such rules are a remnant from the rule-driven approach in the early period of AML. They leave no room for tuning, since regulations require the financial institution to generate an alert and submit a report if the stipulated value is exceeded for cash deposits. For the US this threshold is set to $10,000 and for most countries the amount is the nearest round number in the local currency equivalent, such as 10,000 EUR for the countries in the eurozone.

Apart from these rules with a threshold set by law, there are derivative rules that seek to counter behavior by the money launderers to evade these rules. In the early days of money laundering a Miami attorney coined the term "smurfing" when the DEA (Drug Enforcement Administration) observed a suspected criminal organization sending henchmen into a bank (smurfs), to deposit cash amounts below the threshold to evade alerting and reporting.[1] In response to this modus operandi, the financial institutions created additional rules to detect smurfing, or structuring as it is called more formally. One of these rules seeks to identify (structural) evasion of the threshold by a narrow margin, basically lowering the alerting threshold and being secretive of the delta between the applied threshold and the official threshold. Another common rule considers cash deposits over a period of time (typically a week) and looks at the aggregate value of the combined cash deposits. And a third rule of this type looks at the ratio between incoming cash deposits and withdrawals or transfers, sometimes in relation to the overall activity on the account. These structuring rules are very much open for tuning, and regular tuning may actually be necessary to the cat-and-mouse fight between the financial institution and the money launderers, as the latter, over time learn the pattern behind the structuring rules and they learn how to evade them, rendering these structuring rules less effective or ineffective . . . until the thresholds are adapted and the structuring rules become more effective again.

Statistical Outlier

Some scenarios focus on statistical outliers, whereas others are aimed at finding a specific known abusive behavior. When looking for a statistical outlier, the threshold parameters define how rare and far apart a particular value should be, in order for it to be an alert. A statistical measure is applied to calculate the "rareness" and relative distance from the mean or median of the same value across the comparison population. Those comparison populations can consist of transactions of the

[1] https://en.wikipedia.org/wiki/Structuring

same type by account holders in the same segment (see Chapter 8) or other historic transactions on the same account or accounts of the same customer. In other words, the outlier can be an outlier in terms of a peer group or in terms of the behavior on the account.

Outlier Example

For those not so familiar with statistical measurement, age may serve as an example. For any human population that is not limited by age, older persons become rarer by age. Let's say that in a certain population people die, by whatever cause, on average at the age of 55. The further you move away upward from 55, the smaller the subpopulation become of people aged more than that threshold age. And if you go to the very fringes of your population age-wise, then being of a certain age or older becomes rarer and rarer. You will find not that many people of 100 years old and older, and even less to be 101 years and older. 104 years may be an extreme outlier, let alone 110 years. A sample age distribution pyramid appears in Figure 9.1. Bringing it back to the world of financial service delivery, and now not comparing against a customer segment, but against a single customer's own expenditure history, for most people buying a home is the single largest expenditure and most people only do this a few times, if more than once in their lifetime. So, the incoming mortgage amount and/or the outgoing payment to the escrow account of the solicitor or notary, are extreme outliers compared to the normal day-to-day or month-to-month activity on the account(s) for the customer buying a house.

In a sample aggregate expenditure across a week the number of occurrences in the y-axis drops along with increasing aggregate amount of expenditure denoted in the x-axis (see Figure 9.2).

The above example of buying a home is a simplified example to explain the notion of outlier. First outliers are expressed in terms of n times the standard deviation, rather than an absolute number or percentage deviation from the mean or median. Standard deviation is a statistical measure that compensates for the skewedness in the distribution of a parameter across the population that is being measured.

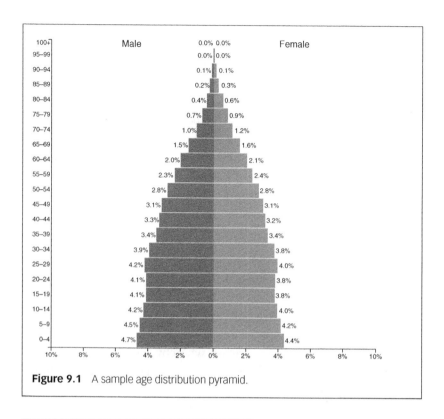

Figure 9.1 A sample age distribution pyramid.

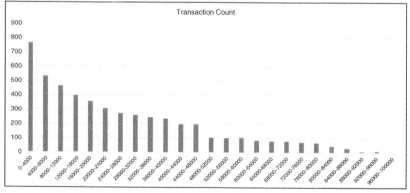

Secondly, money launderers trying to avoid outliers will typically mimic the behavior of legitimate account users and mostly deal with corporate accounts rather than individual accounts, on which outliers may not be as rare and relevant. Moreover, money launderers will try to avoid outliers through a gradual change in the behavior

Skewedness, in terms of our example of age, can be explained by the following: if the population that you measure is being limited to those individuals who are retired, then obviously this will change the average age of that population, but it may also change the relative distribution of age across the population. Percentage-wise, a higher number of people will be above 100. If the population is further limited by country and gender, then, for example, the female population for Japan or Spain may be skewed, because there is relatively high number of women above 90 or even 100 in Japan and Spain, as compared to the rest of the world.

and rather spread evenly any (sudden) increase in funds to be laundered across multiple accounts in the name of different (corporate) account holders.

Outlier scenarios, for their part, look at aggregate alerts and also less obvious outliers. An example of an outlier scenario considering aggregated transactions is a steep increase whereby more than 2 out of at least 5 transactions within the past week represent more than 2 times the average monthly income. A typical modus operandi that such a scenario can be targeting is that of third-party mule accounts, where criminals, under false pretenses, recruit volunteers for make-money-easily schemes, whereby legitimate account holders are being unwittingly "hired" as "mules" to channel funds through their accounts against a commission, often on a don't ask, don't tell basis. What can be observed is a sudden increase of the number of credit and debit transactions and their average amounts; suddenly the account has a turnover of multiple times the monthly income of the account holder. For example a pensioner starts receiving 4 times the value of his monthly pension payout, offset by an aggregate debit transactions of this extra income, minus a bit (the commission). Money launderers are less concerned about detection, since their identity is unknown to the mule and cannot be traced to both the remitter and beneficiary accounts of the credit and debit payments . . . these may be mule accounts as well.

The effectiveness of the outlier scenario depends, therefore, very much on the threshold value, even when expressed in terms of n times the standard deviation. The false positive/false negative rate for these scenarios are commonly higher compared to other scenario types.

Insignificance Threshold

Some scenario rules stress more specific transaction patterns or behavior on the accounts. In these scenario rules, the transaction filtering criteria and processing rules filter a small portion of entities before comparing with numeric thresholds for alerts. Here, the thresholds serve more to prevent alerts being generated where the transactions are of negligible amounts that are not worth investigation. For example, for a scenario rule that looks at the ratio between an incoming wire amount and outgoing wire amount, if the ratio gets a match for alert condition but the actual monetary amount is very small, then it may not be worth the effort of investigating, as it is believed that criminals would not launder such a small amount of money, and if they did they would pose a very low threat to the financial system.

Known risk itself usually has less reliance on numeric thresholds (e.g. being PEP, new customer, customer with STR in past year).

Safety-Blanket Rules

One danger of the data-driven statistical approach is that rules are removed that are deemed to have become ineffective over time. Indeed, whilst the word "tuning" implies that merely the threshold parameters are adapted, part of the wider review of the rules may also lead to the financial institution deciding to stop running a rule when it has not generated any productive alerts for a long time. One has to be careful with that though, as it may be that these rules are mandatory and required by law or regulation (as we discussed above in terms of the cash deposit rule). But the danger lies much more in those rules that are not prescribed by law, but that the money launderers have become aware about and thus have adapted their modus operandi as not to set off the alarm. For a statistician without understanding of what is at stake, this would mean that the rule is not effective and may as well be abolished. But what if the money launderers sense this with a particular financial institution and resume their original modus operandi with that bank? How will the regulator react if, for a period of time, the bank has exposed itself by removing seemingly obsolete rules? The financial institution would be sure to receive a fine. In other words, some rules will need to be kept, despite their inefficacy, as safety-blanket rules. During a review and tuning exercise, one must be careful not to discard and deactivate these rules, unless the risk is mitigated by regular under-the-line analysis. We will explain and elaborate on this type of analysis further below. In a nutshell: under-the-line analysis looks at false negatives, of cases of under-alerting, rather than over-alerting that is the main focus of most tuning exercises.

COMBINING PARAMETERS

Parameters can be stacked and (inter)dependencies can be built into the set of parameters for a scenario.

One scenario parameter threshold can be used by multiple parameter variables for comparison. On the other hand, one parameter variable can be compared against more than one scenario threshold parameter. Let us consider the scenario example we used above.

> For example, a scenario will trigger an alert if over the past **5** days at least **3** cash deposits have been made of at least **$2500** and with an aggregate value of at least **$10,000**.

This scenario and the second example are depicted in Figure 9.2 in a radar diagram with the following data.

	Example 1	Example 2	Example 3	Example 4
Minimum aggregate trx amount (x1000)	10	9.5	10	10
Minimum number of trxs	3	1	5	10
lookback days	5	2	7	5
Minimum single trx amount (x1000)	2.5	3	5	10

When tuning, it would make sense to change the amount thresholds or the number of transactions if the number of lookback days is changed, or one can make a deliberate decision to solely change one of the four parameters. As these four parameters are accumulative

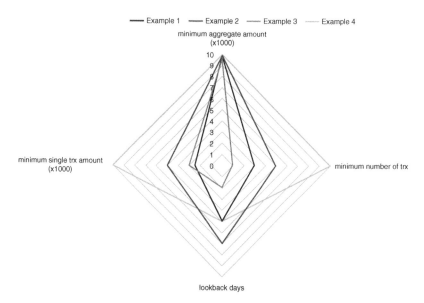

Figure 9.2 A radar diagram.

conditions, a lower number of required transactions, a lower threshold amount per transaction or a lower aggregate amount will make the scenario trigger alerts sooner, hence more alerts are to be expected. For the number of lookback days this is the opposite: the longer the lookback period, the easier the combined scenario decision will be met.

Although it may not be immediately apparent, there is also a dependency between two of the parameters in the above example. Although the brief scenario description does not emphasize it, it is common practice to understand the parameter of minimum number of transactions as the minimum number of *qualifying* transactions. It means that the parameter for the number of transactions takes into account the parameter for the minimum amount per transaction. One could say there is a hierarchy between the two parameters (Figure 9.3).

This concept is important to threshold tuning. Tuning of lower order threshold parameters is different from that for higher order thresholds.

For the above example, assume there are 100,000 customers. Then, for any given day there would be 100,000 numeric values of number of transactions in the past 5 days greater than $10,000 (although most of

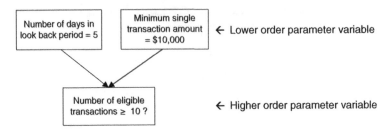

Figure 9.3 Orders of parameter variables.

them would be 0). These 100,000 different values are included as the underlying transactions meet the thresholds of *within the past 5 days* and *minimum value of* $10,000. This number of eligible transactions is the higher order parameter threshold to be tuned using statistical methods.

For lower order parameters, the defining of the value mostly depends on the nature of the scenario rule. The most common numeric lower order parameter is that of the lookback period. The lookback period depends on the target transaction pattern, and the execution frequency. The minimum single transaction amount of $10,000 in example no. 4 may well find its origin in regulations, as argued above. Another example is foreign exchange restrictions. The regulatory stipulated threshold value must be accepted as given and is not open to tuning. That is, not in a way that it widens the ability for money launderers. If a financial institution suspects that *just not* meeting the threshold in certain cases is indicative of money launderers deliberately staying "under the radar" it still has the obligation to report and file a suspicious activity report if they cannot refute that suspicion. It is common practice to have multiple scenarios in place to deal with this situation; whilst one scenario reflects the Currency/Cash Transaction Report and would include the fixed threshold given by law, another scenario with tunable parameters focuses on behavior where this legal threshold seems deliberately evaded either through structuring or by a consistent pattern of transactions just below the threshold.

STEPS FOR THRESHOLD TUNING

The scenario threshold tuning exercise for one scenario rule comprises the following steps at high level.

For discussion and illustration purposes, the threshold is assumed to be a simple numeric value comparison (alert is eligible if value ≥ threshold).

Step 1. Understanding the Patron's Needs

Obviously before carrying out the review it is important to understand (and if necessary, manage) the expectations of the patron. Who is commissioning the tuning exercise? Is this executive management the head of compliance/chief compliance officer the money laundering reporting officer, the IT department? Is it driven by external, i.e. regulatory pressure? What is driving the timelines? Is there a regulatory incentive in place to meet a certain deadline to avoid punitive action by the regulatory watchdog? What is the primary objective: to become more compliant and have a more robust risk-based approach in place, or to become more efficient and decrease cost per productive alert? How will success be measured? Are success criteria measurable? Are they realistic and feasible? What is the view of the workers analyzing and processing the alerts? Are there any specific pain points that they have identified and need to be addressed? Is there a way to narrow the focus of the session to, for example, a certain customer segment for which the system performs relatively poorly? Are there already scenarios identified that perform poorly? What is the low hanging fruit? Dozens of questions can and need to be asked before planning the work and diving into it. And you should not be surprised if the answers to these questions vary hugely from one customer to another.

Step 2. Obtaining General Statistics

Where step 1 focuses on understanding the customer, step 2 is all about understanding the data. This starts with a high-level analysis of the key data, the purpose of which is to understand the data from a statistical perspective and identify potential areas of focus. Examples of such general statistics are

- Distribution of customers by customer segment
- Distribution of (productive) alerts by customer segment

▨ Distribution of (productive) alerts over time

▨ Distribution of transaction types/products

Note that from a measuring perspective you should always distinguish between alerts and productive alerts, because regardless of whether the objective is to become more compliant or to become more cost effective, improving the ratio between productive alerts versus all or non-productive alerts will always be the main aim. (Not the only aim, as avoiding false negatives is often also important and may even prevail over improving the productive alert ratio).

Step 3. Understanding the Scenarios

The next step is to move from the data analysis to a high-level analysis of the scenarios. Which scenarios perform well and which don't? Performing well here means not only producing alerts, but producing productive alerts, preferably against an acceptable "price" in terms of unproductive alerts. Are there any scenarios in which the subject matter experts suspect will be underreported . . . or even stronger, has there been evidence of suspicious transactions that were not picked up by the scenario that should have been picking them up? A scenario producing only false positives (unproductive alerts) will need to be looked at for sure. But likely the scenario that produces hardly any alerts or no alerts at all, although it might be a safety-blanket scenario as discussed above, which serves its purpose without generating alerts, also needs to be looked at. If segmentation is applied at scenario level, then the next level analysis is by scenario by segment. Within a scenario how are the segments performing? Or the other way around, how are the segments performing across the scenarios? This is a slight shift of focus more closely aligned to step 2 where the distribution of productive alerts is measured by customer segment.

Step 4. Understanding the Scenario Parameters

Once the scenarios that will be subject to further scrutiny are identified, the analysis drills further down to the level of scenario parameters. Scenario rule logic will be analyzed and understood by the subject matter experts performing the tuning. And the role of the parameters as part of that logic needs to be understood as well. For each parameter, the type and nature will be understood and, most importantly, its relevance or eligibility will be assessed for tuning. Here, the distinction between higher and lower order parameters can be applied. Whilst, as a rule of thumb, the lower order parameters serve to explain the scenario logic, the higher order parameters, much more than the lower, are subject to tuning.

Step 5. Understanding the Alerts

So far, we have discussed alerts and productive or unproductive alerts in terms of their distribution across scenarios and customer segments. But we can also analyze the alerts in isolation and do an analysis on alert attributes. We can do this across the entire population (or segment) of alerts or grouped by scenario. We'd be looking at the following metrics, which in part are overlapping with the scenario analysis:

- Number of true positives
- False positive rate I (discarded at alert analysis stage)
- False positive rate II (discarded after investigation)
- True positive rate I (investigated)
- True positive rate II (filed for reporting)
- Identifying challenging alerts (which took a long time to close)
- Alert suppression
- Ratio of open alerts, if considerable number of alerts are still left open (not yet investigated)

If the true positive rate is too low, then possibly the thresholds can be raised giving fewer alerts. If the true positive rate is very high, then the thresholds may be worth lowering, giving more alerts for more true positives to be found. These depend also on the positions of true positives. It is possible that some scenarios actually give no alert. One possible cause, other than the scenario being a safety-blanket scenario, is that the customer segment contains too few customers, or the target type of transaction is not applicable for that segment.

Step 6. Statistical Analysis of Each Tunable Scenario Threshold Variable

For each tunable scenario threshold, produce a statistical analysis of the values. This visualizes what values are normal and to what extent the values should be considered outliers and worth investigation. This may also reveal important information about customer segmentation. Normally a threshold variable distribution graph has one "peak." If the graph shows two (or more) peaks, it may indicate that there are multiple heterogenous groups of customers that may better be split into different customer segments (Figure 9.4).

Step 7. Above-the-Line Analysis and Below-the-Line Analysis

Adjust the threshold upward or downward to a certain extent, to see the resulting number of alerts and number of true positives. Normally increasing a threshold makes alerts harder to be generated

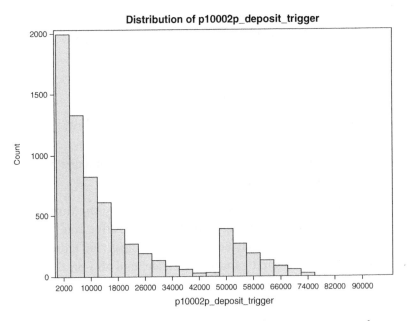

Figure 9.4 A threshold variable distribution indicating heterogenous groups of customers.

(above-the-line), and vice versa for lowering a threshold (below-the-line). The alert volume and true positive rate, as well as the positions of true positives should be looked at during these tests.

Step 8. What-If Analysis (Back-Tests)

Perform real execution of scenario rules on adjusted threshold values to produce different sets of alerts. These alerts are then compared to find out which combination of thresholds is the best. It is good to have a comprehensive user interface to do this comparison.

Step 9. Mock Investigations on New Alerts

During what-if analysis, new alerts may result, which had not been generated before. These alerts should be determined to see if they are new true positives. True positives are alerts which are found to be suspicious after some investigation, or are found to be worth generating as the pattern caught by the scenario may possibly be a suspicious activity, before performing further investigation. However, these new true positives may or may not worth preserving with the new threshold, depending on the false positive rate.

Step 10. Customer (Re)Segmentation

If the result of tuning is not good, then it may be because of the customer group being too diversified. The customer segmentation may need to be reviewed for more efficient monitoring. This may not have been discovered in step 6 above.

Step 11. Report Write-Up

It is important to document the methodology, findings, and results of the tuning exercise. This would be the deliverable to the regulator or auditor, serving as proof of the review exercise.

Some of the above steps are further discussed below.

PREPARATION OF ANALYSIS DATA

Scope of Data

The data needed during the analysis is for reference and comparison on the basis of a target variable. It is very much close to building a statistical model. Here, the target is (i) Has an alert been generated? and (ii) Is it a true positive?

The data must be similar in nature so they can be comparable for the goal of alert generation. For best estimation, the recent historical data should be used. The reference analysis data covered should be

- Recent enough so that it reflects the most up-to-date environment. Transactions that happened a few years before are probably not adequate. However, if the number of customers is too small, then data of longer period would be needed to catch up enough reference data points.

- Long enough in duration to cover transactions at different times of year, levelling out seasonal effects. For example, payroll happens normally at the end of the month; some manufacturers traditionally have more transactions in certain months. This pattern normally repeats itself in a year. Patterns across years are too hard to include. So, normally one or two years' worth of data is taken.

- Covering the type of transactions and business products of concern. If the scenario to be reviewed targets online banking but this business just launched six months ago, it is pointless to take transactions before that for the analysis.

There is no standard or golden rule on how much data must be included. These should all be considered case by case.

Data Columns

On alert generation, one approach is to build denormalized data required for the scenario rule. This is called Analysis Base Table (ABT), which is very similar to that in statistical modelling. Each data row should contain all the data column/field required by the alert generation logic. You may find it very similar to the denormalized data set as discussed in Chapter 7. However, the data in the data set here is

Customer Number	Run Date	Customer Type	Declared Monthly Income	Industry	Customer Since (years)	Agg. Txn Amount	Txn Count	True Positive
0000000101	7/2/2016	Individual	10,000		3	8,000	3	Yes
0000000102	7/2/2016	Individual	25,000		10	1,000	1	No
0000000103	7/2/2016	Corporate		008		200,000	2	No
0000000104	7/2/2016	Corporate		092	2	960,000	2	No

Figure 9.5 An example of an ABT.

per reporting entity instead of per transaction. On the other hand, the data set for threshold tuning contains a target result, which is whether the entity is a true positive or not.

Note also that the data columns are those ready to be directly compared against threshold. This is different from the denormalized data for scenario rules processing. For example, in scenario rules processing each row is a transaction and the scenario aggregates over a lookback period. In the data set for threshold tuning, each row stores the aggregated amount for each customer. In the above example, these would be the aggregate transaction amount and transaction count.

The data set should cover a whole set of reporting entities, and each value to be compared against the threshold (parameter variable) should exist for each entity. Say, the value aggregate amount of cash deposit over the past 7 days should be present for each customer. This is the only way a statistical analysis can be done.

With this data set, one can easily tell how many alerts would be generated if thresholds are set differently and tell how high a threshold is in the population.

One approach to produce this data set is to set all thresholds to 0 and run alert generation. In this way, all data points will satisfy the alert conditions and so an alert is produced for every entity in the population. Note that different alert conditions may have different complications for passing all the conditions set. For example, for a percentage range condition the range may need to be set to 0 ~ 9999, while for a maximum condition the threshold may be set to an extreme high value.

For performance considerations, a computation of the parameter variable is sometimes skipped during implementation, if an earlier alert condition is found to be false.

If that is the case, this cost-saving logic would have to be sacrificed for threshold tuning purposes.

For example, a scenario rule has two alert conditions:

- Aggregate transaction count ≥ threshold 1, AND
- A computed ratio ≥ threshold 2

The computation of the ratio is a costly operation. Therefore, in the implementation, if the condition with threshold 1 is found to have failed, then the ratio is simply not computed to save computation time, because the alert will not be generated anyway. In this implementation, it is not trivial to collect the complete set of ratio values for analysis. The scenario rule logic may need to be modified so that the ratio is computed always, so that the whole set of data is available for analysis.

Quick and Easy Approach

While the above data extraction is quite sophisticated, some financial institutions take a brief approach by indirectly estimating the figures. This sacrifices accuracy but saves lot of effort in preparing analysis data. This could be acceptable if the number of alerts is small and loose thresholds can be tolerated.

Rather than exactly extracting the values to be compared against threshold,

- take the daily aggregate amount value to imply aggregated amount of past X days, and
- use a proportion of target transaction type and imply the target amount.

For example, take a scenario looking at aggregate cash transactions over the past 10 days.

- Capture the aggregate transaction amount per customer over one day. This gives a distribution for all customers.
- In general, ~20% of all transactions are cash-based.
- Thresholds are taken as the 95 percentiles in the distribution and then multiplied by 10 (days) and 20% (for cash).

Analysis of Dates

While a sufficiently long time period of past data is taken for analysis, a long process time and large storage space for this long period may be needed if the customer base is large. It would make the threshold tuning exercise too difficult to realize. With limited time and resources for threshold tuning, a common practice is to do sampling, minimizing the volume of data and thus the time and resources taken.

Still, the more dates picked, the more days selected for analysis, the more accurate the analysis will be. With the constraint of disk space and time, pick the largest set possible. This depends on the data volume and resources available. There is no standard to follow.

For daily executed scenarios, there are a few principles to remember on determining the dates on sampling:

- The dates should be non-consecutive. Money laundering activity usually spans across days. It is common that alerts are generated over consecutive days for same group of financial activities. Taking consecutive days, but not the whole period, may distort the portion of false positives and true positives in the statistical analysis. So the rule is, either the whole period, or non-consecutive days.

- Date selection is diversified for maximum variety:

  - Day of week. Some activity may happen only on Saturdays. The days sampled should evenly covering all days of the week.

  - Month start/end. For example, payrolls may often occur near the end of month. Some transactions may occur at the start of the month.

  - Seasonal factors. Some activity is seasonal. Some kinds of customers traditionally have more activity in certain months than others.

For weekly and monthly executed scenarios, since the frequency is much lower, the number of dates is rather small even though the whole period is taken. There are 52 weeks or 12 months in a year; taking a 2-year period just means $52 \times 2 = 104$ days of weekly executions, or $12 \times 2 = 24$ days of monthly executions. So weekly and monthly scenarios may be taken for all occurrences in the analysis period.

Stratified Sampling

Furthermore, on the selection of analysis dates, the distribution of true positives is also important. If it happens that the dates randomly picked contain no true positives, the analysis result would be distorted, missing the true positive information. In other words, in the sample set of data, we need distributions of certain attributes to be preserved in the whole set. In technical terms, the distribution of the possible values of the data field among the sample set should be close to that in the full set. For the purpose of threshold tuning, the attributes would be:

- Whether the day contains true positive alert (most important)
- The month
- The day of the week

There are 36 days out of a 365-day period that contain true positive alerts. That is, 36/365 = 10% of days have true positive. Then, in a sample analysis of 50 dates, there should be 10% × 50 = 5 dates have true positive. They should also be evenly distributed among the 12 months.

Thus, on picking the 50 analysis dates as sample data:

- 5 of them contain true positive alerts
- Around 50/12 = 4 dates for each month
- For each month, these 4 dates should be spread across different day of the week

STATISTICAL ANALYSIS OF EACH TUNABLE SCENARIO THRESHOLD VARIABLE

Statistical analysis on the threshold variable values help you to understand the distribution pattern of the numbers across the range. The preliminary things to know from statistical analysis are:

- Value range: Minimum value and maximum value. However, the maximum value can be an extreme value that rarely occurs. Therefore, the minimum and maximum values are not very representative, but they give the boundary for presenting the values in graphs.

■ Mean, skewness, kurtosis: These may give you an idea of how concentrated the values are, and how the values lean.

■ Shape of the distribution graph: The shape may help to reveal useful information. If the graph shows multiple peaks, it may indicate a mixture of different customer segments.

The important part is to know the distribution in terms of percentile (%ile). That is, to find out what is the value for the top X percent of the whole population.

Steps to find the percentile:

■ Sort the values in ascending order (first value is the smallest).

■ For data set of N values, the value at position N × k% is the kth percentile of the distribution.

In a set of 10 numbers in ascending order: 1, 3, 10, 200, 250, 400, 1000, 8000, 90000, 100000,

the 90th percentile is the 10 × 90% = 9th value, which is 90000. This means, within this set, 10% of whole population has value greater than 90000.

Note that we are interested in the value distribution for normal, legitimate cases. So, on producing the percentile, the ABT should be filtered out for extreme values of abnormal cases of money laundering data points, if possible.

In threshold setting, the importance of the percentile is that it indicates how extreme a threshold is compared to the whole population. If a threshold is equal to 95%ile of the threshold variable distribution, that means the top 5% of this variable's values are eligible for alerting (meaning, it is just eligible according to this particular threshold, whether an alert is actually generated or may not depend on other alert conditions). See Figure 9.6.

If a scenario rule has two simple numeric value comparison conditions and both must be satisfied to produce an alert (alert if aggregate amount ≥ threshold A and transaction count ≥ threshold B). Then, the subset of data points satisfying both conditions yields the set of data eligible for generating an alert. In the scatterplot in Figure 9.7, each x is a data point with a transaction count as x-axis and aggregate amount as y-axis. The intersection area between the top

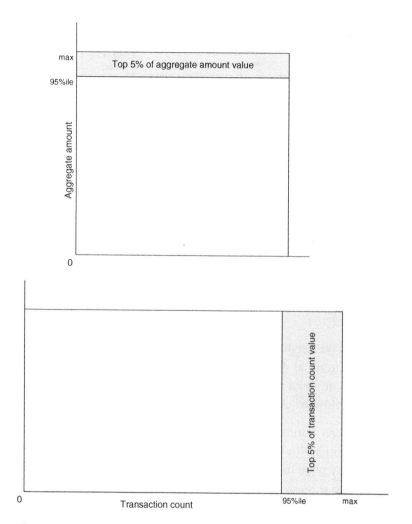

Figure 9.6 5% of population are higher than 95 percentile value.

5% of the aggregate amount value and the top 5% of the transaction count value is eligible for alert, which would be smaller than 5% of the whole population.

Figure 9.7 is just for illustration purposes. For three simple numeric value comparisons as alert conditions, the diagram would be a 3-dimensional space. For more alert conditions, it would not be directly presentable.

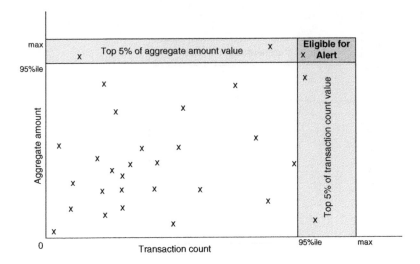

Figure 9.7 Scatterplot for data eligible for alert when over threshold.

Distribution Diagram

Note that in a typical distribution of threshold parameter variable, the values concentrate at a certain range, and extreme values have few data points. Consider a variable of aggregate cash transactions over the past 10 days. How would the values be?

- Less than hundred: Normally, people do not bother to deposit less than a hundred dollars in cash into a bank (homeless people may need to do so).
- Hundreds: Probably a few. There may be some fee payment.
- Thousands: Should be more. In some businesses, cash payments received from clients are deposited in a bank once a day.
- Tens of thousands: Probably less.
- Hundreds of thousands: Should be very few.
- Millions: Should be very rare. Who will have that much cash to deposit in one go? Who needs millions in cash at a time?

Thus, the distribution would be something like that shown in Figure 9.8. The y-axis is the population or frequency of occurrence, against x-axis as the range of values of the variable in concern. There is a peak around the value range where most data values are concentrated. The population diminishes as it approaches an extreme high value. However, the extreme high values have few occurrences so the distribution has a long tail at the right side. This is called a positively skewed distribution.

Putting this into practice, Figure 9.9 shows the distribution of values over the whole range between 0 to maximum of 90000. Each bar represents the number of data points within each regular sub-range. Each bar has equal width for the regular sub-range of values. The height of each bar indicates how many data points have the threshold

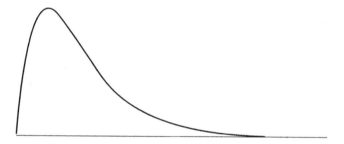

Figure 9.8 A positively skewed distribution.

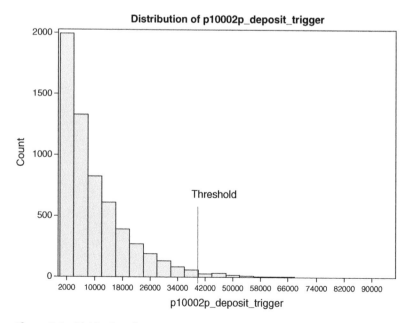

Figure 9.9 Distribution diagram.

variable fall into the particular value sub-range. The area at the right side of the vertical threshold line is the portion that is eligible for alert.

However, note that this diagram visualizes the area as a portion over a certain threshold, but it does not show the percentile values. The position of the bars is evenly distributed along the value range (x-axis).

Population Distribution Table by Percentile (Ranking Analysis)

The population distribution table in Figure 9.10 shows the population split for 100 percentiles. Each row shows the value range that are between p percentile and $p+1$ percentile, the number of data points in that range, and the number of true positives in that range. This percentile rank table gives a rough idea on the alert change when one threshold is adjusted. For example, the threshold for 97th percentile is at the value 96832. There are 11 (1+2+3+5) true positives with value greater than 96832. If the threshold is raised to 98th percentile, which is 97788 (+956), fewer alerts will be generated (1% less are eligible) and 5 true positives will be lost (not alerted).

Value Range	Percentile	True Positives	True Positives (%ile)	
98769-99993	100	1	100	
97789-98763	99	2	91	
96833-97788	98	3	73	
95500-**96832**	97	5	45	← Data > 96832 as threshold are eligible for alert
94594-95631	96	0	0	
93718-94593	95	0	0	
93451-90407	94	0	0	
...				
17657-17651	6	0	0	
15254-16486	5	0	0	
14311-14280	4	0	0	
12345-13356	3	0	0	
11427-12337	2	0	0	
10987-11411	1	0	0	

Figure 9.10 Population distribution table by percentile.

If the threshold is lowered to 96th percentile, which is 95631 (−1201), there would be more alerts (1% more are eligible) generated. It should be noted that the above statistical analysis is not applicable for lower order scenario parameter variables. For example, for the scenario parameter defining the lookback period (e.g. past 14 days), to each data point or customer on an analysis date, it is always 14 days with no variance for analysis. This is dependent on some higher order variables that need tuning.

DISTRIBUTION DIAGRAM COMPRESSED AS A SINGLE LINE

In Figure 9.9, you can see the area nicely presented. In reality, if there are a large number of data points, it is common that the diagram is compressed as a single line as in Figure 9.11 because most values are concentrated on a narrow value range and there are few data points near the maximum value. In this case, the diagram would become meaningless as no area can be observed. Therefore, this diagram can be used for reference, but one should not rely only on the diagram to draw a conclusion.

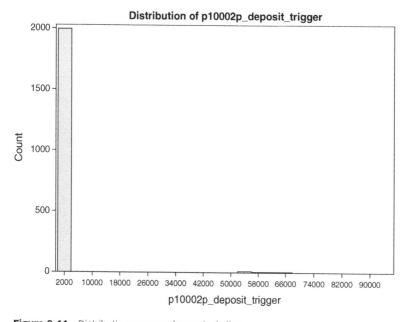

Figure 9.11 Distribution squeezed as a single line.

Multiple Peaks

If the distribution diagram contains multiple peaks as shown in Figure 9.12, then it probably means there are multiple customer segments mixed together, in which each segment exhibits very different behavior. In this case, further customer segmentation should be split so that an appropriate threshold can be applied to each individual distribution.

Zeros

On extracting data for analysis, all customers and accounts are covered in producing the distribution. However, the portion of accounts that exhibit the target transactions can be small. For a bank of 100,000 accounts, the majority of accounts likely have no cash transaction over the previous 10 days. For a given day, the variable of *aggregate cash transactions in the past 10 days* may have a value of zero for 50% of accounts. Therefore, the frequency for a value of 0 would be very

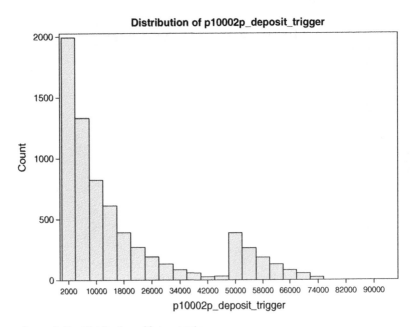

Figure 9.12 Distribution with two peaks.

high. These empty data points occupy the population making the analysis result less accurate or less visible.

In other words, we focus on those data that have action. In the above examples, the distribution is effectively aggregate cash transactions in the past 10 days, *if the customer has SOME cash transactions.*

ABOVE-THE-LINE ANALYSIS AND BELOW-THE-LINE ANALYSIS

After understanding the distribution, adjust the threshold to see how many more or less alerts would be generated. Remember, the goal is to reduce false positives and identify true positives.

Above-the-line (ATL) analysis refers to an increase in the threshold so that fewer unproductive alerts (fewer false positives) are generated. In contrast, below-the-line (BTL) analysis refers to a decrease in the threshold to see if more productive alerts (true positives) are generated.

Above-the-Line Analysis

For a threshold for simple numeric value comparison, all data points higher than the threshold are eligible for alert. Primitively, we only wish to be alerted to the true positives. Therefore, the threshold can be adjusted to just under the first true positive above the current threshold. This can be observed from the percentile rank table. The immediate percentile with a non-zero true positive number is the *highest threshold to catch all known true positives.* Setting the threshold higher than that will lose some true positives (thus making them false negative).

If at the initial threshold setting, the scenario rule has not yet been put to productive use, there is no true positive from the production transaction monitoring system. The investigator then needs to pick the data and determine which ones are true positive. If there are too many data points, then some points should be sampled out to check.

In Figure 9.13, **x**: False positive alert (unproductive alert), **T**: True positive alert (productive alert).

Remember that thresholds are best estimates; there are always false positives and false negatives. If there are a lot of true positives right above a threshold, there is a high chance that data points that appear

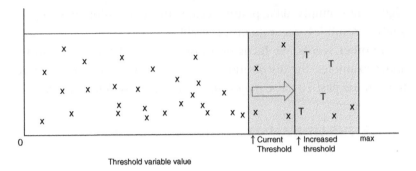

Figure 9.13 Above-the-line analysis.

right under the threshold in the future may also be true positives. This may happen in the future although there is no true positive according to historical data for analysis. Therefore, the threshold should not be set too close to the first known true positive. Moreover, if the increase in the threshold does little to help in reducing false positives, then it is not worth increasing it because it also increases the risk of false negatives. (See Figure 9.14.)

The above figures illustrate the idea with 2-dimensional graphs. Putting into practice, from the percentile rank table, one can tell which percentile catches all true positives. If the number of true positive at that row is large, this leaves more room for possible future true positives that are immediately lower.

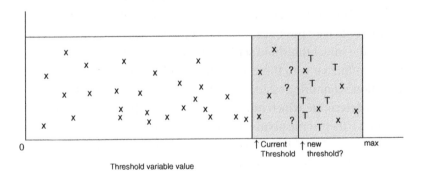

Figure 9.14 ATL analysis, consider the ? that are close to new threshold next to many true positives (T).

Value Range	Population (%ile)	True Positives	True Positives (%ile)	
98769-99993	100	1	100	
97789-98763	98	2	91	
96833-97788	97	3	73	
95500-96832	96	5	45	← Highest threshold to catch all true positives
94594-95631	95	0	0	
93718-94593	94	0	0	← Current threshold
93451-90407	93	0	0	

Figure 9.15   Consideration in threshold – lowest true positives.

If the population is large, the resolution of this table may need to be increased. That is, instead of 100 × 1 percentiles, produce 1000 × 0.1 percentiles. Then, the analysis can be done at 0.1 percentile intervals so that the adjustments can be more accurate. See Figure 9.15.

This operation can be much more convenient with a visual analysis tool with which the user can plot graphs and zoom in and out to get accurate figures immediately.

Below-the-Line Analysis

Below-the-line focuses on considering a decrease in the threshold to see if more true positives can be found while keeping false positives at a manageable level.

First, lowering the threshold will surely produce more false positive alerts. How much lower can be tolerated? This is also related to the resources to investigate the added alerts. There are always false negatives no matter how low you set a threshold. Note that the change of threshold value and change of resulting alert is not a linear relationship. Lowering the threshold by 100 may produce 20 more alerts, while further lowering the threshold by another 100 may then produce 200 more alerts as the threshold comes closer to the peak of the distribution (Figure 9.16).

To determine the lowest threshold tolerable for false positives, the percentile rank table can give you an idea of what threshold would give how many percent (of whole population) more eligible entities.

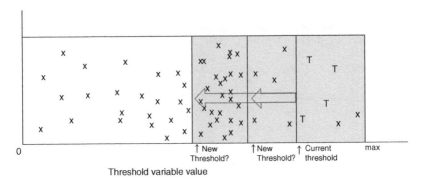

Figure 9.16   BTL analysis, lowering a threshold for the same extent may increase different number of alerts.

Value Range	Population (%ile)	True Positives	True Positives (%ile)	
98769-99993	100	1	100	Whole population is 10000 accounts
97789-98763	98	2	91	
96833-97788	97	3	73	
95500-96832	96	5	45	← Current threshold
94594-95631	95	0	0	← Threshold here: 1% x 10000 = 100 more alerts
93718-94593	94	0	0	← Threshold here: 2% x 10000 = 200 more alerts
93451-90407	93	0	0	

Again, if there are a high number of true positives around the threshold, lowering the threshold probably can yield more true positives.

Value Range	Population (%ile)	True Positives	True Positives (%ile)	
98769-99993	100	8	100	
97789-98763	98	7	91	
96833-97788	97	10	73	
95500-96832	96	19	45	← Current threshold, lot of true positives around
94594-95631	95	0	0	Lowering threshold may reveal new
93718-94593	94	0	0	productive alert
93451-90407	93	0	0	

In contrast, if there are few true positives around the threshold, lowering the threshold probably gives no more true positives.

Value Range	Population (%ile)	True Positives	True Positives (%ile)	
98769-99993	100	8	100	
97789-98763	98	16	91	
96833-97788	97	2	73	
95500-96832	96	0	45	← Current threshold, little true positives around
94594-95631	95	0	0	Further lowering threshold probably give no
93718-94593	94	0	0	new productive alert
93451-90407	93	0	0	

Note that this is just talking about eligible entities for this particular parameter variable. Actual alert results also depend on other alert conditions.

Effect of Open Alerts in Historical Data

The above discussion assumes all historical alerts in the analysis period have been investigated and closed. That means all of them are determined as false positive or true positive. Sometimes, the alerts generated by the transaction monitoring system are more than the investigators can deal with. Upon scenario review, there are still ~50% of alerts still in open state. This would affect the accuracy of the tuning result, as the positions of true positives play an important part in determining the thresholds. It is not certain at which point of threshold would all the true positives be captured. Of course, one can still investigate the alerts during the scenario review, but if the alerts were too much to handle in the past, they must also be too much to handle during scenario review.

Use of Scatter plots and Interactions between Parameter Variables

The deficiency in above-the-line analysis and below-the-line analysis is that they only focus on one single parameter variable. Very often, a scenario has just one or two significant thresholds that needs sophisticated analysis with data. If multiple parameters are equally important, a further look into the interactions between variables is needed. Each data point is a combination of all parameter variables. A data point satisfying one threshold may not satisfy another threshold, so one cannot tell the change of alert result by looking at one variable.

This is illustrated in Figure 9.17. In this diagram, both point A and B has an x value below x_1. Therefore, if the threshold for x is lowered from x_1 to x_2, both points are eligible for alert by looking at the x value.

However, point B has a y value higher than A. With the threshold of y being y_1, point A is never eligible because the y value of A is lower than threshold y_1. Here, lowering the threshold for x from x_1 to x_2 just gives one more alert (if there is no other alert condition to be considered). This is illustrated in Figure 9.18.

Analysis with a scatterplot is therefore useful in revealing the actual alerts when the threshold changes. It shows the data points against two variables. You can then see more clearly how many data points would become eligible when the thresholds are adjusted. Typically, this type of analysis is done with 2, at maximum 3, variables that can be tested in combination. When there are many different parameters to consider, this analysis has to be repeated many times to cover all angles of the combined scenarios.

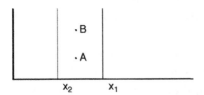

Figure 9.17   Lowering the x value yields 2 data points eligible for alert.

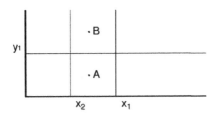

Figure 9.18   Considering another variable, lowering the x value actually yields 1 data point eligible for alert.

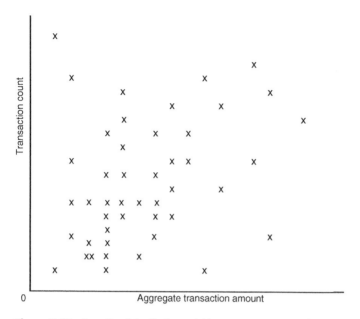

Figure 9.19 A scatterplot with the variables aggregate transaction amount against transaction count.

In a scatterplot, each data point is presented by a dot (or other symbol) on a 2-dimensional space. The x and y axes are the measurement of two parameter variables. So, the position of each point reflects the value of these two parameter variables. In Figure 9.19, a data point is (aggregate transaction amount, transaction count).

Often there are too many data points to show in a human-readable pane; usually sampling is done to minimize the number of points visible (see Figure 9.20).

To find out whether a threshold should be increased or decreased, the following steps can be followed:

1. If true positives are *close* to the threshold, the threshold should be considered for lowering as there is likely more true positives (suspicious) data points below the threshold (see Figure 9.21).

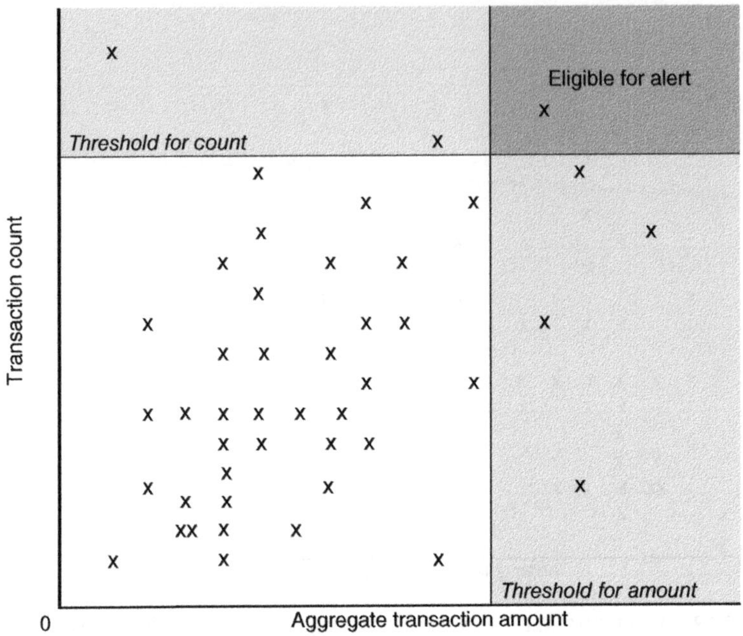

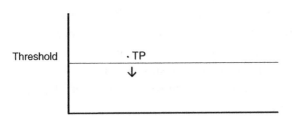

Figure 9.20 With threshold lines, the upper right rectangle is the area eligible for alert under these two parameter variables.

Threshold | · TP
↓

Figure 9.21 True Positive close to threshold.

However, if the threshold is lowered, would a lot of false positives appear?

(i) If decreasing the threshold causes a gentle increase in false positives, then decrease it to capture more possible true positives (Figure 9.22).

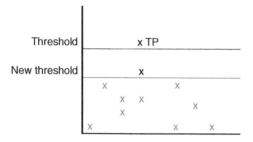

Figure 9.22 Decreasing the threshold causes a increase in false positives.

(ii) If decreasing threshold causes a sharp increase in eligible data points, then further analysis needs to be done (Figure 9.23).

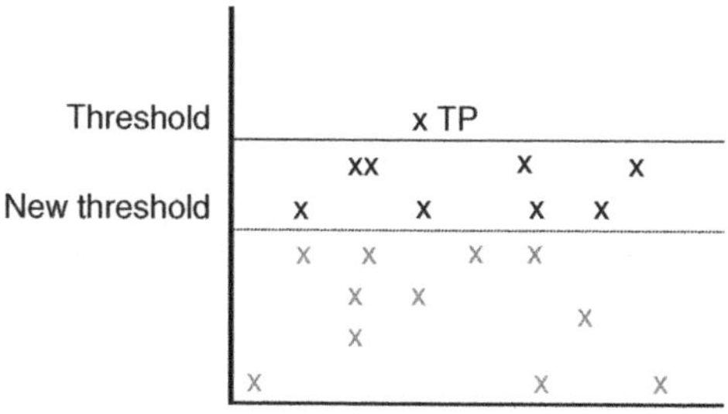

Figure 9.23 Deceasing the threshold causes sharp increase in alerts.

(iii) Look further with another parameter variable; if the newly covered data points are filtered out by another parameter variable threshold, then it is safe to decrease the threshold. That is, the false positives are bound by the threshold of the other variable (Figure 9.24).

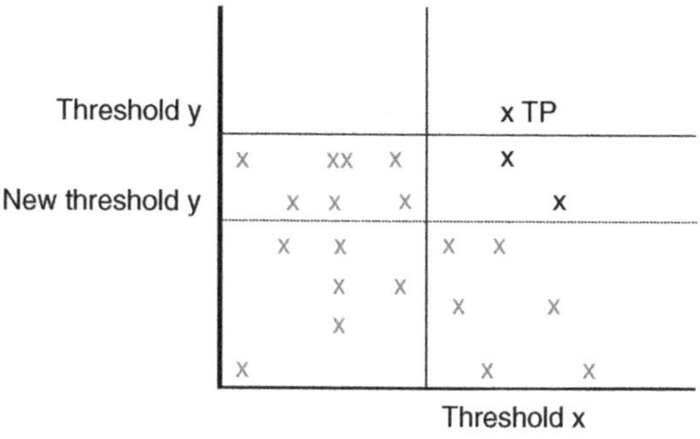

Figure 9.24 Cross with another parameter variable.

(iv) This should be done with all other parameter variables. If it turns out that a decrease in this threshold causes a sharp increase in false positives by itself, and no other variable binds the false positives, then consider holding the decrease of threshold, or expect an increase in the staff's workload for handling the additional alerts. It also means that "reducing false positives" cannot be achieved solely by threshold tuning. There may be common false positive alerts that may be filtered out by adding additional alert conditions into the scenario logic.

Figure 9.25 summarizes the process.

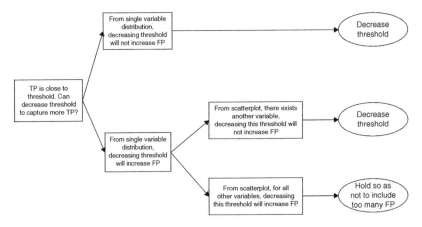

Figure 9.25 Process to decide whether to increase or decrease a threshold.

2. If true positives are *far* from the threshold, the threshold can be considered for raising, as it can decrease false positive alerts see Figure 9.26).

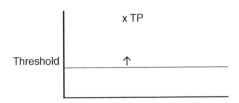

Figure 9.26 True Positives far from threshold.

However, if the threshold is raised, would a lot of false positives be saved?

(i) If increasing the threshold does not help much in minimizing false positives, then keep the threshold in order to capture possible true positives (Figure 9.27).

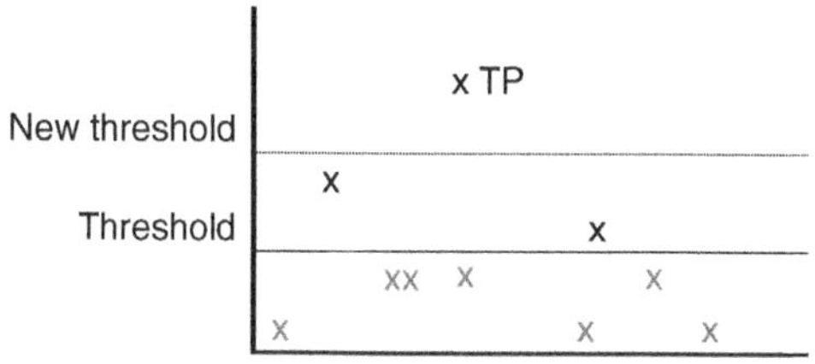

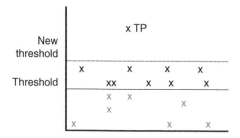

Figure 9.27 Increasing the threshold does not help in minimizing false positives.

(ii) If increasing the threshold causes sharp decrease in false positives, then further analysis should be done (Figure 9.28).

Figure 9.28 Increasing the threshold causes sharp decrease in false positives.

(iii) Look further with another parameter variable; if the eliminated data points are filtered out by another parameter variable threshold, then increasing the threshold actually does not help in reducing false positives. The false positives are already bound by the threshold of the other variable (Figure 9.29).

If increasing the threshold causes a sharp decrease in eligible false positive data points, and it is true considering all other parameter variables, then increasing this threshold contributes to the reduction of false positives.

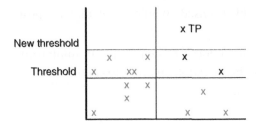

Figure 9.29   Cross with another parameter variable.

The decision chart in Figure 9.30 summarizes the process.

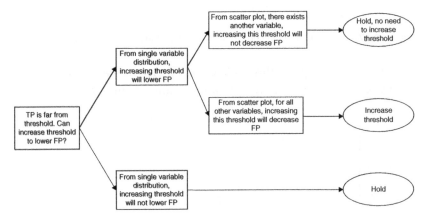

Figure 9.30   Process to decide whether to increase or decrease a threshold.

Binary Search

A scatterplot is not easy to implement. On the other hand, the threshold parameters are not equally important. Therefore, besides using a scatterplot against all parameters, one may identify the most essential parameters and work on those first. On testing with one parameter, other less important parameters may be lowered to a reasonable tolerance level. This varies case by case and the scenario rule has to be well understood to decide how the thresholds should be reasonably adjusted.

If one refrains from using a scatterplot, there are alternatives available in the form of above- and below-the-line analysis. But these methods come with their own drawbacks. One can only do one test at a time and how would one know which (combination of) threshold values to use for the tests? A regular interval, say, original threshold ×0.9, ×0.8, ×0.7, . . . ×0.1 is not very meaningful as the alerts may vary a lot between one bucket, say, between ×0.9 and ×0.95. And probably there will be a lot of time and effort wasted with tests that ultimately transpire as meaningless.

One approach called a *binary search* may provide some consolation. Underlying the binary search is the same idea of a basic search algorithm in sorted array. Let us first apply this approach to below-the-line testing. There is a target optimal value to be found between the current threshold and an implausible or infeasible other end, which can be zero or a value that is low enough to be unreasonable. The search consists of a repetition of tests whereby the testing threshold is moved across the spectrum between the current threshold and the implausible threshold, and the next testing threshold splits the segment in two where the highest concentration of productive alerts were found. One must look for the alert number and true positives caught, until it converges to an optimal. This allows the target to be reached within a few iterations (see Figure 9.31).

For example, a current threshold is $1000 and below-the-line is to be done; it ends up at $812.5 with new true positive and acceptable number of alerts (see Figure 9.32).

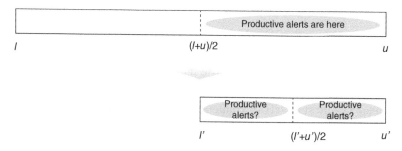

Figure 9.31   Binary split of value.

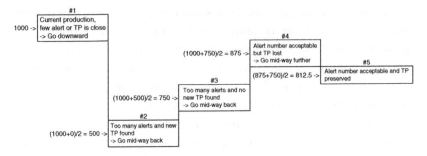

Figure 9.32 Moving towards the goal by binary search.

Note that for a "binary search" to work, the input value and output value should be of a "monotonic" trend (not necessarily linear) within the value range (binary search works in a "sorted" list of values). That is, the higher the input, the higher the output. Or the other way round: the higher the input, the lower the output. The input and output here are the "threshold value" and "number of alerts" respectively.

WHAT-IF TESTS AND MOCK INVESTIGATION

The above analysis gives direction on whether each threshold should be increased or decreased, by looking at the change in the number of alerts. Adjusting the scenario thresholds downward may produce new alerts that had not been encountered before. We do not know whether these new alerts are worth producing or not until the actual alerts are assessed. A more realistic test needs to be done to simulate the situation IF the parameters are changed.

What-If Tests

The most definite way to reveal the alerts is to actually execute the scenario rules, under the new parameter settings. We call this *what-if* tests against different sets of challenger parameter values. This would be more costly compared to the above statistical analysis and scatter-plot, because now the alerts and the information needed for supporting the investigation must also be produced. Moreover, results are not instantly available. Therefore, we wish to minimize the number of executions for these what-if test cycles. Thus, what-if tests and mock investigations should be done after the statistical analysis and scatterplot, when the scope of tuning is narrowed down. Of course, one may jump directly to what-if tests without statistical analysis, but they would lack the proper corroboration and justification of the challenger parameter values.

Any what-if testing would be the last analysis to be done before the tuning exercise is to be completed. The technical implementation of this step is not difficult. The production data has to be replicated to a testing environment and then the alert generation process must be manually run after the scenario parameter thresholds are adjusted. The alert results must be stored for comparison and review.

Multiple rounds of what-if tests would be required, each with differentiating scenario parameter values. It is an iterative process and needs to be repeated until the alert results are satisfactory. Batch job execution performance is a common concern in alert generation; running the batch alert generation multiple times could become a challenge, as it would consume much time. There are multiple scenario rules and multiple scenario parameters and each requires multiple executions before coming to a final result. Optimizing this process is critical, especially when the team is working towards a hard and tight deadline.

In some software solutions, there are tools developed to facilitate the fast generation of alert results. This cannot be done without trade-offs. In this optimized alert generation, non-tunable parameters are made to be fixed values and alerts are just selected from the data set filtered by the thresholds as selection criterion.

The new alerts generated, if any, should be investigated and be determined if it is a new true positive. Be aware that a true positive means the alert is suspicious enough and worthy of investigation, but it does not necessarily need an STR.

Sample Comparisons of What-If Tests

For one scenario rule, several rounds of what-if tests are conducted with different sets of parameter threshold values. The results would be a different set of alerts generated. What is interesting is how many alerts are reduced (or increased) and how many of them are true positives.

Parameter Set	Threshold Min Agg. Amount	Threshold Transaction Count	Number of Alerts (Change)	Number of True Positives (Change)
(Production)	5,000,000 (97%ile)	200 (95%ile)	100	5
Set 1	5,300,000 (97.2%ile)	200 (95%ile)	90 (-10)	5 (no change)
Set 2	5,700,000 (97.7%ile)	200 (95%ile)	80 (-20)	4 (-1)
Set 3	5,300,000 (97.2%ile)	220 (96%ile)	90 (-10)	5 (no change)

The above table lists the different sets of parameters under test. The parameter values and the resulting number of alerts are compared against the production result that had occurred in the production system. For each row, if the threshold had been set under these parameters, what would be the number of alerts and number of true positives? The percentile value in the threshold column indicates the position of the threshold under the statistical distribution. That is, how extreme the parameter threshold is over the population. In the number of alerts column, basically fewer alerts are desirable in terms of human resources for handling, but note the considerations in above-the-line and below-the-line analysis for the risk of potential loss of true positives in the future. The number of true positives should best be preserved so that all true positives are still captured after tuning the thresholds.

Qualifying Results of What-If Tests

Among the multiple parameter sets, one of them has to be chosen as the best to replace the current production setting. We called it the champion parameter set on this tuning exercise. The key performance indicators of a parameter set are:

■ The number of alerts resulted, in comparison with production (less is desirable).

■ The number of true positives (desirable to remain the same or increased if threshold is lowered and new true positive found during mock investigation).

More detailed comparisons may include:

- Missed true positives that appeared in production but were lost in the parameter set. Sometimes, it is tolerable to lose true positives in production for reducing lot a of false positives. It may happen that a criminal practiced a very normal transaction pattern that was not worth an alert, even though he/she was laundering money.

- Number of new alerts appear from parameter set but had not appeared in production.

- Number of new true positive alerts that had not been caught in production.

- Number of production alerts that are not generated by the parameter set.

What If I Can't Just Do "What-If"?

In certain situations, the institution may not be able to do the statistical analysis and all the scientific investigations. What is available is the alert generation system. Then, the procedure is basically to test out the thresholds to the level desired.

A scenario normally has multiple threshold parameters but usually there is one or two being most sensitive to the actual data. Focus on that parameter and apply binary search as described in this chapter to find out optimal value. Some threshold values may need to be determined with other business reasons like "relativity between customer segments," "according to experience," "reference from outside figure," etc. Usually those sensitive to actual data are "aggregate amounts," while ratios and percentages are less sensitive.

Again, it would lack the proper corroboration and justification of the challenger parameter values.

SCENARIO REVIEW REPORT

The scenario review report summarizes the results and the rationale behind the approach. This serves as proof of what had been analyzed and considered before the new scenario thresholds are proposed. Normally this report has to be reviewed and endorsed by chief officers before being applied to the production system.

Figure 9.33 is a summarized review of a scenario, with a list of active scenarios analyzed. Each scenario has multiple tunable threshold parameters. For each parameter threshold statistical analysis, above-the-line/below-the-line analysis, and/or scatterplot analysis are conducted. After that, rounds of what-if tests are conducted for one scenario. One parameter set is chosen for a scenario after considering the true positive and false positive alerts.

Typically, a scenario review report may contain the following sections:

- Overview
- Findings and general statistics
- Scenario review approach
- Scenario review results
- Recommendations

Addressing the problem is like :

The Suffering → Finding Out Cause → Eliminate the Cause → Establish Proper Way

Here,

- The suffering is either too many alerts being generated, i.e. too many false positives, and/or reportable behavior not being identified, i.e. insufficient hit rate or too many (assumed) false negatives.

- A scenario tuning review aims at finding the root cause, which may be threshold too high/low, customer segments not properly defined, data quality issue, human operation issue, resource issue, etc.

- To eliminate this root cause we can then adjust thresholds, redefine customer segment, employ new rules, employ new technology, address data quality issues, operational issues and/or resource issues, whichever fits the root cause.

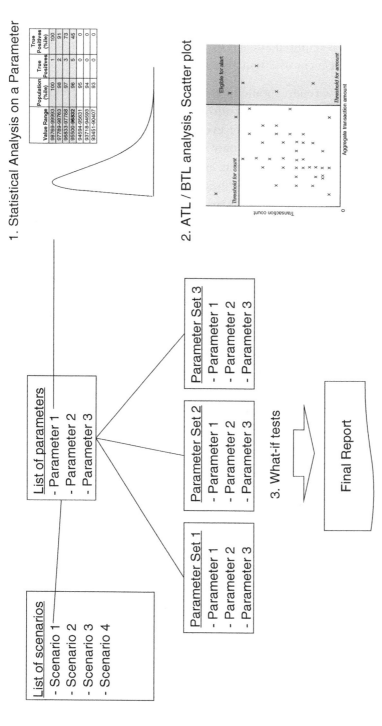

Figure 9.33 High-level flow for adjusting scenario parameters.

▓ To ensure ongoing operation efficacy, reviewing on a regular basis is required and a proper workflow must be established to ensure a consistent quality of the review.

The review report should now incorporate these four elements.

During the review, it is not uncommon that the scenario execution frequency, lookback period, or even the alert condition and parameters need to be changed. A new threshold parameter may need to be added. These must, of course, also be reported in this document.

The overview section describes in general the background of the scenario review exercise. What are the major issues, or pain points, of the current transaction monitoring system? It may also introduce the different sections of the report.

While the areas of concern that needs further attention can be identified by first pass data analysis, sometimes subject matter expertise provides the best basis for the next step: drilling down deeper into the root causes of underperformance. However, this depends very much on the reviewer's or consultant's experience and knowledge on this subject matter, and also a deep understanding of the transaction monitoring system in question. The investigative approach can or must be corroborated by continued statistical analysis in which, ideally, multiple methods are combined.

The section on general statistics gives an overview of the environment with data and statistics. It gives the reader an understanding of the current transaction monitoring from different angles, from a data point of view. From this section, the reader should have a picture in mind as to how the transaction monitoring system is performing, and from which area would most problems come.

Some basic statistics may contain the following. The list is to be adjusted according to the individual environment.

▓ Distribution of customers by customer segment, by risk level

▓ Distribution of alerts by customer segment

▓ Distribution of alerts by scenario rules

▨ Distribution of alerts over time

▨ Distribution of transaction types/products

▨ Distribution of true positives – among different scenarios, among customer segments

As an example of findings, a scenario rule looking at ATM withdrawals has been giving no alerts. The reason may be that ATM withdrawal transactions never happen in the segment of corporate customers. So the scenario rule should exist but it is natural that it seldom gives any alert.

Examples of statistics

Alerts by Scenario

Scenario	Alerts	% of alerts	True Positives	True Positive Rate
001 Large cash transactions	9671	18.5%	92	1.1%
002 High velocity wire	6208	12.8%	55	0.89%

Alerts over Months

Month	Scenario 001	Scenario 002	Total
Jan 2016	20	12	32
Feb 2016	18	12	30
Mar 2016	19	17	36
Apr 2016	14	12	26
May 2016	12	6	18
Jun 2016	9	5	14
Jul 2016	13	7	20
Aug 2016	17	8	25
Sep 2016	22	10	32
Oct 2016	21	12	33
Nov 2016	23	15	38
Dec 2016	25	16	41

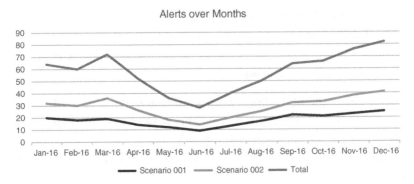

Figure 9.34 Sample statistics – alerts over months.

Scenario Review Approach

In this section, the analysis techniques and procedures are described. It prepares the reader to understand how the analysis results should be interpreted. With the causes of the issues identified, it discusses a suitable approach considering the constraints in the environment. It should always include the rationale behind the approach. Various approaches may be listed and the pros and cons between them discussed. On the other hand, the limitations in the review exercise should also be mentioned. These limitations may be that open alerts that are not yet closed may be causing inaccurate outcomes, because they are (dis)counted as true or false positives. It should include the length of analysis period, how the analysis dates are chosen, sampling methods adopted . . . anything that is considered in the review exercise.

Scenario Review Results

This is the main content of the scenario review report. For each scenario rule, document the detailed findings and statistics. The analysis and tests that have been performed are listed. Also, the final set of parameters chosen is documented with supporting rationale.

Overview

An overall summary of all scenario parameter tuning results follows. It consolidates all results to show the final outcome at a glance.

Scenario	Current Production			After Tuning				Parameters Tuned	Old Values	New Values
	No. of alert	No. of productive alert	% of Open Alert	No. of alert	No. of productive alert	Alert change	Productive alert change			
S001	9215	93	54	8478	93	-8%	0	amount min_large_tran	18,000,000 2,000,000	18,700,00 2,100,000
S002	5858	105	55	5741	105	-0.02%	0	deposit_min withdraws_today	9,500,000 300,000	9,700,000 390,000
...										

Various scenarios can be compared in a table format. Further detail comes after this overview. Some readers may just look at this section; only those who are technical enough would drill into detail at the following section.

Example:

Detail Results for each Scenario

A basic overview of the scenario is present so that readers of this report quickly know what this scenario rule should do.

- Description of the scenario.
- Entity level (by party/account/household).
- Scenario execution frequency.
- List of parameters, with descriptions and current threshold values in production. It should also be indicated which parameters are tunable parameters.

Example:

S001 Large aggregate cash transactions (Individual)

Description: Large aggregate cash transactions . . .

Entity Level: Party

Execution Frequency: Daily

Parameters:

Parameter Name	Description	Current Value	Tunable
num_day	Number of days in interval	10	No
min_agg_amount	Minimum aggregate transaction amount	150,000	Yes
min_amount_today	Minimum amount transacted on current day	20,000	Yes
transaction medium	Medium of transaction	CASH	No
customer_tier	Customer Tier	INDIV *(for individual customers)*	No

Alert Statistics is a summary of alerts from the scenario throughout the analysis period:

- The analysis period
- Number of alerts
- Number of true positive alerts
- Percentage of true positives (high TP rate means this scenario is effective)
- Number of open alerts
- Percentage of alerts that are still in open state (high rate of open alert may mean the TP rate is less accurate)

Example:

Analysis Period	1 Apr 2015 – 31 Mar 2016
Number of Alerts	9125
Number of TP	91
TP %	1.00%
Number of Open Alerts	506
Open Alert %	5.55%

For each parameter variable, the results of basic statistics as described in the section in this chapter called "Statistical Analysis of Each Tunable Scenario Threshold Variable" are documented.

- Mean
- Standard Deviation
- Kurtosis
- Skewness
- Range
- Which percentile the current production threshold value is at
- The percentile ranking table
- Above-the-line analysis and below-the-line analysis results
- Scatterplot analysis results

Example:

Variable for parameter min_agg_amount	
Mean	19,653
Standard deviation	90,285
Kurtosis	31,281
Skewness	7,328
Range	2,301 – 8,431,250
Current Production Threshold	150,000
Current Production Threshold at Percentile	99%ile

Variable for parameter min_amount_today	
Mean	8,057
Standard deviation	7,985
Kurtosis	7,281
Skewness	88
Range	100 – 6,090,821
Current Production Threshold	20,000
Current Production Threshold at Percentile	42%ile

Percentile ranking table for parameter min_agg_amount

Percentile	Aggregate Cash Transaction Amount	Productive Alert
100	8,431,250	
99.9	421,562	23
99.8	301,116	19
99.7	240,893	27
99.6	192,714	22
99	120,446	
95	37,639	
90	18,819	
75	9,409	
50	4,700	
25	1,568	
10	940	
5	500	
1	100	

A conclusion on this scenario is shown listing the detail of the champion parameter set after rounds of what-if tests.

	Current Production	Suggested Parameter Set
Number of Alerts	9,125	9,024
Number of Productive Alerts	91	91

Parameter	Production Value	Current Ranking (%ile)	Suggested Value	New Ranking (%ile)
min_ agg_amount	150,000	99	190,000	99.6
min_ amount_today	20,000	42	(unchanged)	(unchanged)

Other Recommendations

During the scenario review, there may be issues that cannot be resolved within the review exercise. Recommendations may be made in this report to tackle these issues in the future.

These may include:

- Some deficiency on monitoring; a new scenario rule is needed. It would take time to design and develop this new scenario.
- Data required for a scenario is not available in the source system. It would take time to enhance source system
- Data required for a scenario is not accurate in the system because of data entry in front line human operation. Staff training is needed, and operation guidelines may need to be updated at branch level.
- Business areas that should be included for transaction monitoring, but this would require a change in source system.

Above are the steps for tuning thresholds for an existing scenario rule that have been effective in the production system. Active scenarios have alerts generated and true positives identified. In the above analysis, these true positives play an important part in determining the thresholds.

If talking about a newly developed scenario rule:

- The available analysis period would be much shorter, maybe just a few days.
- There are no readily available true positives.

The above scenario tuning exercise can still be employed, but some points need to be adjusted.

- Scenario running in production has months of historical data for analysis. For a newly developed scenario, this takes only a few days. This is not desirable because of not enough variations such as for seasonal factors. However, it is the best that can be done.
- In statistical analysis, there is no true positive information. One should then focus on the percentile, or portion of population covered by each threshold parameter.
- Above-the-line, below-the-line analysis, and scatterplots can be done focusing on the change of alerts. With mock investigation, the data points can be identified as true positives for analysis.
- What-if tests are used to compare the alert results, while the true positives are from mock investigations.

SUMMARY

For any new scenario, these initial thresholds are a best guess, based on experience and expertise or test data. These initial thresholds are, ideally, to be replaced by thresholds based on the analysis of production data fed into and produced by the very same system and scenario. This is called scenario tuning, or more specifically, threshold tuning. Unless the system has an auto-tuning in place (machine learning), the first tuning exercise is typically scheduled 6 months after go-live of the (new) system, but this is subject to the strategy adopted by the financial institution. Parameter variables are meant to be changeable and therefore usually a user interface is provided, like dedicated screens for authorized staff to make changes. Regulators nowadays require institutions to have solid supporting on all scenario thresholds, with proper documentation discussing how the thresholds are established. As a result, a decent threshold tuning exercise needs to be conducted. There are many approaches to (data-driven) scenario tuning, but all of them looking at the performance, or productivity, of the scenarios in terms of the ratios between true and false alerts. Data is analyzed to predict the outcome if certain parameters were to be changed, and to calculate the optimum values. This can be done by scenario, but also by segment. Data-driven scenario tuning is typically in the realm of statistical analysis that typically looks at ways to sample the data, do supervised analysis (based on the actual disposition of historic alerts), and look at distributions for each scenario and/or segment. The outcome will be captured in a performance review report, which may contain suggestions for changes to the parameters to optimize the performance of the scenarios in production. Occasionally the recommendation may include the removal of a scenario, although one has to be careful not to remove a safety-blanket; even though the circus artist rarely loses his grip and falls down, this does not necessarily make it wise to remove the net beneath.

Index

Printed and bound by CPI Group (UK) Ltd, Croydon, CR0 4YY

16/04/2025

14658513-0005